THE BOAT OWNER'S FITTING OUT MANUAL

THE BOAT OWNER'S FITTING OUT MANUAL

Jeff Toghill

VAN NOSTRAND REINHOLD COMPANY
NEW YORK   CINCINNATI   TORONTO   LONDON   MELBOURNE

First published in Great Britain, 1980, by Stanford
Maritime Ltd., 12–14 Long Acre, London WC2E 9LP

Printed in Great Britain

Published by Van Nostrand Reinhold Company
A division of Litton Educational Publishing, Inc.
135 West 50th Street, New York, NY 10020, U.S.A.

16 15 14 13 12 11 10 9 8 7 6 5 4 3 2 1

Contents

This book originated in Australia as a guide to planning and carrying out the work of fitting out bare hulls, and calls on the experience of the author, Jeff Toghill, and others, with a number of such projects. However, because of differences in terminology, boatbuilding practices and certain regulations, the text was considerably revised for this edition and the publishers wish to acknowlege the assistance of Anthony Siggery in its preparation.

CHAPTER 1

The Basic Hull

BOAT HULLS come in all shapes and sizes. Timber, fibreglass, steel, aluminium and even concrete, motor-driven, sail-driven or both; round, square, planing, deep keel—you name it, there's a hull to fit it!

Which all adds up to a pretty confusing prospect when looking at fitting out the different types of hulls. But in fact it is not as complicated as it looks, for many of the fitting-out techniques can be applied to more than one type of hull or hull material. The secret lies in selecting the technique best suited to the hull you are fitting out, and—while compromises must be made with any technique—following the guidelines as closely as possible to achieve the most suitable yet most economical results.

FITTING-OUT PROCEDURES

Most boat manufacturers nowadays offer their product in different stages of completion, starting with the bare shell and adding fittings and furnishings in stages up to the finished luxury craft.

As a general rule structural members in the hull are included and fitting out will involve one or more of the following stages:

Interior furniture and furnishings
Motors and ancillary machinery
Mast, spars and rigging
Deck fittings and gear
Electrical circuits, instruments and plumbing
General hull fittings (rudder, keel, bulkheads, etc.)

The hull may have been delivered without deck or cabin, in which case there is another stage to add to those listed above. But this work is more along the lines of boatbuilding and can really be considered a part of the hull construction. So we shall assume that our work is to be confined mostly to fitting out the completed shell and, while dealing briefly with laying a deck or fitting a cabin trunkway, we shall be concerned more with such fittings as windows, hatches and the wide range of deck hardware.

TRANSFERRING THE STRESSES

When a boat works in a seaway the hull flexes and moves. For this reason great care must be taken in fastening any fittings to the hull structure so they do not break away. Also, since many of the interior fittings, particularly some of the furniture, add greatly to the structural strength of the boat, the fastening point between fitting and hull must be well secured.

Modern fibreglass (GRP) yachts often have much of their interior furniture moulded and secured in place as part of the hull construction, eliminating the need for heavy stringers and other structural members. However, there are still many fittings, both internal and external, which require strong fastenings to take the load which will be placed on them, and great pains must be taken with fastenings to ensure that the transfer of stresses between the fittings and the hull will not cause structural failure or 'hot spots' of stress.

STRUCTURAL ZONES

For this reason it is vitally important before one even thinks about fitting out a boat to know something of her construction. The hull is designed to cope with severe stresses when the boat is moving in a seaway and what to the eye may appear as just a simple shell is in fact a complex structure designed to withstand these stresses. To remove even a small piece of a vital structural member could weaken it to the point where the whole hull could collapse. While this may not be obvious at the time of fitting out, when the boat gets into a seaway and the weaknesses show up, the danger is severe and could result in the loss of the boat and perhaps the loss of lives.

Far too many amateurs, used to fitting out a kitchen or bedroom in the home, tackle the fitting out of a boat with the philosophy that providing what you cut doesn't collapse, it's got to be okay. This may work in the kitchen because it is static, and may also be effective in a boat as long as she sits at the dock. But once the hull starts to twist and wrack—and hulls do twist and wrack in a seaway—the partly sawn stringer into which a bunk is fitted, or the rebated beam taking the cupboard upright, will be unable to take the strain and will break at the weakened joint.

The loss of one beam or one stringer places extra load on other structural members and so the damage progresses and the boat will at best suffer severe structural damage, at worst break up and sink.

Similarly, much of the strain on a hull may be designed to be taken by some of the interior fittings. Bulkheads are the classic example, since they offer structural strength in a number of directions, helping to hold the hull together as it wracks in the seaway. Removing a bulkhead, or cutting holes in it to fit radios, cupboards or doorways, or not fitting it correctly in the first place, leaves the boat structurally very weak in this area. In her first bad seaway she may strain other structural members which have to carry the extra load created by the weakened bulkhead.

This demonstrates the need for the amateur to know what he is about before he starts to chop and change the interior of his boat. To know which members are structurally vital to the boat's construction and which can be cut or replaced is to ensure that when the fitting-out job is done the boat will be in as seaworthy a condition as she was originally.

The bulkhead holds the sides and top of the hull 'tube' together and must not be weakened by cutting large doorways or other apertures.

TRANSVERSE MEMBERS

The main structural members concerned with thwartships strength are those which serve one of two purposes—preventing the 'tube' of the boat's hull from collapsing and preventing it from wracking. They form the cross-sectional 'shape' of the boat around which the skin or shell is wrapped, and thus literally form a circle of strength to hold the shape of the hull in place against all stresses. Basically, the requirement is for some structural strength to support the sides of the hull and some to prevent the sides collapsing inwards or outwards.

In timber boats, a more complete picture of structural transverse strength can be seen, in that *ribs* (or *frames* as they are more correctly called) run down each side of the boat joining the deck to the keel. These are strong structural fittings, often placed close together, which take the full stresses which come on the hull when moving in a seaway, both in the form of wracking and

pressure on the hull. Obviously, they must never be cut or even rebated as any weakness in a frame could result in collapse of the hull shape.

Plywood boats tend to have fewer frames than clinker or carvel boats, but they are usually heavier in construction and rely on the laminations of the ply to help take some of the strain. Frames may never be cut, but there is no reason why they cannot be used to support interior fittings and, indeed, it is often to these frames that much of the interior furniture is secured.

Metal boats also require fewer frames and they are therefore farther spaced. Fibreglass yachts often have no frames at all. In order to support interior fittings *landings* need to be fitted. If moulded furniture is already secured in the hull it is probably an integral part of the boat's construction and must not be removed or weakened.

The sides of the boat are held apart at the top by deck beams. Once again this is best illustrated in timber craft, where fairly heavy gauge beams are spaced close together to take the transverse stresses. These beams may sometimes be cut, such as in the case of a cabin or trunkway, but when this is done compensation must be made by fitting beams to the cabin roof or fitting adjacent bulkheads or some other form of structural transverse strength.

In order to make a solid structural unit and prevent the hull wracking, the beams are joined to the frames by angles known as *knees*. Like the deck beams themselves, these are a vital part of

Deck beams close in the tube of the hull form and complete the circle of transverse strength. Note the location of bulkheads giving added strength to the beams.

The bracing effect of floors on a power boat can be seen here. High speed motor yachts require heavily reinforced floors.

the structure of the boat and must not be cut or weakened without some form of compensation. They are particularly noticeable in timber and metal boats, less so in fibreglass boats where there are fewer beams and the main transverse stresses are taken by the bulkheads.

The floors, often small in a yacht but larger in motor cruisers, complete the structural circle. They act as the deck beams of the lower areas of the boat, bracing the bottom part of the transverse hull section. They may be butted against the keel and the ribs (chine hulls) or carried right across the boat in her bilge area (deep keel yachts). Either way they prevent collapse of the hull and take the ballast weight and the stresses on the keel.

The bulkhead is probably the most important transverse structural member in the boat. It forms the complete 'structural circle' and thus does the work of beams, frames and floors. It goes without saying that bulkheads are essential in any boat, and they must not be weakened or their effectiveness will be ruined. However, they are also rather a nuisance in terms of breaking the boat into sections, and doors must be cut to provide access between these sections. Providing reinforcement is added and the doors do not weaken the bulkhead to too great an extent, doors are acceptable. A good shape for a door is the curved or oval shape which offers good access yet creates minimal weakness.

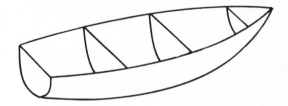

Bulkheads stiffen the hull shape and prevent it from collapsing or wracking in a seaway.

There are, of course, other areas of transverse structural strength, but these are fairly obvious and in any case unlikely to be concerned with fitting out in the normal course of events. Where alteration to such an area may occur in some special case—such as recessing a mounting for an outboard motor into the transom—the question of structural hull strength will be discussed where details of the work involved are described.

LONGITUDINAL MEMBERS

Most of the longitudinal strength of a boat is involved in preventing the hull from bending. Imagine a boat in a seaway with her bow and stern supported by consecutive waves. Because of the trough between the waves the midships section of the hull will be unsupported and will therefore tend to sag badly. Indeed, the term given to this type of stress is just that— *sagging*.

11

Now imagine the midships section riding the crest of a wave. Because of the troughs on either side of the wave, the ends of the boat will be unsupported and tend to sag. The term given to this condition is *hogging*. It follows that because waves follow one another in succession, a boat working in a seaway is subjected to a series of hogging and sagging stresses, and to prevent the hull from breaking up under these stresses strong longitudinal structural members are necessary.

The two principal members are located at the top and bottom of the hull, running its full length. They are the *beam shelf* and the *keel* respectively. The keel, of course, is the traditional 'backbone' of any ship and is every bit as important in small boats as in ocean-going liners. The sheerstrake and the *beam shelf* are equally important.

Depending on the size and construction of the boat, additional longitudinal members may be added to the hull. A *keelson*, for example, is usually fitted in motor yachts—it is, in effect, a

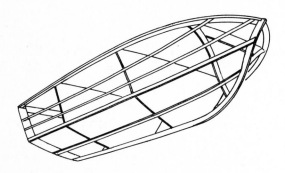

The longitudinal strength of a boat is formed by keel, beam shelf and stringers. The chine of a planing boat is a type of stringer.

second keel. *Stringers*, similar in construction to the beam shelf, are often fitted at different points up the sides of the hull, although the trend in some forms of fibreglass construction is to replace stringers with an extra thickness of hull skin.

Particularly is this the case with GRP planing hulls which may have no internal stringers at all. Instead the thickness of the fibreglass skin is increased considerably at the chine and towards

the keel. In some forms of construction this type of craft may have a series of stringers built into the flat bottom section of the hull. These serve a twofold purpose of strengthening the bottom skin against the pounding of seas when the boat is at speed and of providing added longitudinal strength to prevent bending due to the enormous stresses of climbing over or leaping off a wave at planing speed.

It follows that because of the vital part these longitudinal members play in ensuring the strength of the hull they must not be damaged or cut in any way during fitting-out activities. There is no reason why they cannot be used as supports for interior furniture—indeed, they can be very useful in this regard. But no form of attachment or fastening must interfere with the basic strength of these members.

COMBINED STRESSES

Between the extremes of transverse and longitudinal stresses lie a host of other strains which may affect a boat's hull. These conditions are too involved and numerous to cover in a book such as this, but to illustrate the point, perhaps the best known strain arises as a result of what is known as *yawing* or *corkscrewing*. Here the hull is subject to both transverse and longitudinal stresses, alternating in a wracking action which brings pressure to bear on almost every structural member in the hull. This means that not only must the structural makeup of the hull be at its maximum strength, but also that fittings such as bulkheads which form an integral part of that makeup must be in position and properly secured.

It all boils down to one basic maxim—*when fitting out the interior of the hull be very careful not to cut into any of the structural members unless adequate compensation is made.* And when using structural members as supports or attachment points for fittings, be very careful with drilling or any other technique which may reduce their total strength. It's one thing having a beautifully appointed yacht which everyone admires when sitting aboard, and quite another having nothing but beautiful appointments left when the hull disintegrates in a seaway!

CHAPTER 2

Materials for Fitting Out

SINCE FITTING OUT a boat involves a wide range of activities, it also involves the use of a wide range of materials. It is not my intention to detail them all in this chapter since I lay no claim to being an expert in, say, furnishing fabrics or melamine plastics. These and many other materials are used infrequently and outside expertise should be called in when their use arises.

But it is important for the amateur to have a working knowledge of the more important materials used in fitting out boats, if only to make the work easier and the results more rewarding. Only three basic materials are in general use—timber, fibreglass and metal—although there are varieties of these three which can be useful. A brief rundown on the types and characteristics of each will create a useful background to the work that will convert these materials into useful fittings on your boat.

TIMBER

Without doubt the most common material used in fitting out pleasure craft is timber. Quite apart from its versatility and ease of use, the warmth and attractive appearance of timber finish enhances the interior of any boat. Providing it is well maintained, it also adds a quality to exterior finishing, particularly when the vessel is constructed of metal or fibreglass. The neat finishing touches of timber trim on a metal or synthetic boat give it a sophisticated look which cannot be achieved by other materials.

The ease of working timber makes it a great favourite among amateur handymen and although, like all materials, it has its limitations, there are few people who cannot make some sort of a job with timber when they put their hand to it. Shaping is easy, cutting is easy and timber can be fastened in a whole variety of ways. You need only a basic knowledge of the timber and the tools used for working it to achieve results that are strong and attractive.

This basic knowledge, however, is all important. Knowing something about the timber before using it can make or mar the job. Too many amateurs buy just any old bits of timber

Timber makes an attractive and practical finish to a boat in many different ways. Rails, steps, wheel, decking and trim are all timber on this GRP boat.

and then wonder why the finished result is not as attractive as that done by a professional shipwright. Quite apart from the different levels of skill, if the timber is not right for the job it will present all kinds of problems which even the shipwright himself would find hard to cope with.

For this reason, it is worth spending some time at this point examining the different types of timbers, the ways in which they are cut and how these factors affect the work of fitting out a boat. Quite apart from obvious strength factors—and these are vitally important in some fittings which come under load when the boat is working in a seaway—one must consider shrinkage, expansion, warping and, in the case of plywood, delamination. Imagine, for example, the frustration of fitting a section of timber immaculately into place, finishing and polishing it, only to find some weeks later that it has warped out of shape or cracked.

The grain

The strength of timber and its tendency to alter shape depend greatly on the way in which the grain is running. Crooked grain, for example, will change shape if it expands or shrinks and is of limited use for fitting out. Straight grain is also susceptible to change but is more predictable. Changes such as swelling or shrinking are always greater across the grain than along the grain (a useful piece of know-how when securing a tight-fitting section into place).

The way in which the timber is initially sawn will also affect its swelling/shrinking characteristics. Where the grain runs horizontally across the end of the plank (*slash sawn*) the swelling and shrinkage is greater than where the plank is cut with the grain running vertically up and down the end of the plank (*rift sawn*). The strength of the timber is also affected by the way the plank is cut. It is easy to imagine that a slash sawn plank would be more susceptible to bending stresses than would the vertically-grained rift sawn timber.

Apart from the straightness of the grain, the location of knots is an important factor, since knots create weak points in the plank. While timber that is free of knots is obviously preferable for many kinds of work, it is absolutely essential where any stresses are to come on the timber. By the same token, of course, the knots in some types of wood can be most attractive in terms of finished appearance. So in selecting timber for a particular job the choice will be governed by the stresses it will encounter. All timber must be seasoned before use, as it tends to warp during the seasoning process, and you should check with the timber yard to ensure that it has been correctly done.

Hardwoods and softwoods

Although hardwoods are used quite extensively in boatbuilding, they are confined mainly to the structural areas. They are not used greatly for fitting out other than, perhaps, for purposes such as mounting winches and providing structural supports to bulkheads or engine beds. Most hardwoods, as well as being difficult to work,

Long, clear-grain softwoods are ideal for structural work such as deck beams.

have crooked grains and are somewhat brittle.

Softwoods, by contrast, are mostly fairly pliable. The long, straight-grained softwoods offer the best material for fitting out boats. These timbers are also usually lighter in weight than the hardwoods and while weight is not an adverse factor for the structural parts of the boat, fitting out should be done with light timber wherever possible. Pine is ideal for this type of work and is probably used more widely than any other. Long-grained clear Oregon pine is hard to beat for general fitting out purposes, offering easy working and an attractive finish.

The following is a guide to the types of timbers most widely used in marine work:

Hardwoods

IROKO: Often known as African Teak, it may also be used as an alternative. It is more easily worked than teak, but for planking requires careful selection to ensure a straight grain.

TEAK: Considered by many to be the ideal timber for marine use since it is highly resistant to rot and weather. Hard to work and very stable, it contains a natural oil which may be supplemented to maintain a good finish. Today its use is largely confined to interior and exterior fittings, but in the right lengths it is considered the best timber for planking.

OAK: The traditional boatbuilding timber. Susceptible to rot and hard to work, so is usually confined to structural members where its strength is its main advantage. Not widely used in fitting out.

MAHOGANY: Used mainly for its superb finish. Varnished hulls are often built from this timber which is fairly easy to work. There are a number of different types of mahogany, of which Honduras is the most widely used.

ELM: Hard and strong with a degree of elasticity, Rock Elm is the traditional timber for frames, strakes and bent work. Takes a smooth finish and varnishes well.

Softwoods

OREGON: The most widely used timber for boat work, particularly for fitting out as it does not shrink or swell as much as other timbers and is fairly resistant to rot. Easy to work, can be obtained in long, clear-grained lengths, and can be brought to a most attractive finish by means of varnishes or oils.

SPRUCE: Also a good timber for marine work, being very light in weight yet very strong. Mostly used for making spars or similar load-bearing members. Not widely used in fitting out.

CEDAR: An easily worked timber with good resistance to rot. Widely used for fitting out in the days gone by when cedar panelling was a must for luxury yachts.

ASH: White ash offers a most attractive finish to the interior of a boat. The blond wood is ideal for panelling or for any interior fittings where finish is important, particularly where contrast with the darker teaks and mahoganies is required. Fairly strong and easy to work.

MAPLE: Another timber with a most attractive finish for interior work, but suffers from brittleness due to its short grain. Not over-resistant to rot, and will splinter easily if bent. Mostly used in cut sections which will not come under any form of stress. There are many different types of maple, and advice from the lumber yard, or preferably from a shipwright, should be obtained before purchase.

Plywood is the ideal panelling material for all boat jobs. A light framework is all that is required and in some interior work even this is not necessary. The cut ends of the ply are vulnerable to damage and must be covered.

Plywood

Made by laminating thin layers of wood and bonding them with a waterproof glue, marine plywood is both strong and easy to use, providing an ideal material for fitting-out purposes. It can be obtained in all kinds of finishes, and thus enhances the interior decoration of the boat while at the same time providing good strength where it may be required. If it is of good grade and correctly waterproofed, it will withstand saturation for a surprising length of time. For this reason all plywood used for fitting out must be of correct marine grade.

Earlier plywoods were very susceptible to rot, particularly dry rot, but modern techniques have developed a system whereby impregnation of the timber fibres with anti-rot chemicals renders them very resistant to rot. This impregnation may create a tint or 'blush' in the surface veneer, but as a general rule this tint will not spoil the appearance, even of polished finishes.

Plywood comes in a variety of thicknesses and can be used for almost any type of fitting. It is ideal for lighter fittings such as tables, cupboards and bunks and, providing it is of the correct strength, is equally suitable for stressed areas such as bulkheads and hatches. It can be fibreglassed, glued, nailed, screwed or bolted. For these reasons it is the most useful form of timber for the major part of fitting out the interior of the boat, and is also useful for a number of exterior purposes.

Because of plywood's cross-grained construction, the ends of the sheets are particularly

15

vulnerable to damage. The laminations tend to be easily splintered when worked, and care must be taken when sawing or planing to reduce this tendency as much as possible. Broken edges may give rise to rot or similar problems unless correctly sealed.

Rot

Rot is the bugbear of timber work on boats. It cannot be avoided since all forms of rot are related to moisture and by virtue of their environment boats are constantly in contact with moisture. However, preventive measures taken during building the boat can do much to ward off rot attacks in the hull structure and by the same token a little extra care and prevention during fitting out will eliminate much of the problem in the interior areas.

There are two basic forms of rot—wet and dry. The former is probably the most familiar since it comes about through constant saturation of the timber. The fibres gradually break down and disintegrate and the wood becomes a mushy, sodden mess which collapses completely. Dry rot is more insidious in that often it cannot be seen until it has progressed to a dangerous point. It is a form of fungus which attacks the fibres of the timber and causes complete collapse but, unlike wet rot which is usually very visible, dry rot can germinate in a piece of timber with little or no outward indication of its presence.

The prevention of both forms of rot must begin at the very beginning—before the timber is secured in place. No matter what the fitting, if it is to be located in a position where it will be constantly saturated and thus prone to wet rot it must be waterproofed. Painting is the simplest method of achieving this.

Preventing dry rot is more difficult since it may attack timber in virtually any location. It is particularly prevalent in interior timber work, but can just as easily attack exterior timber. The only real solution is to treat every piece of timber before it is secured into position, particularly if it is eventually going to be concealed or located in a position with difficult access. Once dry rot gets a hold in timber it spreads like the proverbial bushfire and the only cure is surgery—not a pleasant prospect in any circumstance, but particularly unpleasant if half the boat has to be ripped apart to get at the affected part.

All timber, whether exposed to the air or not, should be treated with one of the anti-rot chemicals before being secured in place. Paint and varnish are not protection against dry rot, as the insidious fungus can move beneath these protective coatings. The vulnerability of laminated timber to dry rot is such that most marine plywoods are impregnated before they are sold.

FIBREGLASS

Aside from its widely accepted use in the construction of boat hulls, fibreglass has become the wonder material of the century for many other shipboard uses. Its versatility and strength plus its maintenance-free properties make it ideal for the construction of fittings, for repair work and even for alterations on almost any craft. And its ease of use puts it within reach of even the most ham-fisted amateur. Indeed, providing certain basic techniques are followed, using fibreglass for many aspects of boat work, particularly fitting out, is easier than using the traditional timber.

The key lies in the term *basic techniques*. For although fibreglass is the simplest material in the world to use, success with it will only be realised if exactly the correct techniques are used. The techniques are in themselves quite simple and therefore there is no excuse for anyone with even moderate ability as a handyman to make a mess of fibreglass construction. In this case, a little knowledge is *not* a dangerous thing, for it can be the difference between success and failure with this excellent material.

GRP

An alternative term for fibreglass is Glass Reinforced Plastic, commonly abbreviated to GRP. The plastic is a cold-setting resin, the most useful variety of which for marine use is polyester resin. Reinforcing is provided by glass fibres which, generally speaking, can have a higher tensile strength than steel. Just as steel mesh provides the reinforcing for concrete construction, so the glass fibres, often woven into a mesh or mat form, provide the reinforcing for the polyester resin.

It is important to note that the form in which the glass fibre reinforcing comes can make a considerable difference to the strength of the finished product. While obviously the final strength of the GRP will depend on the glass/resin ratio, there are vast differences in both the tensile strength and the strength/weight ratio between glass rovings, glass cloth and glass

Chopped strand mat is the most popular form of glass fibre for boat use. It is cheaper than cloth and more practical than rovings.

mat. Rovings are usually random fibres often sprayed in place, the mat is a loose weave of chopped strands, while the cloth is a tight weave not unlike a material such as linen. The strength of relative types of fibreglass reinforcing can be gathered from the following:

Material	Tensile Strength (pounds/square inch)	Strength/ Weight Ratio
Glass rovings	120 0000	63
Woven cloth	45 000	26
Chopped strand mat	15 000	11
Mild steel	60 000	8
Timber (approx)	15 000	22

From this it can be seen that claims that GRP has a greater tensile strength than steel hold good in some cases and not in others. However, in terms of strength-to-weight, it far exceeds that of steel even in the mat form. Since weight is quite an important factor in boat construction and fitting out the advantages of GRP can easily be seen. Another misconception is that fibreglass is weaker than timber, whereas the figures above indicate that only the strand mat produces a finished GRP with a lower strength/weight ratio than average timber.

Choice of the type of glass fibre material obviously depends on the particular requirements of the job. In hull construction, where

highest possible strength factors are required, rovings are normally used, probably in conjunction with woven mat. By contrast, where small fittings or units are to be moulded or built, the strand mat provides a more convenient material to use.

Resins

A number of resins are available on the market and it is important to use the correct one for the job concerned. *Marine resin* is a superior quality resin with high water resistance, high strength and good adhesion to wood and is the most suitable for fibreglass which will be exposed to water. It is used widely for marine work and also for swimming pools. Gelcoat resins are specially formulated to make tough resilient films and are designed to form the outer coating of a GRP moulding. If thicker resins are required, such as may be the case when laying up a vertical or overhead job, *thixotropic resins* are available which are merely a normal resin to which a thickener has been added. These resins rarely justify their special price since for the odd occasion when a thick resin is required, it can be made up by adding a suitable thickening agent to normal resin.

Catalyst

The catalyst or hardener used with polyester resin is usually provided with the resin but can be purchased separately. As a general rule, methyl ethyl ketone-peroxide is used in liquid form although other catalysts can be obtained in paste or powder form. The addition of the catalyst to the resin immediately commences the curing action. Setting takes place in four stages:

1 *Pot life*—during which the resin/catalyst mixture remains in a workable liquid form although it may begin to thicken.

2 *Gel time*—during which the resin becomes 'rubbery'.

3 *Hardening time*—during which the rubbery feeling gives way to firm, hard cured GRP, and the moulding can be removed from its mould.

4 *Curing time*—during which the finished GRP continues to gain hardness and stability.

Pot life and gel time are governed by the amount of catalyst and the temperature. The higher the air temperature or the greater the proportion of catalyst added to the resin, the faster the GRP will set. Under normal conditions pot life can be as little as 15 to 20 minutes and gel time even less, but apart from the variables of the temperature and catalyst, different products may also vary in this way. Hardening time can vary also, depending on the size and thickness of the moulding as well as the air temperature. With a small moulding and reasonably warm temperatures hardening time may be an hour or even less. With a large moulding it may be twelve or twenty-four hours before the moulding is hard enough to be removed from the mould.

Curing time is all important if any likelihood of sagging or other distortion is to be avoided, and therefore it is always better to err on the side of over-curing rather than under-curing. The curing time can also vary according to the use for which the moulding is intended. For normal applications, curing time can be a few days if the moulding is stored in a warm, dry atmosphere. Where the product is to be used for such items as water tanks, which must have a good chemical resistance, the GRP must be extremely stable and a curing period of as much as one month may be necessary.

Releasing agents

When a mould is made it must be finished to a high degree of polish if the resultant moulding is to have a high quality finish. In order to release the moulding from the mould when the job is finished a release agent must be applied to the mould before the gelcoat is applied. The most common type of release agent is a wax polish of the type known as carnauba wax followed by a coating of polyvinyl alcohol. Wax on its own may be effective, but the risk of any sticking is best eliminated by covering the wax with PVA.

Pigments

Where colour is required a pigment is added to the gelcoat resin. The minimum amount of pigment should be mixed to achieve the required degree of colour as pigments tend to cause some deterioration in the properties of the resin. Ready prepared pigments can usually be obtained in the form of resin pastes. This is the best way to obtain them since the paste mixes readily with the gelcoat resin prior to application.

Dermatitis

The application of resin is a messy business and the use of disposable rubber gloves to prevent too much contact between resin and the skin is recommended. Similarly glass fibres can cause irritation in some skins so before commencing the job prepare yourself against the possibility of contact with either material.

Brushes

Two types of brushes are used when applying a resin to the mould: flat, soft bristle brushes are ideal for gelcoat application while stiff bristle brushes are more suitable for working the resin into the glass fibre layers. The flat brush can also be used for applying resin in quantity to the fibreglass, but the stiffer stipple brush or a roller is best, ensuring complete saturation of the fibres. Brushes can be cleaned in acetone or polyester solvent cleaner and can be left standing in them for some time if required. Water must never be used.

A flat brush to paint on the resin and a stipple brush to work it through the glass fibres cover most GRP jobs.

Rollers

Rollers are particularly important wherever a large area of GRP is to be laid up. They produce a better penetrating effect than brushes, which tend to lift the fibres a little. Rollers are also much faster and can cover large flat areas quickly before the resin begins to gel. As a general rule, metal or nylon washer-type rollers are considered best as these chop into the laid-up resin, grooving it to allow better saturation when the next application of resin is made. Rollers can be cleaned with the same material as brushes.

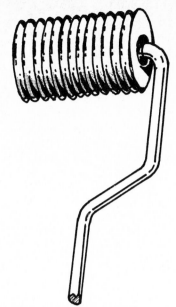

A washer roller makes quick work of saturating the cloth and drives out air bubbles.

Trimming tools

When the resin is firm but not hard set, scissors may be used to trim overlays or other unwanted areas. Once the resin has set, however, heavier equipment such as tin snips or hacksaws will be necessary to tidy up loose edges. Surface finishing is invariably done with wet and dry sandpaper used wet and rinsed off frequently. Initially 240 grade can be used but finer grades down to 600 should be used for final smoothing. The final showroom finish so attractive on a good fibreglass moulding can be achieved by polishing with a metal polish or polishing compound and finishing with a wax polish.

Laying up

Having cleaned and prepared the mould and applied the release agent, the first step in laying up a GRP unit is to select the materials required and prepare them prior to beginning the job. Once the resin is mixed with the catalyst things will happen fairly quickly, so it is important that all glass fibre mat or woven cloth is ready and all tools at hand to prevent delay and avoid the risk of the resin setting before it has been properly worked. The quantity of glass fibre should be measured and an extra few centimetres allowed around the edges to be on the safe side and allow for edge trimming. The number of layers for the moulding will depend on what product is to be made. The amount of resin required can be estimated as follows:

1 *Gelcoat*—2 oz per sq. ft. of surface area to be laid up.

2 *Resin*—this is best done on the basis of weight. Weigh the total amount of glass fibre to be used and estimate the corresponding weight of resin required on the basis of 30:70 glass:resin ratio for normal mat, increasing to around 50:50 glass:resin ratio for woven cloth. This is only a general estimate, but one widely used by professionals. The strength ratio can be increased by reducing the amount of resin but a better saturation will be achieved by using more resin providing it does not reduce the strength of the finished GRP.

Air temperature

The air temperature should not be below 10°C when laying up. Humidity is also important; the air should be as dry as possible since the moisture in a humid atmosphere will inhibit the setting.

The gelcoat

The gelcoat resin is first prepared by mixing with the required colour pigment paste. It is most important to thoroughly disperse the pigment through the gelcoat resin if you expect to get an even colour throughout the moulding. This will involve considerable stirring which in turn may create air bubbles. Any air bubbles must be removed before the resin is used or the finished product will be pockmarked with air-bubble cavities. When the catalyst has been applied to the resin and well mixed, the gelcoat should be brushed across the mould using a wide soft brush and *single sweeping strokes* in one direction only. It is important that a good layer of gelcoat is in place before laying up begins. If sufficient coverage is not achieved in the first painting, the gelcoat should be left to dry and a second coat applied later. No attempt should be made to paint over the first coat until it has hardened or the entire effect will be ruined.

Main body

When the gelcoat has hardened the process of laying up the main body of the GRP can begin. A coat of resin is painted over the gelcoat and the first layer of glass cloth or mat laid onto it. A stipple brush should now be used to dab the fibreglass cloth down into the resin. As soon as the reinforcing glass fibre is well set into the first

resin layer, a second layer of resin is painted over it and again worked in hard by dabbing with the stipple brush. At this point rollers may be brought in to assist in saturating the reinforcement with resin. An indication of saturation is that the fibreglass loses its white appearance and becomes transparent. White patches indicate that saturation has not taken place or that air bubbles are trapped beneath it. All air bubbles must be removed or cavities will result in the final product, thus weakening it.

If further layers of glass reinforcement are required, these are placed in turn on the first while the resin is still wet and another layer of resin applied over the top. Indeed, from this point on the laying up procedure is mere repetition until the required number of layers have been completely saturated. It is best to finish all the layers before setting starts to take place, as this will produce a more homogeneous moulding than laying successive layers after one has hardened.

The inside surface of the moulded product can be finished by the addition of surface tissue while the final layer is still wet. Alternatively, when the moulding has cured, the inside surface can be painted with a suitable sealer.

After an initial layer of resin beneath it, the CSM is thoroughly saturated using a dabbing action with the brush to force the liquid through the fibre.

Additional layers of mat thoroughly saturated with resin build up the GRP. Here CSM is being laid over woven cloth.

As the glass mat is saturated it becomes transparent. White areas indicate insufficient saturation or air bubbles.

Moulds

Fittings such as interior furniture (particularly iceboxes, lockers, tanks) can be made simply by GRP moulding. It is rare that fibreglass can be just built up to a suitable shape because of its wet and floppy nature before it cures. Once cured, of course, it is rigid and remains so. Thus any sizable fitting to be made in GRP must be laid up in a mould. The mould may be of male or female form, depending on which side is to be the smooth or finished side, this being the side in contact with the mould. If the exterior is to be smooth, as is the case with hull mouldings, then a female mould is used. Where the smooth surface is to be on the inside, as with basins, iceboxes and similar items, a male mould is used.

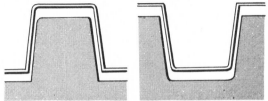

Male mould (left) and female mould.

Moulds can easily be made from almost any material, the only difficulty being in the shape itself. The shape of the mould must be faithful if the finished product is to be accurate, and the finish of the smooth side must be as near to perfect as possible.

Clay, plaster, wood, metal, even plasticine, can be used to make a mould. But without doubt the best material for making up a good rigid mould is fibreglass itself. Particularly is this the case with a female mould, in which case the process is two-staged, the first stage being a plug made to full size and the second a mould taken off this plug by laying up over it with GRP.

This is an ideal system where a repetition of the product is required or it is of fairly small size and

Fibreglass makes an excellent mould but must be reinforced to prevent it twisting out of shape.

simple shape. But cost is high using the female mould when only one or two fittings are moulded in it. A male mould is much cheaper and easier to construct, particularly where large objects are concerned. Bear in mind that many items in ordinary household use, such as buckets, can be pressed into service as a mould if they fit in terms of size and shape.

Where a large male mould is required—for example a large tank—it can be constructed from a number of materials, the shape being obtained firstly by the use of, say, a wooden framework overlaid with mesh or material and the finished shape achieved by use of plaster. The final coat of plaster must be smoothed out as much as

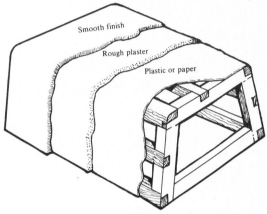

Male moulds can be built up and shaped from a number of different materials. Plaster is useful providing it is well smoothed back and sealed.

possible and finished to produce a uniform, smooth surface. Because plaster is porous it will require sealing before it can be used as a plug, and for this job cellulose fillers are probably the best, although any sealing type of varnish or shellac laid on in a number of coats will achieve the same result.

It is important when moulding large GRP fittings such as tanks to round the corners to avoid weaknesses. Also, where the fitting is to carry a considerable weight or be placed under any kind of stress, it should be reinforced with stiffeners constructed of timber, plywood, balsa or any other forming material overlaid with several coats of GRP during the lay up process. It is important that these stiffening or bracing pieces are well glassed into the main structure of the moulding.

21

'Potch' (fillers)

Because of the complex curves in a boat's hull there are many occasions when a fitting, no matter how carefully shaped, will not sit completely flush with the hull skin. Indeed, even the most astute tradesmen will allow that occasionally a gap must be filled. In some cases, particularly in fibreglass hulls, the bonding will cover any such irregularities and similarly slight errors in joinery or other structural work may be covered by the finishing panel. But often it is necessary to use some sort of filler, both from the point of view of appearance and also to prevent cavities which may later develop pockets of rot or moisture.

A typical example is when fitting the chain plates to a hull. If the chain plates are made up as a separate unit, then it will be very difficult, when fitting them in place, to flush them exactly against the hull skin.

In timber hulls they may be bolted down fairly tight to structural members, and in metal boats they may be welded into place, in which case the welding will cover any irregularity. But in fibreglass hulls there may be considerable gaps where the chain plates do not flush against the skin which must be filled before the chain plates are bonded in place. Apart from the finished appearance of the job, when the plates are bonded to the hull with an overlay of GRP filling is necessary to prevent resin running down through the gaps between the chain plates and the hull skin.

This is only one example, however; there are cases where gaps must be filled in all types of material. There are a number of patent fillers

Potch is simple to mix and can be used with almost any material. Its thickness can be controlled by the agent used in the resin.

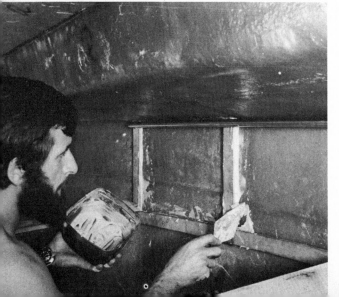

which range from (in the case of timber) plastic wood through to prepared epoxy fillers for fibreglass work. Epoxy metal fillers may also be used with metal craft, while ferro-cement hulls can usually be treated with resin paste compound. Always double check that the filler you use is adequate for the job.

Outside the patent brands, one widely used filler is a concoction sometimes known as *potch*. This is particularly useful for fibreglass hulls, but can be used on almost any material, and is more useful than most since its density can be varied by the use of different thickening materials. Basically, potch is simply a mixture of the normal polyester resin with a thickening compound. The best resin is gelcoat resin, although almost any resin will do.

In order to make a thixotropic paste the resin is mixed with plaster of paris or sand or some similar material. Plaster of paris is probably the easiest to use and is excellent for most fitting out purposes where a fairly thick filler is required. Sand or other coarse materials can be used where a larger area has to be filled and a composite of thicker consistency is required. In all cases, of course, the thickness of the final potch can be controlled by the amount of thickening material added. In the case of plaster of paris, it is simply mixed with the resin to the required consistency and then the catalyst added as normal. It goes without saying that the life of the potch is limited by the amount of catalyst used, but this will be obvious from experience or from the manufacturer's instructions.

While the plaster of paris/resin mixture makes the best potch for general purpose work in filling cavities in the interior of a boat being fitted out, the sand/resin mixture is also quite commonly used, particularly in the early stages of fitting out when a ballast keel or some similar large area is being filled. A sand/resin mixture is often used to level off the surface of the lead ingots or other ballast material dropped into the keel of a yacht prior to glassing in the whole keel section. Providing the surfaces are clean, potch will adhere to most materials and fill unwanted cavities in most parts of a boat's hull. Since its pot life is limited it must be used fairly quickly, but can be mixed in small portions prior to use if the filling work is liable to be slow.

Potch can be finished like any resin surface by sanding back flush with surrounding surfaces. It is often better, however, to secure a filling in place by sealing over the potch with fibreglass, in which case perfect adhesion can be obtained between the filler and the surrounding surface. Potch can also be used to temporarily hold fittings in place while they are being aligned correctly. This is particularly useful when making difficult templates or fitting difficult items into awkward corners. A few touches of potch around the edges will hold either the template or the fitting in place.

METALS

Metals used for fitting out can be divided into two categories—those employed for fittings, and those for fastenings. The latter are dealt with separately in Chapter 3.

Metal fittings may range from large, heavy-duty winches of stainless steel to the aluminium alloy framing around a window or brass catches on a locker door. Whatever the fitting, two basic factors must be borne in mind: that the metal used is strong enough for the job, and that as far as possible it is free from the effects of corrosion.

Corrosion may be caused by a number of factors, but the end result is the same: wastage of the metal. The two common forms found in small craft are rusting and electrolytic corrosion.

Rust

Rust is the oxide of iron formed in the presence of oxygen and water, and is thus confined to the ferrous metals, of which steel is the most common. One approach to the problem is to avoid using mild steel fittings wherever possible, and there is now a wide variety in acceptable grades of stainless steel. But given care, mild steel can be effectively galvanised, and where the fitting is not subject to abrasion or friction, the protective coating will last for upwards of ten years. The advent of epoxy-based paints has also favoured a

The step of this aluminium mast was of a different metal. Corrosion has set in and eaten away the alloy. Insulation would have prevented this.

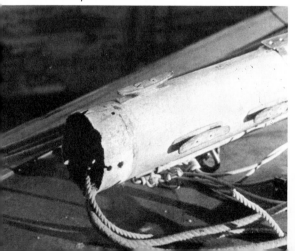

return to this less expensive metal, and where the newly galvanised surface of the fitting is treated with one of these products it should be possible to completely inhibit corrosion from rust.

It is worth mentioning here that, cost apart, a further reason for choosing mild steel, and in certain cases wrought iron, is strength. These metals do not have the chromium and nickel of the stainless alloys, additives which in certain cases can induce a degree of brittleness. The incidence of fractured stainless steel fittings may in fact be fairly small, and certainly less than that for the equivalent drawn steel wire, but for items such as chainplates, stanchions, pulpits and the like, galvanised and epoxy-painted mild steel can be as strong and corrosion-proof as its stainless cousin, albeit a fraction less smart.

Electrolytic corrosion

This is a form of corrosion which takes place when two dissimilar metals come into electrical contact and are immersed in an electrolyte. If that sounds too technical, let us take the practical example of a brass winch, bolted to an aluminium mast. The electrical contact is made where the two dissimilar metals touch and all that is needed to start the corrosive action is an electrolyte. This is provided by salt water, either as spray or as salt-laden moist atmosphere. An electric current which runs between the two dissimilar metals is immediately set up, causing one to waste away.

The process is most simply illustrated by the standard school physics laboratory experiment demonstrating the first stages in the making of a battery. A container filled with an electrolyte (acid) has two rods lowered into it, one of copper and one of zinc. If these two rods are joined by a piece of wire to create electrical contact an electric current immediately begins to flow through the acid from the zinc (anode) rod to the copper (cathode) rod. After a period of time the zinc rod begins to waste and eventually disintegrates altogether. This is what happens when any dissimilar metals are in contact on a boat.

The metals most prone to this sort of corrosion are alloys such as aluminium and brass which are low in the galvanic series and become anodic in the presence of more noble metals such as steel, and particularly its stainless alloys. In our basic cell you'll note we use copper and zinc, respectively noble and base metals at opposite ends of

23

the galvanic series, and it is this *difference* which in the presence of an electrolyte causes a current to flow. By the same reasoning, therefore, where metals are the same or near neighbours in the galvanic series there will be no current flow, and therefore no corrosion.

Here then is the first clue to prevention—the use of similar metals; but while in theory this would be fine, in practice it can rarely be carried out. The first line of defence is therefore to prevent the formation of an electrical circuit between dissimilar metals by insulating them from one another. Heavy fibre gaskets and Tufnol are common materials for this. The second line of defence, normally used on the underwater hull, is to attach a small piece of base metal which we *know* will corrode; in other words, it will always be the anode in our electrical circuit. This is the familiar sacrificial zinc anode.

CANVAS

Cotton canvas is rarely used for boat work these days. Apart from its vulnerability to rot, it is heavy and hard to work and easily stained. Modern canvases are usually made of some synthetic material such as nylon cloth impregnated with plastic. These materials are more durable, less likely to rot, and can be worked more easily than traditional canvas, and in addition can be obtained in a range of colours.

There are many uses for synthetic canvases, particularly in terms of covering material for

Awnings and covers are best made from synthetic canvas if they are to withstand severe weather conditions.

deck fittings, for cockpit cushions and for awnings or covers. Indeed, synthetic canvases can be used for almost any type of covering except deck and cabin top sheathing where the traditional cotton canvas is still preferable. Bags for holding deck tools or, for that matter, sails are also commonly made of synthetic canvas as also are spray dodgers and any kind of screen which may be used to make life on board more comfortable.

FABRICS

A wide range of fabrics may be used in furnishing the interior of a boat. The choice of fabric is obviously a personal one since different boat owners have different preferences for curtains, cushion and bunk covers and so on. However, it is important to note that fabrics used for home furnishings may not be entirely suitable for use in a boat, particularly if they are liable to get wet, and more particularly if they are likely to be saturated with salt water. A good example is denim, without doubt one of the most versatile and useful materials available. However, denim stains badly when saturated with salt water and the stains are very hard to remove. For this reason it should not be used in a boat unless you can be certain that it will always remain dry.

The sort of fabric which is less vulnerable to water damage (nylon, terylene, etc.) is often not entirely suitable for furnishing purposes. Cotton and wool, which suit the interior of a boat far more, can be used providing they are not liable to be thoroughly saturated at frequent intervals. Minor water damage, as from spray coming down a hatchway, can be prevented by spraying these materials with synthetic water-repellant sprays which are readily available on the market. In fact, this is probably the best way to go about furnishing the inside of the boat—use the material of your choice and spray it thoroughly with water repellant before placing it in position on board. I have found from experience that wool fabrics when sprayed in this manner make ideal cushion and bunk covers and cotton can be used for curtains and similar purposes. Remember, however, that this only applies where water damage will be limited to light spray. Where the furnishings could be thoroughly soaked from time to time a water resistant material must be used. Vinyl will do the job, for it will withstand heavy saturation and will wipe dry quite easily. However, there is a problem even with vinyl

Fabric covers give a warm cosy look to the inside of a boat. They should be sprayed with water repellant before installation.

where it is used as covering for bunk mattresses or cushions, for although the vinyl will soon dry out the stitching may rot and the interior foam remain saturated and very difficult to dry out. There is really no answer to this problem except to ensure that the furnishings remain dry and if that is not possible they must be stowed away in plastic bags while the boat is at sea.

PERSPEX

Glass is one material that should never be on board a boat in *any* form. Shattered glass is extremely dangerous and almost impossible to completely remove. Even a tumbler broken by falling from a table can leave splinters of glass in the bilge or other areas where it is difficult, perhaps impossible, to remove them. As a result, for months afterwards your crew will be picking up splinters in their feet or in their fingers as they attempt to clean areas where the broken glass lies.

Perspex or other forms of non-shattering plastics are acceptable and are widely used on board boats. Windows, hatchways and other fittings as well as normal domestic utensils can be made of these materials and a wide range of items in both perspex and plastic is available at most boat chandlers. While plastics may not be acceptable in principle to boat owners who pride themselves on the appearance of their boats, a little searching will generally find fittings which are not only practical but also aesthetically acceptable.

Hatches and skylights made of perspex can be covered with aluminium or stainless steel grills to prevent the plastic being scratched.

However, toughened, armoured and other specially treated glasses are used in quality work, for hatches and windows especially. They do not craze, change colour or tend to get scratched. Obtaining such glass and having it properly cut and drilled may be somewhat difficult, and a better alternative is then presented by polycarbonate plastics such as Makrolon. These recently developed products are more readily worked with, and extremely tough if used in suitable thicknesses. And as far as external openings are concerned, actual failures are very often caused by poor installation or weak frames rather than by the glass or plastic breaking initially.

CHAPTER 3

The Basic Work

THERE ARE SEVERAL basic techniques, apart from correct tool-using procedures, which must be employed in fitting out a boat if the finished job is to be sound and able to withstand the working of the hull in a seaway.

Fastenings provide a typical example. A fitting fastened with screws may hold together without any signs of stress while the boat lies quietly to her mooring, but when she wracks in a seaway the screws will probably pull out and the fitting collapse. The appropriate fastening technique for such a fitting would probably have been bolting, unless it was a timber fitting, when it should have been jointed and glued as well as screwed.

Other techniques with which you should be familiar include making templates for difficult fitting pieces, bending timber into curved shapes, and setting up levels inside the hull, to name but a few. They are all basic procedures, but without them you will encounter great difficulties in fitting out the boat properly. They cannot all be described here, but the techniques most commonly encountered in fitting out a boat are included.

ATTACHMENT

The more commonly used methods of fastening fittings or landings to hull, deck or structural members of different types of craft are listed below.

Fibreglass hulls

1 *Bonding*—this method uses fibreglass tape or woven cloth impregnated with resin to bond the fitting or landing to the hull. Used mostly for lightweight fittings and furnishings, only occasionally suitable for fittings which will come under load.

2 *Bolting*—fittings which come under heavy load need to be through bolted. A wood or metal 'pad' is usually used to spread the stresses over the fibreglass skin.

3 *Pop riveting*—used mostly for fairly light fittings, again with a washer or plate backing.

4 *Screwing*—used occasionally instead of bolting, with a timber pad on the opposite side to give the screw 'bite'. Tap screws also sometimes used.

Timber hulls

1 *Bolting*—where possible, through bolting is the most secure means of fastening, particularly where fittings are liable to come under load. May need a metal pad on the opposite side to spread the load.

2 *Screwing*—suitable for lightweight fittings, particularly for interior work. Should not be used where there is any great movement or where the fittings come under load.

3 *Riveting (roving)*—used widely for securing planking, particularly in clinker construction. Copper nails are *roved* by placing a cap over the end and drawing up tight with a riveting action. Can take moderate loading.

4 *Nailing*—used also for fastening lightweight fittings. Copper nails must be *clenched* over at the end. Not really suitable for fitting-out work except where the finish will not be visible. Anchor nails are more secure.

5 *Gluing*—an excellent form of fastening for fittings, especially interior furnishings, joints, etc. Usually used in conjunction with screwing.

Steel hulls

1 *Welding*—the best general means of fastening steel to steel in boats. Used for all structural work and often for heavy duty interior work, particularly landings.

2 *Bolting*—mainly used for securing timber to steel structural members, particularly landings. Tap bolts may be used where through bolting is not possible.

Aluminium hulls

1 *Welding*—the most suitable form of fastening aluminium to aluminium, but requires special skill on the part of the operator.

2 *Bolting*—the easiest and best form for internal fittings but can lead to corrosion problems. Tap bolts may be used where through bolting is not possible.

3 *Tap screwing*—can be used for light fittings. Mainly confined to light interior work. Can create corrosion problems.

4 *Riveting*—any form of riveting is good for aluminium, the most common form for fitting out being pop-riveting. Not really suitable for fittings under heavy stress.

Ferrocement hulls

1 *Bolting*—as with fibreglass, this method is ideal for most fastening work provided a pad is used on the opposite side. Essential for fittings that will come under load.

2 *Welding*—sometimes used to secure brackets or landings to parts of the pipe construction of the hull.

3 *Epoxy-bonding*—if correctly done, the concrete breaks away before the resin or timber.

FITTINGS UNDER LOAD

One of the most important factors in securing a fitting is the amount of load that will stress the fastening. In some cases the load will be obvious and an estimate of the strength of the fastening easily determined—for example, sheet winches, secured through the deck or cockpit coaming. It does not require a very technical mind to be aware of the sort of stresses that will come on the winch, the deck and the fastenings when sheeting home a big genoa jib. The only fastening that could cope with such strain would be large diameter bolts, through fastened to a metal or timber pad. Other cases, however, may not be so obvious—the fastening of bulkheads to the hull skin, for example. Some boats wrack badly in a seaway, depending on their structural makeup. When this is the case considerable stresses will be put on the bulkhead fastenings, particularly in the corners, and there will be a certain amount of working around the edges also.

These are both extreme cases. Generally speaking a modest amount of common sense, together with a basic knowledge of the boat's construction and the sort of stresses the hull will encounter, will enable you to judge the sort of fastening to use. The following table offers a guide to the sort of fastening best suited to different types of fittings. The estimate of size and gauge of fastening will vary according to the size of the boat and the fitting.

Fitting	Fastening
Sheet winches	bolting
Engine beds	bolting, bonding (GRP), welding (metal)
Mast step	bolting, welding (metal)
Chain plates	bolting, bonding (GRP), welding (metal)
Hatch covers	bolting, screwing and gluing, jointing
Landings	screwing, bolting, bonding (GRP), welding (steel)
Rudder fittings	bolting, welding (metal)
Cleats	bolting
Navigation lights	screwing, bolting, pop riveting
Bunks	screwing (and gluing), bonding (GRP), jointing
Galley	screwing (and gluing), jointing
Toilets	bolting
Lights	screwing (pop riveting)
Shelves	screwing (and gluing), bonding (GRP), jointing
Bulkheads (timber)	screwing (and gluing), bonding (GRP)
Bulkheads (metal)	welding
Tanks	bonding (GRP), welding (metal)
Window frames (metal)	bolting (or pop riveting)

This random sample of typical fittings demonstrates that the fastenings may vary according to the material from which the hull is constructed as well as the size of the fitting. The examples indicate the sort of fittings which, because of their load factor, require heavy fastening and those which need only be secured with fairly light fastenings.

FASTENING TECHNIQUES

Through bolting

The most common form of through bolting is used when deck hardware fittings—winches or cleats—are secured to a deck or cabin top. Because these fittings will come under heavy stress the fastenings must be strong and secure, which means that they cannot be simply fastened into a few millimetres of deck. There must be some form of strengthening on the underside of the deck which will not only add strength to the fastening itself, but spread the load over as great an area as possible.

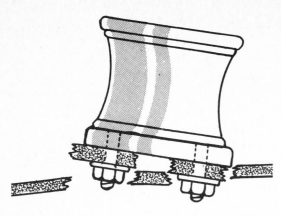

With only washers beneath the nuts the load is concentrated on small areas and the fastenings are likely to pull out.

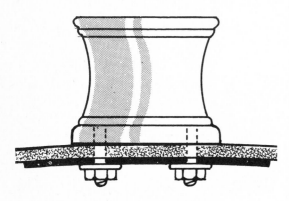

A metal pad spreads the load over a large surface area and, if secured properly, will withstand all stresses.

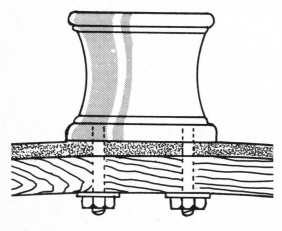

A deck beam or similar structural member is the ideal anchoring medium, spreading the load throughout the hull structure.

Imagine a winch, for example, secured through a cabin roof by four bolts. Perhaps each bolt has a washer beneath the nut to spread the load. For most of the time this might suffice but come a sudden heavy load the bolts will pull right through the cabin roof. Spread the load by securing the bolts through a wide metal plate and the cabin roof will pull off before the winch will go. This is the principle on which through bolting works, although the means of spreading the load may vary beyond metal plates. The important factor is the large surface area over which the load is spread.

Much depends on the construction of the boat. A timber boat will have far more structural members which can be used to support through bolting than will a fibreglass boat. A deck beam, for example, is ideal for this kind of work in a wooden boat since it not only provides a strong base through which to fasten the fitting, but spreads the load for a considerable distance across the boat's structure. Fibreglass boats, by contrast, have fewer structural members and consequently a greater need for artificial pads or plates to spread the load.

There are a number of ways in which strengthening can be done. The area in which a stress fitting is to be secured may be strengthened during manufacture. Particularly is this the case with fibreglass where it is quite common for winch mounts to be specially strengthened with heavy GRP layers during the moulding of the deck. Similarly, chain plates may have heavy reinforcing moulded into the hull or deck, often in the form of a metal plate integrated into the fibreglass construction.

But strengthening is usually carried out only where known heavy-duty fittings are to be mounted. If the location of strengthening does not suit your ideas on fitting out your boat, or if you decide to add other fittings in locations that have not been pre-reinforced, then the basic procedure of spreading the load must be followed. Thus, the most important part of a bolted fastening is the pad on the underside. This must be directly related to the stresses that will be placed on the fitting, and some idea of the strength factor required can be gauged from the fact that some shipwrights place a pad beneath every nut, even if it is secured through a structural member such as a beam.

Pads not only spread the load—which may be adequately done by the beam—but may also prevent the bolts being pulled into the beam

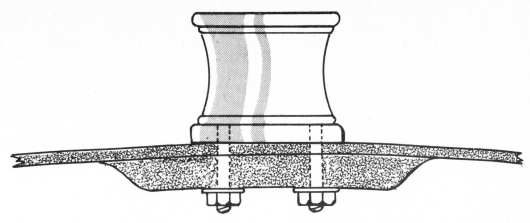

Thickened GRP can act as a load spreading pad, but must be tapered at the edges to prevent hot spots where the stress is transferred to the deck.

itself. Small diameter washers can easily be pulled into a timber or GRP beam, and large diameter washers can buckle under extreme loads, so a solid metal plate may be necessary to spread the strain over a larger area of the beam.

In determining the size of a suitable pad to withstand the pressures and spread the load it is always safer to err on the cautious side and select a heavier rather than a lighter plate. If the stresses are likely to be no more than moderate, a wide plywood pad may be sufficient. Fastenings designed to secure plate racks, lights, life buoys, instrument panels and similar lightweight gear fall into this category and there is rarely any need for metal plates to back this sort of fitting. But winches, cleats and sheeting tracks which will be subjected to heavy strains will need heavier solid timber pads or metal plates of good dimensions.

Tap bolting

It sometimes happens that through bolting is not possible since there is no access to the underside of the mounting surface and the nut cannot be

fitted to the bolt. A typical example of this is a mast, where fittings anywhere but adjacent to the open ends of the mast cannot be bolted since you cannot reach far enough into the tube to fit a nut. Short of through bolting right through the opposite side of the mast, the only alternative is to tap the bolts into the mast wall. This may not be strong enough for some fittings, such as tangs, where bolting right through the mast becomes essential, but for lighter fittings tap bolting is often satisfactory.

The holes for the bolts are drilled slightly under the bolt size and a high tensile steel tap the same size as the bolt is used to cut a thread into the hole. Where heavy metal such as thick steel is involved, a tapered tap must be used first to start cutting the thread, and the full-sized tap used to finish the cutting. The tap should be lubricated with oil, in the case of steel, and for aluminium the best lubricant is kerosene.

Any type of bolt may be used when tap bolting, providing, of course, it is compatible with the metal into which it is tapped. The most

A timber pad beneath a GRP deck. The edges of the pad should be chamfered and the corners rounded to prevent hot spots.

Threading drilled holes in an aluminium mast wall to accommodate bolts.

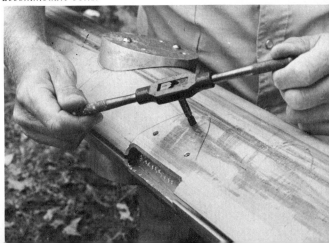

commonly used bolts are of stainless steel, but for tapping into mild steel, bolts of the same material can be used. The choice of bolts with hex or screw heads is optional.

Screwing

The secret of successful fastening with screws is matching the drill to the screw. Nothing makes for a weak fastening more than a screw which can wobble around in its drilled hole. The drill should always be fractionally smaller than the size of screw to be used when drilling the top piece of timber, and smaller again when drilling the lower piece of timber. This enables the threaded section of the screw to bite into the bottom timber and thus draw up the joint as tightly as possible. A countersinking bit widens the drill hole at the top to enable the screw head to be recessed.

Another secret of screwing is to ensure that the screwdriver matches the screw head. To drive home a screw firmly, good leverage is essential— this can never be obtained with a screwdriver that keeps slipping or jumping out of the screw head. The blade of the screwdriver should fit the slot in the screw head in terms of thickness and also in terms of width. A blade which is too narrow for the screw head will tend to burr the slot while one which is too wide will not permit the screw to be driven home hard.

Screws

Although interior fastenings are rarely subjected to weather or sea water, moisture is always

Drilling both top and bottom timbers to match the size and shape of the screw ensures a firm fastening.

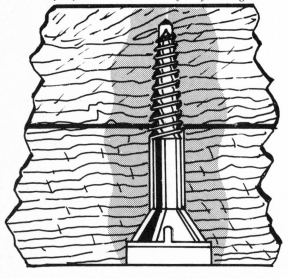

present. For this reason steel screws should never be used when fitting out a boat—not even galvanised screws—since over a period of time there is a tendency for a rusty 'bleed' to appear at the screw head which mars the appearance of the work. Nothing looks worse than streaks of rust either inside or outside the boat, so avoid steel screws regardless of the fact that they may be somewhat cheaper.

Brass and bronze are commonly used for screws used in fitting-out work although by far and away the best fastenings are stainless steel or monel screws. These are expensive, however, and except where considerable strength is required, do not justify the cost. Brass screws are not over strong and must never be used where they come into continuous contact with salt water (below the waterline) or they will corrode quickly.

Tap screwing

Tap screws are used widely with fibreglass and similar synthetic materials, but they may also be used with metals such as aluminium and fine gauge steel. However, with thicker metals, tap bolting is preferable, as described on page 29. The difference between tap bolting and tap screwing is, basically, that the tap screw cuts its own thread while tap bolting requires a thread to be cut before the bolt is inserted.

A drill matching the *core* diameter of the tap screws to be used must be chosen to drill the hole. The core diameter is slightly less than the diameter of the whole screw—including thread— and must be matched up very carefully. Since the thread is to cut into the surrounding material, too large a hole will not allow it to bite and the screw will pull out, while too small a hole will cause it to bind and the head of the screw will probably break off.

With the hole drilled, the screw is inserted and screwed home using a correct sized screwdriver (head shape). This is very important, for much greater stresses will be placed on the screw head as it cuts its own thread than would normally be the case. Particularly is this so with metals. Choice of the correct screwdriver will minimise the possibility of damage to the screw head or failure of the metal.

Tap screws are specially constructed to cut their own threads and ordinary screws cannot be used for this purpose. For boat work, stainless steel tap screws are best, particularly where they are used with other metals. If corrosion problems are likely to occur it may be necessary to use some other type of tap screws.

The dowels on the left are poorly matched with the colour of the timber, while those on the right will blend in when flushed off. But note how badly executed joinery will mar the effect of this detail finishing.

Dowelling

Where a good finish is required in timber which has been screwed or bolted, the head must be well countersunk and then covered with a dowel. Plastic filler will also do the job, but the finish will not be as attractive. A matched dowel plug, with the wood grain aligned with that of the surrounding surface, offers a superb finish to a job fastened by bolts or screws and is standard practice where quality timber is used.

The screw or bolt is countersunk to a depth of at least 5 mm and a matching dowel cut from an identical piece of timber, fitted to the hole and glued into position. The grain of the dowel should be aligned with that of the surrounding timber and all dowels must be aligned before the glue sets. When the glue has cured the protruding dowel is planed off flush with the surrounding surface and finished by hand sanding.

Glues

As with most synthetic materials, the composition of glues changes almost daily as new formulae with better adhesion and easier application are introduced. In a book of this type it would be virtually impossible to indicate one particular type of glue as being superior since by the time the book hits the stands a better type may have been produced. Sufficient at this stage to discuss the types of glues generally available, their qualities and their use.

The glues used for bonding two surfaces—usually timber—together are the ones most used when fitting out. Other glues can be used for such work as caulking decks but this work is more of a maintenance nature and although described in the section on laying decks, glues of this type are of no concern when adhesion is required.

Urea formaldehyde is perhaps the best all round glue at a reasonable price. Phenol and resorcinol formaldehyde glues are supposed to be stronger but are also more expensive. Since strength is not as important in fitting out as in, say, hull construction, urea formaldehyde is most widely used for this work.

Synthetic resin glues are usually supplied in two-pack form and must be mixed just prior to application. Because of the variety of commercial formulae available it is not possible to generalise on instructions for mixing them and each manufacturer's instructions should be followed closely. It is important to point out here, however, the need for accuracy in mixing the two packs, particularly if only small quantities are mixed at a time. The effectiveness of the glue will be controlled by the accuracy of mixing and if needs be small scales should be used (for powder) or a pipette or similar measuring device for liquids.

Once mixed the glue must be used quickly as it will tend to harden from the moment the two packs are joined. Most glues have a pot life of something around 8-12 hours under normal temperatures; this may be increased by placing the glue in the refrigerator. The fresh mix is preferable and small quantities, carefully measured, are better than a total mix retained for the extent of a long gluing job.

Conversely, heat can speed up the curing process and a temperature of around 30°C can reduce the pot life of a glue to less than an hour. This factor can be used to advantage in speeding up the curing process where a fast job is required and many workshops use heat curing. This is not usually possible for the amateur handyman, particularly on the interior of a boat, but since these glues cure perfectly under normal room temperature there is no problem providing the temperature does not drop below, say, 15°C.

Under normal temperature conditions resin glues may take a week to reach their maximum bonding strength and therefore clamps should be left on as long as possible. Where there is no great stress on the bond the glue will probably have cured sufficiently in 24 hours to allow the removal of the clamps. Screwing is an excellent method of holding a glued bond together and, indeed, gluing and screwing is probably the most widely used form of joinery on board yachts and similar boats.

The procedure for gluing is simple providing the surfaces to be joined are clean and free of grease, oil or dirt. Timbers such as teak, which may have an oily surface, should be cleaned with trichloroethylene and all timber should be dry with a moisture content not greater than 12 per cent. The surfaces should not be too smooth, as a 'key' for the bonding makes for better adhesion—slight roughing with sandpaper may be necessary on very smooth timber to give the glue something to bite on.

A palette knife or squeegee is ideal for spreading the glue evenly across both surfaces to be joined, after which they should be left for a short while to enable the glue to penetrate the timber fibres and create a better bond. The two surfaces should then be placed together and clamped under pressure for the required time. Be careful not to apply too much pressure or the glue will be squeezed out but, by the same token, there must be sufficient to ensure that the two faces are firmly joined together.

While it is important to lay on sufficient glue to ooze from the joint this must be cleared off before the glue sets or it will need sanding to remove it.

Clamping

G-clamps are the ideal means of clamping together two glued surfaces. However, it is important to note that clamping can, and probably will, mark the surface of the timber. If, as is the case with much fitting-out work, the surface is to be visible later the clamp marks will show up and spoil the appearance of the work. In this case plywood pads must be used between the clamp and the timber surface to spread the load and prevent surface damage.

When the glued surfaces are clamped together, timber pads must be used to protect the surfaces from gouging by the clamp jaws.

Nailing

Nails are not widely used in fitting out other than for light trim or for areas which will be concealed when the work is finished. This is due mainly to the fact that as the boat works in a seaway fastenings that have nothing more than nails holding them in place can work loose. Unless the nails are clenched or roved, or are a special anchor type, they do not offer as secure a grip as screws or bolts.

Clenching the nail simply means driving it completely through the join and then turning over the tip by means of hammering. The final touch can be added by means of a punch which will drive the nail shank back into the timber.

Roving is really a form of riveting in which a copper nail is burred back over a special rove in much the same way as an iron rivet is secured. Because the copper nail is soft a hole must be drilled before it can be driven home. The shank protrudes well beyond the joined timbers when the head is driven flush with the top surface and a matching rove is inserted over this protruding shank. The nail is then cut off a few millimetres above the rove and the whole unit riveted fast by placing a 'dolly' under the nail head and tapping down the remainder of the shank until it is flushed over the rove.

Anchor nails are ideal for boat work. They have a serrated circumference for much of their length which enables the nail to grip firmly in the timber. Indeed, once they are well embedded in a join, it is virtually impossible to remove these nails without severely damaging the surrounding timber. They may be of a number of different metals, phosphor bronze, monel and stainless steel being the most common, and while they are more expensive than galvanised iron nails their cost is more than justified where a tight join is required.

Countersinking of nails can be achieved by tapping the head with a ball head hammer or a punch. However, care must be taken not to damage the surrounding surfaces.

Extracting nails that have gone wrong or for some other reason need to be removed is easily done with a claw hammer. However, in prising the nail loose care must be taken not to damage the surrounding timber surface, especially if it is to be painted or varnished later. A small plywood pad inserted beneath the hammer head will prevent damage and at the same time offer better leverage for extracting the nail.

Riveting

There are two principal methods of riveting—standard hammered riveting and the easier pop riveting. Both have their uses, pop riveting being confined mainly to fastenings that will not experience too high a stress factor. For the most part both forms are confined to securing metal to metal, although this is by no means their sole use.

With the toughness of modern synthetics it is quite common for light fittings to be pop riveted into place on fibreglass boats.

Hammered riveting is mostly used when a great deal of stress is to come on the fastenings. Winch brackets, for example, may be riveted in this way, as may any deck plates which are to take fittings that will come under heavy load. However, in modern boats this type of riveting is rarely used since the convenience and ease of pop rivets makes them a more popular choice, particularly with amateurs.

Hand riveting employs the use of cold rivets, usually of aluminium, and an exactly matching drill. Unless the rivets are tight in the drilled hole the fastening may move under stress and the rivets will shear. With the holes drilled the rivets are tapped into place after first being dipped in a zinc chromate solution. A flat anvil or dolly is placed under the rivet head and the shank hammered back on itself with a ball head hammer.

If a watertight join is required the rivets should be countersunk at both ends and a sealer of epoxy resin placed in the countersunk recess before hammering the rivet closed. The diameter of the rivet should not be less than the thickness of the join and where two plates are joined the rivets should be not less than two diameters from the edge of the plate.

Pop riveting is an easy process using a special tool and specially manufactured rivets. The

Whatever the type of rivetting, the secret lies in careful matching of rivet to the drilled hole.

Pop rivetting requires a special tool but is quick and effective with fittings that will not be heavily stressed.

rivets are usually of aluminium or monel and encompass a stainless steel pin, the head of which is balled to prevent it being pulled through the hollow rivet. As with all forms of drilling, the hole drilled to take a pop rivet must be the exact size of the rivet or working will take place and the rivet may shear. The great advantage of pop riveting over the standard method is that no dolly is required on the opposite side and thus fittings can be fastened to virtually any object regardless of whether or not the opposite side is accessible. Securing fittings to an aluminium mast is a classic example.

The fitting is placed in position and the rivet inserted with the pin outwards. Some form of epoxy resin should be used if the join is to be watertight. The pop riveting gun is then placed over the pin, securing it in a matching nipple. When pressure is applied the pin is drawn into the hollow rivet, the ball end forcing the rivet outwards and securing the join. The pin snaps off when the action is completed. Because of the pressure required, particularly with large-sized rivets, there are a number of different types of pop riveting tools available and it is advisable to check carefully the size of rivets to be used on a fitting-out job before purchasing the riveter.

Welding

Although aluminium welding requires sophisticated equipment and greater expertise, steel welding is a simpler process and more easily learned. Courses in welding are available from technical colleges and companies concerned with welding materials, and are suitable for amateurs. Equipment for arc welding has been simplified in recent years and now home welding units which plug into the household circuit are obtainable at quite reasonable cost. For this reason we shall deal only with steel welding in this book.

Probably there will be only little call for welding in fitting out the average boat. Particularly is this the case if her hull is of timber, fibreglass or concrete construction. Most handymen prefer to eliminate the need for welding equipment altogether in these cases and have the odd requirement made up in a factory or professional workshop. Fitting out a steel hull, however, will probably justify the purchase or hire of a welder since attachment of landings to the hull may require the use of such equipment.

There are a number of different methods of welding two pieces of steel together, the most common—and the one dealt with here—being arc welding. The electrodes used should be carefully selected not only to suit the thickness of the metal to be welded but also to suit the composition of the metal. A table of sizes is available with most instructions concerning welding and the correct electrode selected from this table. A general purpose electrode which can be used in many different positions should be chosen rather than one which requires a special welding angle.

The electrode is fitted into the handle and the correct current selected on the welding machine. The amount of current is controlled by the size of the electrode and, again, a table is usually provided with welding equipment to guide the uninitiated in these matters. Excessive current will cause overheating and spattering of the weld. Insufficient current will make the weld hard to work and the arc hard to strike.

Striking is the action of getting the arc started and is achieved by tapping the surface of the metal with the electrode. A scratching action may be necessary to remove surface dirt and make a good electrical contact but care must be taken not to allow the arc to fire with the electrode in long contact with the surface of the metal or it will stick to the weld. Tapping is the best way to prevent this. If the surface is covered with any material, such as paint, it must be wire brushed to bare a patch of metal so that the arc can fire. Once welding is under way, however, the heat of the arc usually takes care of any dirty or overpainted surfaces.

Good welding is an art and a considerable amount of practice is necessary before starting work or damage may result. A correct shield, to protect eyes from glare and the face from spattered metal, is essential and in any case permits the operator to see how the weld is progressing. A slow, even progression along the join, allowing the weld to form a level or slightly convex surface, is the ideal to aim for. Since much of the welding in fitting out will be concerned with only light fittings, spot welding may be used quite frequently. Where stress comes upon a welded join, however, full welding along the seam will be necessary.

The Basic Weld Joints

1 *Fillet weld*—the most common weld joint used in fitting out, this is the means of securing two pieces of metal at an angle. The angle is determined and the metal clamped into place to hold it while the touching edges are welded. Landings for interior furniture and all forms of fittings can be easily made by this method when working on a steel hull.

2 *Butt weld*—in this joint two pieces of metal are joined end to end. The butts may have parallel faces or be shaped into a V, the latter being

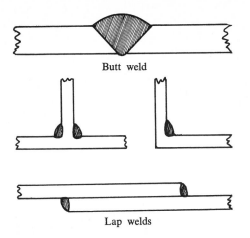

Butt weld

Lap welds

used only in heavy gauge plate. The plates are located with their ends slightly apart (about half the width of the plates) and clamped into position. Welding should be done on both sides unless a backing plate is used behind the weld and left in position afterwards.

3 *Lap joint weld*—as its name denotes this is a joint which requires the two plates to be joined to overlap. When in this position the ends are welded on both sides of the joint.

Soldering

Unlike welding, soldering is a low-temperature process which does not fuse the joint between two metals; a compatible alloy—the solder—is melted between them and forms the join. As such, solder is suitable for many types of light engineering work, and since copper and brass are good conductors of heat these are the metals with which it is most frequently employed. To produce a sound joint the work must be at the flow point of solder, hence the need for good heat conductivity, and since copper and brass are frequently used in electrical and pipe work this is where it finds its greatest use.

The solder and heat are applied to the job with a soldering iron, which normally has a solid copper bit to retain heat, while the source of heat may be a gas flame, or the iron may have an integral electrical element. Where soldered fittings for piping are concerned, however, the pipe run will tend to conduct heat away from the job at a rate greater than can be maintained by an iron, and here heat is normally applied direct to the pipe adjacent to the joint with a portable propane or butane torch.

The essence of good soldering is cleanliness and the prevention of oxidisation at the joint, and for this a flux is necessary. For electrical work the flux is normally included as a core in the strip of solder, while for structural jobs it is usually applied separately. Other aids to cleanliness are a fine file and emery cloth with which the job and the iron can be cleaned up before work begins.

To make a joint the solder is first applied as a thin surface coating to the separate items to be joined, a process known as tinning. At the same time a similar thin coating is also applied to the iron. Heat the iron, apply a drop of flux, followed immediately with a dab of solder which should flow smoothly over the copper point. Now repeat the process on each half of the job, heating with the iron, or if necessary with the gas torch, applying a drop of flux, and then a dab with the solder so that it flows nicely over the area to be joined.

The join may now be formed by bringing the two surfaces together and heating them *both* to the melting point of solder. This is sometimes the tricky bit, and if one half is too cool a 'dry' joint results—you can tell if it easily breaks.

Bending

It is sometimes necessary to bend lengths of steel or timber to fit a required shape. In the case of steel this can be achieved either by heating or by the use of pipe bending machines of the type used by plumbers. Timber, however, is not as easy to bend and depending on the degree of bending required and the type of timber involved one of two methods can be used—steaming or laminating.

Steaming

Where the timber to be bent is required to remain in its original form—that is, it cannot be cut or laminated—then it must be steamed before it can be bent to shape. The steaming process is one of the oldest boatbuilding practices still in existence and consists simply of immersing the timber in a steam (or hot water) bath until it becomes pliable and can be bent to shape. Hot water can be used if the piece is relatively small, but where long lengths are to be bent steaming is more common.

The simplest basic method of steaming timber, particularly if there is only the odd piece to be steamed, is to make up a steaming tube from a piece of downpipe. One end is closed off, the piping half filled with water, and the timber to be bent inserted into it. The whole unit is then placed at an angle over a fire so that the water boils, creating a steam tube around the timber

Severe curves will cause splitting of the timber or excessive strain on the fastenings unless the timber is steamed into shape.

which should, after a while, saturate it sufficiently to make it pliable. If the timber is required to retain its curved shape and is not to be fastened directly into position a 'mould' must be made around which it can be bent and clamped to harden. There will still be a tendency for it to spring back to its original form, and steaming is not always the most satisfactory method unless the bent timber can be secured in position in the boat while it is still in a pliable state. Where the shape of the curve is to be retained without support, laminating is a more satisfactory method.

As with all boatbuilding techniques, steaming will require quite a lot of patience plus a certain amount of trial and error to attain the right degree of bend. The amount of steaming required will vary from timber to timber and this is where the trial and error part comes in. To attempt to bend too early will risk breaking the timber, and therefore it is better to err on the side of over-steaming rather than under. The best type of mould is one that is pegged or nailed out on the floor or on a board to accept the curve of the timber between rows of nails or pegs. Once again, a certain amount of trial and error will be necessary to obtain the shape required.

Laminating

Laminating timber has a twofold purpose— shaping and strengthening. To this could be added a third—beautifying, for attractively laminated timber fittings can enhance the appearance of a boat considerably. A combination of dark and blonde timbers laid up in a lamination can make a most attractive addition to the interior (or exterior) decoration of any craft and is widely used for this purpose—a laminated tiller is a practical example.

The main use for laminating is to bend or shape timber into difficult angles without losing strength. Hence its appearance in such areas as beam knees, deck beams and floors. The lamination adds greatly to the strength of the timber, as witness the strength of marine plywood which is a lamination of thin timber sheets.

Thin strips of wood must be used for laminating or there will be a risk of fracture when bending them into shape. If it is necessary to use thicker timber for some reason or another then the strips will probably have to be steamed to shape before the lamination can be commenced.

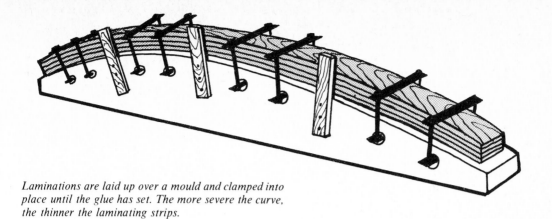

Laminations are laid up over a mould and clamped into place until the glue has set. The more severe the curve, the thinner the laminating strips.

The average thickness of laminations for general fitting-out work would be in the region of 3 mm to 5 mm. If the bending is not severe thicker strips may be used and, similarly, if a severe curve is required the thinner the timber strips the better.

A good waterproof marine glue is required plus a number of G-clamps. A mould must be made up to the shape of the required lamination and this is usually done in the workshop rather than on the job itself. Because the curve in fittings such as deck beams may be difficult to obtain by template it will be necessary to scale up the plans (unless they are lofted) so that a mould can be made. Laminated deck beams are ideal for yachts where there is considerable camber in the deck as they not only offer good shape, with relative ease of construction, but excellent strength in an area where it is badly needed.

The timber strips must be clear grained, with the grain running along the length. The first strip is placed in position on the mould and a thin layer of glue applied to its surface and also to the surface of the next strip. The two strips are then clamped in position and time allowed for the glue to cure. The process is repeated until the required thickness of lamination has built up, when the whole piece is clamped up tight and allowed further extended gluing time.

Apart from its strength, laminating can enhance the appearance of a fitting by careful choice of timbers. This is an ideal method of building a tiller.

Once finished the laminated timber will remain in shape regardless of the conditions under which it is placed. Unlike other methods of bending timber there is no likelihood of a good lamination springing back to its original shape. Indeed it would be impossible to physically bend it out of its laminated shape. Hence the strength factor of this type of work.

When the glue has thoroughly cured the fitting can be planed and sanded to shape like any other piece of timber and then finished to suit the area in which it is to be fitted. While it can be painted if so desired, the attractive appearance of a neatly laminated section usually calls for a clear finish with varnish or shellac. This, of course, is a matter of personal preference.

The uses of laminated sections are unlimited. Wherever timber is required, but particularly where strength or appearance is also a requisite, this method is undoubtedly the best. Almost any curves can be formed, even reverse curves if required. And the process is simple yet strong and effective and most types of timber can be used with it. Needless to say it is an equally effective method of making a straight section and this is often done where appearance calls for the attractive finish of laminated timber, but for the most part it is the sweeping lines of a curved lamination, as well as its strength, that make it most popular in fitting out a boat.

JOINTS AND JOINTING

The basic method of joining two pieces of timber is to nail, screw or glue them together. If they are fastened together at right angles, as is mostly the case when fitting furniture or similar pieces of equipment in a boat, then the join is termed a *butt*

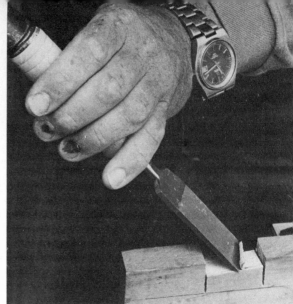

Careful jointing, gluing and screwing makes for an extremely strong framework. Basic joints will need to be adapted for difficult corners such as these.

The success of a joint depends on close fitting. Great care must be taken when marking up, sawing and chiselling as a loose joint will not glue or screw tight.

joint. The weakness in this form of jointing is obvious. Regardless of how well the joint is made, eventually the stresses which fall upon it will cause it to break up. If it is glued and screwed and the timber is fairly thick it may have a reasonable chance of holding together, but generally butt joints are not used other than for simple basic work such as making a box, and even then are used only if the joint is not intended to be permanent.

There are a number of different types of joint which are stronger and more suitable for permanent work, although probably most are only a development of the basic butt joint. There is no room in a book such as this to detail all the various joints, but I have included the more basic ones commonly used for boat furniture and similar onboard uses.

Chisels, together with the tenon saw, are the most important tools used for jointing. The fastenings may be of any type—nails, screws or glue—but more commonly joints are glued with screws used for additional strength. However, here again there is no set pattern and much depends on the individual item that is being constructed.

Before setting out to build an item of furniture in the boat, a great deal of preparation should be done in order to speed up the work and reduce the possibility of errors. Assuming at the outset that you have chosen the timber and designed the unit on paper with appropriate measurements,

then the first step is to start marking up.

First mark the pieces of wood to length. Knife lines should be used in preference to pencil as these make good guidelines for the saw. Any reference marks made with the pencil should be made on the outside surface as they will then be visible throughout the entire procedure. Do not saw the wood to length too early. If the first joint is not successful there may be sufficient timber remaining to cut another without affecting the original dimensions. When the wood has been cut to size then the joints must be marked. It is a good idea to hatch in the waste areas of the joint with a pencil before starting to cut, for if you remove the wrong part you will wreck the piece of timber completely.

The housing or rebate for a lap joint should be made by using the tenon saw blade flat along the surface of the timber and exactly vertical to it and sawing carefully along the knife mark to the required depth. The waste is then chipped away carefully with a chisel. It goes without saying that care in chipping away the waste will ensure a firm joint with faces touching as much as possible.

Now fit the joints together using either a hammer and a block of wood or a clamp to press them together. Do not glue or screw yet for all the joints will need to be cleaned up to·fit smoothly. When all the joints have been fitted and you are happy with the job, take them apart again and clean up the inside surfaces with a smoothing plane and glass paper. This will be the last time you will have a chance to adjust any misalignment, so ensure that not only do the joints fit tightly but that all surfaces are in good contact or the glue will be ineffective.

When gluing up each joint, use clamps to hold the timber in position but place small pads of waste timber under the clamp jaws to prevent them marking the work. Gluing is then carried out as described on page 31, which also describes the types of glues available and methods of gluing up joints for secure jointing. There are many types of joints, and we have space here for only a few, but the following are the principal joints used for shipboard work.

The half lap

There are many different types of half lap, the most common being the *corner half lap* where two pieces of timber are rebated together at right angles to form a secure joint. This is commonly used in all types of joinery, particularly for cupboards, benches, berths. A similar joint, not used at corners, is the *tee half lap*. This often joins together two structural members, such as the

tops or sides of berths, and can also be used to create door posts for cupboards or wardrobes. Yet another and even stronger half lap joint is the *cross half lap* which is probably the best joint of all in terms of strength but is a little more involved in the making. A *straight half lap*, not widely used, is somewhat akin to a scarf in which the butt ends of two pieces of timber are jointed together to make them one long piece.

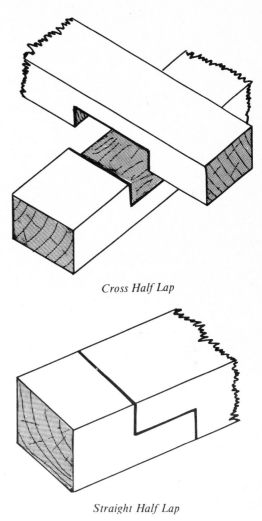

Cross Half Lap

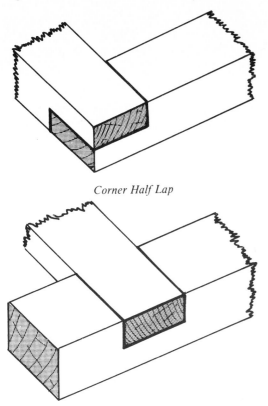

Corner Half Lap

Tee Half Lap

Straight Half Lap

The dovetail joint

The dovetail is perhaps one of the strongest of all corner joints and can be constructed in much the same way as a half lap. However, it is a quite difficult joint to make unless you are familiar with your tools and your jointing work for it requires the matching of angled pieces of timber. Single and double dovetails may be used, and in

39

some cases of strongly constructed box formations a number of dovetails may be involved in making the joint.

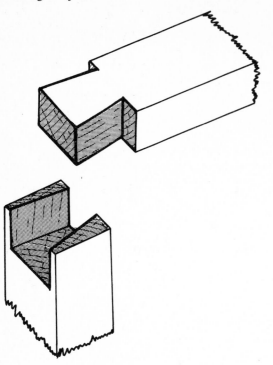

Single Dovetail

The *dovetail tee half lap* is similar to a normal tee half lap except that the rebated section is dovetailed. The wedge-action of the dovetail adds a great deal of strength and this is undoubtedly a joint to use where great strength is required and appearance is not so important.

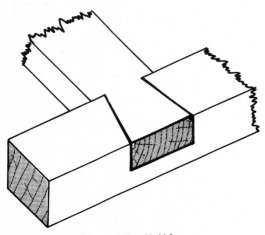

Dovetail Tee Half Lap

Mortice and tenon joint

The strongest of all joints is the mortice and tenon where a large surface area suitable for gluing is combined with the interlocking of the pieces. However, this is a difficult joint to make and requires chisels of the correct size and good sharpness as well as considerable expertise to ensure accurate cutting and close fitting of the joint.

There are two forms of mortice and tenon—one used for corners and the other elsewhere. The timber is divided approximately by three so that one third of the wood is taken away to allow the insertion of the tenon. The importance of fitting correctly so that all available surfaces are bearing together and thus glue firmly cannot be over emphasised. Unless all surfaces glue firmly together the joint will be weakened. Of the two, the *corner mortice and tenon*, or *bridle joint* as it is sometimes termed, is the easier to make and can be done wth relatively little experience.

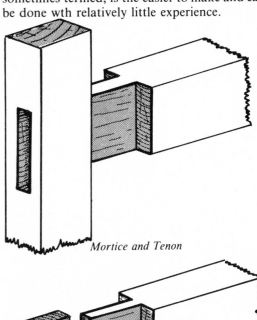

Mortice and Tenon

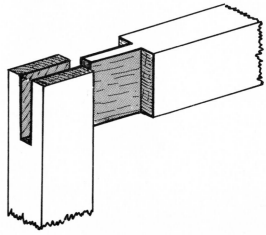

Bridle Joint

Mitre joint

This is an angle joint in which the butt end of each timber is cut to an angle half that of the finished angle of the joint. The two ends are then butted together and fastened and glued. To strengthen the joint, which is normally fairly weak, a tongue of timber or metal is often inserted into it.

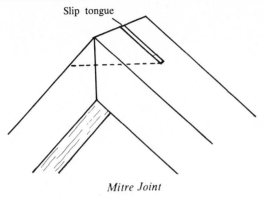

Mitre Joint

Box joints

The box joint is, as described earlier, a simple butt-ended joint in which two pieces of timber are brought together at right angles and secured. Although it is a fairly weak joint used only for temporary work, it can be improved by rebating one piece of timber and fitting the butt end of the other into it rather in the fashion of a sort of half lap. This offers more faces to glue together and a right-angled rebate to add strength. It is termed the *rebated joint* and is often used for work which will not receive overmuch stressing.

The strongest of all box joints is the *dado joint* which has rebates in both ends as illustrated. It is almost a combination of half lap and mortice and tenon in that the timber pieces fit into each other and there are many surfaces for gluing. However, it is not widely used since a half lap or mortice and tenon is more suitable for jointing.

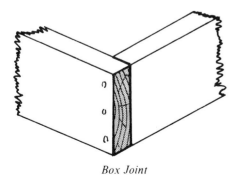

Box Joint

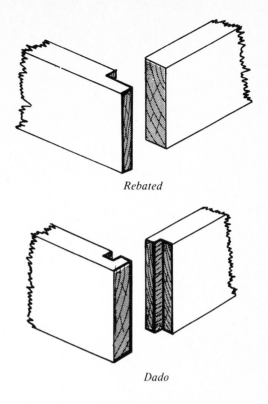

Rebated

Dado

SCARFING

Scarfing is used to overlap and join two pieces of timber at their ends, forming a very strong bond. It is mostly associated with long lengths of timber such as masts, toe rails and rubbing strakes. Where a length of timber has to be fitted and sufficient length cannot be purchased in one piece, a second piece will need to be scarfed on to obtain the required length.

The methods used vary from timber to timber and from purpose to purpose. For example, scarfing a piece of plywood would involve a different technique to scarfing a long toe rail of teak. For this reason, I will offer the basic formula for scarfing here which will need to be adapted for individual purposes.

The basic intention behind scarfing two butt ends of timber is to increase the surface area in contact and thus increase the fastening and gluing surfaces to obtain a better bond. Obviously, two right-angled butt ends of timber would be very difficult if not impossible to glue or fasten together. As soon as the timber was bent out of alignment the bond would break. So the surfaces of each butt are increased by angling the faces as much as possible.

41

The two butt ends are brought together and an acute angle marked on one by means of a sliding bevel. This angle is then transferred to the second piece of timber and both cut carefully so that the angled faces fit flush together. Sometimes the angle is right across the timber, sometimes small butts are left at each end of the cut. The important factor is that both faces meet exactly and flush together perfectly. A liberal coat of glue is applied to each face and the scarf clamped together firmly until the glue has cured and a good bond achieved.

Through bolting or screwing may be used to strengthen the scarf if it is likely to come under heavy stress. Bending is the greatest problem where a scarf is concerned and scarfed timber which has to be bent severely may require additional fastening.

The lipped scarf, pictured on the left, when bolted and glued should have a length of joint about six times the width of the timber, but this ratio will vary depending on the job. For masts and spars, for instance, where there may be no additional fastening, the ratio should be increased to at least 12:1, while planks and sheets of ply without fastenings are normally scarfed at an angle giving a ratio of 8:1. Where a scarfed length of timber is subject to bending, for instance in the fitting of a rubbing strake, the ratio of 12:1 can be usefully increased.

LANDINGS

Most interior fittings must be attached to some part of the hull and yet, for the most part, the interior of a boat shell is smooth and round. Exceptions to this are the interior of a wooden hull which has a fair number of structural members inside the skin and, to a lesser extent, steel and ferro-cement hulls which usually have at least a few stringers or cross members. In the case of a timber boat, of course, these structural members provide the ideal landings for interior fittings. Usually the only additional material required to provide a securing point for these fittings is in the form of spacers between the structural members or flat landing pieces to level out the curves in the hull.

Metal hulls have only a few structural beams

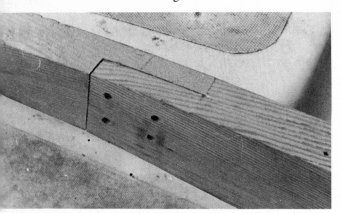

A typical short scarf. The basic method must be varied according to the type of timber being scarfed and the stresses it will encounter.

Landings may be in different forms. Here small angled landings glassed to the hull support the main framework of the lockers.

and stringers which can be used as landings and fibreglass hulls have even fewer, relying mostly on the longitudinal strength of the hull skin construction and the transverse strength of bulkheads for their structural makeup. In these cases some form of landing must either be attached to the hull skin or fitted between such structural members as are available to provide a base or platform onto which fittings can be mounted.

A landing can be literally of any shape or form or, for that matter, of any material. Internally, particularly in the case of furnishings, timber is the ideal material as it permits screwing (and gluing)—the easiest form of fastening—and is very easy to work. Externally, however, and in particular where securing a fitting that will be under stress, metal may be the most suitable material. In many cases both timber and metal may be necessary, depending both on the size of the fitting and the amount of stress it is likely to encounter.

Platform landings
The most common use for a landing is to provide a flat base onto which a fitting is fastened. Boats are literally curved in all directions and since almost all fittings come with a flat base, or at least a base which is unlikely to exactly fit the curve of the boat, a landing must be made on which to mount it. As mentioned, the versatility of timber in this regard places it well up on the list of suitable materials since it can not only be readily shaped to match the curve of the boat but if needs be can be laminated into all kinds of configurations in order to fit into difficult corners.

Take, as an example, the fitting of a bunk into the saloon of a round bilge yacht. The top and sides of the bunk, viewed in section, will be respectively horizontal and vertical. Yet there will not be one part of the boat's hull or structural construction which will be either vertical or horizontal or even, for that matter, at a consistent flat angle. The curve of the hull will create problems in securing the structural parts of the bunk no matter at what point they are fastened. Before the bunk itself can be fitted landings must be made which reduce the complex curve of the hull to basic horizontal and vertical planes.

Another example is that of fitting a sheet winch to the cockpit coaming. The coaming is usually curved and thus a flat landing must be

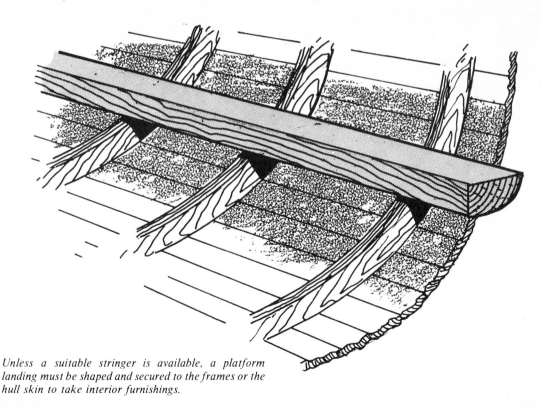

Unless a suitable stringer is available, a platform landing must be shaped and secured to the frames or the hull skin to take interior furnishings.

No matter what the fitting, a landing must be made to level the curves of the boat's construction and create a platform on which it can be landed.

fitted to match the base of the winch. In addition, the winch often has to be angled to provide a good lead to the sheet and thus the landing must be shaped to provide such an angle. Metals can be worked to produce landings of this kind but timber is an easier material and providing it has sufficient strength to cope with the stresses that may be experienced will generally be found to make the job simpler.

Such landings as these are known as platform landings for the obvious reason that they reduce the complex curves of the boat to a flat platform onto which a fitting can be easily mounted.

Interior landings

Because the interior of the yacht's hull is the most curved part of her anatomy, and because most internal furniture needs to be horizontally level, it is often necessary to fit platform landings through much of the internal area before any sort of fitting out can commence. Even structural members with square or rectangular section are rarely suitable for direct fastening as they are fitted to the boat's side at an angle, the acuteness of which depends on the exact location of the member.

A deck stringer, for example, may well lie in the vertical plane and therefore be suitable for fastening a fitting without need for a landing. The subsequent stringers down the side of the boat, however, will be at an increasingly greater angle to the vertical and thus quite unsuitable for any form of fastening where a horizontal plane is required.

It may, of course, be possible in a timber boat to level off the uppermost edge of the stringer to form a horizontally flat surface onto which fittings may be directly fastened. If the stringer is sufficiently heavy to permit this it is quite a good method and certainly an easy one. But planing often reduces the strength of the stringer and a more suitable method would be to build a platform landing onto the stringer, thus reducing its angle to the horizontal without reducing its strength.

A fairly simple way to form landings in a steel hull is to weld a horizontal flange onto the metal stringer or hull skin; in fact this is a widely used system. Failing this, however, platform landings of timber can be bolted to the metal stringer to provide a flat surface in the horizontal plane.

With GRP hulls the best method of forming landings is to shape a timber landing to the curve of the hull and then bond it into position with fibreglass. The horizontal top of the landing can be left free of glass if required for gluing, but if covered with the resin screwing is simply a case of drilling through to the timber.

Ferro-cement hulls create problems since often it is bad practice to drill into the plaster in order to secure a landing. In most cases landings or attachments for landings are built into the construction of the hull in the form of flanges or shelves to which fittings or landings can be attached.

Fibreglass boats are perhaps the easiest of all

A shaped landing glassed to the hull skin makes an excellent furniture base for GRP boats.

to fit with landings as this versatile material can be used to level almost any angle simply by moulding (often by hand) a horizontally flat surface onto or around the stringer. However, to make for easy fastening it is better to construct landings of timber, particularly for interior work, and in this case fibreglass is used to bond the timber landing to the hull or stringer.

CURVES AND CORNERS

There is an old saying among seamen that a carpenter is not a shipwright. This is an absolute fact and, indeed, it is more often than not very easy to detect by eye when a boat has been fitted out by a carpenter and not by a shipwright. The reason lies in the multitude of curves in a boat's hull, and the way in which fittings and furnishings must be matched to those curves if the result is to be accurate and strong. The interior fittings of a boat can add greatly to her structural strength and in fact are often an integral part of that structural strength. Curves which do not match leave gaps which allow movement and thus weaken the strength of that particular area.

Imagine a full bulkhead, for example, designed to add structural strength to the boat,

Every fitting must fit snugly to the shape of the hull or hot spots and areas of weakness will be created. This particularly applies to bulkheads and other fittings that fit into the curve of the hull.

resisting pressure on the hull from the outside, preventing wracking and twisting in a seaway and, in the case of a yacht, probably supporting the mast. It takes no great mental effort to imagine what would happen to that boat if the bulkhead were so badly fitted that it only touched the shell at certain spots. Enormous stresses would be put on these spots and other areas, being unsupported particularly if they were in some key position such as under the mast step, would allow the shell to buckle inwards. If the corners were badly fitted the whole hull would wrack and probably fatigue or collapse in a big seaway. An extreme example, but one nevertheless illustrating the need for extra care in making fittings such as bulkheads match the curve of the boat's lines.

Less dramatic examples would be careless matching of hatch covers or windows which would be a permanent source of leaking in bad weather as the seals would not meet the hull in a watertight joint. Or skin fittings which, because they were not correctly matched to the surrounding hull, allow leakage as the hull flexes in a seaway and squeezes out the sealing material.

So what it amounts to basically, then, is that any fitting, from a bulkhead to a porthole, must be accurately and correctly fitted into place to match the curves and contours of the surrounding hull to provide a strong, even bond. This will add strength, if needs be, or at least carry out its intended purpose and not distort or move out of position when the hull works in a seaway. Of course this is no mean feat. You have only to look at the complex curves in certain parts of a hull to understand the difficulty of making an accurate fitting. Curves of any kind are hard to measure and cut exactly, and when they are complex curves such as encountered in round bilge yachts then the problem becomes a very acute one.

Cutting templates
One way to overcome the problem is to measure as accurately as possible, cut the piece to be fitted a fraction oversize, and then gradually work it into place, filing and sanding the edges until an exact fit is obtained. There is nothing wrong with this method and, indeed, a certain amount of adjustment in terms of sanding and filing will probably always be required. But a simpler method is to first make patterns or templates.

These can be made initially from the boat's

plans, but if plans are unobtainable you will need to make up your templates from measurements on the boat. A flexible curve as used by naval architects is ideal for getting the shape of any curved surfaces and transferring them to the templates. Probably the best and most commonly used method is to cut the templates *in situ*. This is not always easy, but for the amateur it is often less tricky than other methods and if a mistake is made then only the template has to be recut and expensive timber or plywood used for the fitting is not spoiled.

The best example of the need for a good template comes with fitting a bulkhead. If the boat is a chine-type motor cruiser the problem is less acute as the sides of the bulkhead will probably be straight or only slightly curved. But even so getting the exact angles at the deck/hull join and the chine will be easier with a template than by measurement. If the bulkhead has to be fitted to, say, the forward section of a deep keel

Where awkward curves or large areas are involved, the template can be made up in sections and fastened together prior to cutting the final shape.

yacht, however, then the curves are going to be positively hair-raising and only a template will do the job with the required accuracy.

First approach to cutting a template is to mark up the hull or location where the fitting is to be placed. This must be done very accurately for the finished job will depend on the accuracy of the measurements at this stage. The material used for the template can be literally anything, but cardboard or masonite is probably as good as any. Where a big fitting such as a bulkhead is to

be cut the template will need to be fairly stiff to enable it to be fitted into place without bending. In some cases where a very large bulkhead or one with very complex curves is to be fitted the template may have to be cut in sections and joined.

This will also be the case if the boat is decked and the whole template, once shaped and cut, cannot be removed through the hatchways. When the template is made in sections it goes without saying that a great deal of care is necessary to ensure that all the sections fit together exactly. To eliminate the problems associated with fitting large bulkheads and other interior sections which may be long or of difficult shape, this work should preferably be carried out before the hull is decked in.

With the board template cut to approximate shape and size it is then fitted into the hull and adjusted with a plane or knife to the exact shape required. Absolute certainty can be obtained by securing the template in position with adhesive tape and examining the edges from both sides for exact fitting. At this point it may be expedient to mark any fastening points so that they may be drilled before the fitting is placed in position. This also applies to any rebates or holes to carry other fittings, wiring, etc. which should be cut while the bulkhead is in a convenient spot to work on easily and accurately.

What it all boils down to, basically, is that the template is simply a pattern, and in just the same way that a seamstress will cut her dress from a paper pattern, so you can cut your fitting pieces accurately from templates prior to putting them in place. This avoids all the problems of working

Templates are just like any other pattern. For light work they can be cut from paper or cardboard then taped onto a sheet of plywood for final cutting and shaping.

in difficult corners with hand tools, to say nothing of the expense and inconvenience of cutting incorrectly and thus wasting material.

Templates can be used for a number of different jobs when fitting out. A transparent sheet of paper placed over an area to be fastened can provide exact locations of drill holes. If a bracket of stainless steel or similar material has to be made up at a nearby workshop the business of trying to draw the bracket to exact measurements or endeavouring to explain to the dealer exactly what shape and size of bracket you require can be eliminated by using one or two templates, cut from cardboard to an exact fitting. Similarly, trying out any new idea can best be done by experimenting with cheap templates before settling on the final plan.

Templates are used by shipwrights in all facets of boatbuilding and fitting out, so it follows that if professionals find them useful amateurs who use them will reduce their problems a hundredfold and save themselves a lot of wasted time, effort and expense.

The stick-marker method

Sometimes, due to tight or awkward corners, it is very hard to shape even a template *in situ*. A method which overcomes this problem is one known as 'stick marking'. It requires only a large piece of plywood—say one metre square—and a long straight-edge batten which is pointed at one end.

Assuming you are cutting a bulkhead template, then the procedure is as follows: the plywood sheet is secured in the place of the bulkhead, close to the edge (one sheet will be used per side, of course). The batten is then placed across the ply so that its point touches the beginning of the difficult shaped area (say the carline). A pencil line is drawn along the edge of the batten on the ply and numbered. At the same time the point at which the batten crosses the edge of the ply is marked on the batten and similarly numbered.

The procedure is repeated any number of times around the edge of the hull, after which the plywood sheet is placed on the template material and the process reversed. When the batten is aligned along, say, position 1 pencil line and the mark on the batten aligns with the edge of the ply, the point of the batten is marked on the template. When all positions have been marked the template will carry a series of points indicating the exact shape of the difficult curved areas. These points are joined to outline the edge of the bulkhead, after which the template can be cut and checked into position.

STIFFENING

It frequently happens when fitting out a hull that an area needs to be strengthened or stiffened before a fitting can be mounted onto it. This is not related to spot stiffening directly behind the fitting but to a general strengthening of the whole area. A good example might be a foredeck onto which a windlass is to be fitted. While the immediate strengthening under the windlass may be sufficient to prevent it pulling out of the deck, the whole foredeck itself may buckle when the load comes on the windlass unless strengthening members are so located that the strains are correctly transmitted to the structural parts of the hull.

Bulkheads are also sometimes subject to this problem since they are not designed for heavy load on one particular area, and if a fitting is to be attached to the bulkhead which will create considerable stresses the whole area of the bulkhead must be strengthened in order to transmit those stresses to the structural makeup of the hull.

Probably fibreglass hulls are the most prone to this sort of problem since they have larger areas of skin—or deck—unsupported by structural stiffeners, and the material is very flexible. However, it is by no means unknown for all

Stiffening of timber sheets is usually achieved by fastening rigid structural pieces to them. Here the side decking of a hull has been stiffened by timber battens.

materials to suffer from this problem. Plywood in particular, because of its flexibility, often needs to be stiffened.

Stiffening of timber surfaces is done by using beams, frames or uprights of dimensions suitable to create a solid unit when fastened into position. Obviously, the exact dimensions will vary according to the stresses experienced and even more so in terms of the area to be stiffened. The shorter the stiffening timber the less its dimensions, although it is obviously better to use strengthening members too large rather than too small. A glance at the associated structural members in the hull will offer a guide as to the dimensions of the stiffeners.

A certain amount of stiffening will be achieved even if the members are not run right out and secured to structural members of the hull, but the ideal system is to have the stiffeners fastened to suitable structural members in the hull in order to transmit the stresses throughout as great an area of the hull as possible.

If the stiffeners are straight, the type of timber used is not over important, but if curved surfaces are to be stiffened or if the stiffener has to be curved to cover a specific area, then softwood must be used and steaming or laminating may be necessary. It is important never to butt the end of a stiffener against a hull skin or deck area as a stress spot will occur with possible damage to the skin when the boat is working in a seaway. If it is not possible to secure the end of the stiffener to a structural member of the hull a gap must be left between the butt end of the stiffener and the skin.

The material most prone to flexing is fibreglass. However, it is also the most easily stiffened since it does not require through fastening or welding, but simply a section of timber or of the fibreglass material itself. In some cases merely thickening the skin will solve the problem, particularly if the area is fairly small. But where larger surfaces need to be stiffened timber beams or formed GRP girder sections must be used to transmit the stresses right out to the hull.

The formation of a fibreglass girder can be done in a number of ways. It can be moulded in the workshop and bonded in place, or it can be built up in its exact location on the surface to be stiffened. It may be solid in the sense that it may be formed around timber or foam which is left in place, or it may be hollow, being formed around some other material which is later removed. It may be angular, U-shaped, semi-circular or

round. So versatile is this material that it can be built to literally any shape required.

Probably the most common is the enclosed U-girder (which is also known as the Top Hat section) as this offers considerable stiffening and also permits two edges to be bonded to the surface, thus creating a solid, stiff unit. And without doubt the best form of U-girder is one formed over a core of timber or foam which is left

The popular 'Top Hat' girder form is easily achieved using a timber stiffener glassed to the surface. Both timber and GRP girders add structural strength.

in place. Where the surface is level timber can be used, but where difficult corners are encountered, or curved surfaces have to be stiffened, the core material can be almost anything from strips of polyurethane foam to rope, rolled paper or metal strip. Polystyrene foam is not suitable as it reacts with the resin.

One of the easiest methods of forming the girder is to first stick the core material in place on the surface to be stiffened, then to build up layers of resin and mat to the required thickness. It goes without saying that the strength of the member comes from the GRP, not from the core (although some strength may come with a timber core), and therefore it must be built to a fairly heavy section and well bonded to the surface.

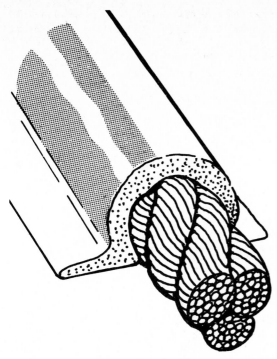

Almost any material can be used as the core of a formed GRP stiffener. Rope and rolled paper allow it to curve quite considerably.

The bonded area should be tapered out to avoid the stress spots that may occur if it is finished too sharply.

It is important when forming a GRP girder, particularly around a piece of timber, to reduce the angles as much as possible. The corners of the timber (or foam) must be planed down so that the fibreglass 'flows' over them and does not create a sharp angle. Much the same applies at the base where the material will form a 'soft' angle between the timber core and the hull skin. Fibreglass does not take kindly to forming right angles or any acute angles.

SETTING UP LEVELS

Building cupboards and wardrobes for a house is relatively simple because you can take your measurements and levels from the floor and walls, knowing they are all exactly horizontal or vertical as the case may be. Not so with a boat, for apart from the fact that the hull is curved in many directions, there is no guarantee that she is sitting level in her cradle or on her chocks and, if she is not, then using a spirit level is pointless.

Imagine the result of fitting furniture into a hull using a spirit level if the hull were listed to one side. When the hull is launched it will settle to its correct level in the water, leaving all the furniture leaning to one side!

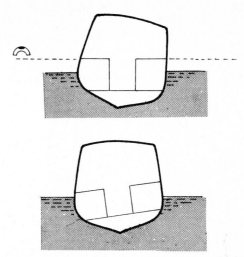

If the boat is not level when the furniture is installed the furniture will not be level when the boat floats on her normal waterline.

So the first and vitally important step in preparing to fit out a hull is to ensure that it is set dead level, both longitudinally and transversely, on its cradle. This can be achieved in a number of ways depending on the way in which the boat is set up. On dry land, for example, it is relatively easy to adjust the cradle or chocks until she is level. In the water it is more difficult, and worst of all is when the hull is sitting on an angled slipway or hard. A basic method for levelling the hull in each of these conditions follows.

In the water
With all the complex curves that exist in a boat's construction, finding a level is not easy. Indeed it is decidedly difficult, particularly if the boat is in the water during the fitting out operation. The slightest amount of list, hardly detectable to the eye, will render the spirit level useless, since the horizontal plane found by using this instrument will not be the horizontal plane of the boat's interior.

One method is to measure equal distances up each side of the boat on the inside of the hull from the keel and then set up a base level from which other levels can be obtained. But this is rarely satisfactory, and in any case only offers transverse levels. It is also sometimes suspect because of the possibility of irregularity of the surface in the keel if it has been filled with lead or some other ballast. And then again, although the sides of the boat *should* be symmetrical, errors can creep in during construction that may cause them to be slightly out of alignment.

A more satisfactory way of obtaining levels when the boat is in the water is to float her at her exact waterline (or at least parallel with it) as scribed into her hull. This is the level the designer has used in drawing the hull, so what better base to start from? It may mean shifting weights around and generally trimming the hull until she floats level with her waterline all round, but having achieved this, the scribed waterline can then be transferred to the inside of the hull and used as a base level.

Transferring the waterline can be done in a number of ways. If the hull is of GRP construction it will be translucent enough for the outside waterline (or water level) to be sighted from the inside and marked on the inside of the hull skin. With opaque hulls this method will not be possible and transverse and longitudinal levels will need to be constructed from planks. When the boat is floating *exactly* on her waterline these levels can be checked with a spirit level then secured into place as base levels.

Be careful when securing these levels, however, since your own body weight may affect the trim of the boat and if the planks are fastened into position when the boat is in trim other than her exact waterline all interior fittings will be out of alignment.

Failing either of these methods, the outside waterline must be transferred to the inside of the hull by careful measurement all round. This is a laborious task and difficult to do accurately unless the hull is open. Whatever the method used, a base level should be constructed not only as a reference point for other levels, but also to enable frequent checks to be made with the spirit level to ensure that the hull has not moved out of waterline trim.

On dry land

If the boat is ashore the problem, although tackled in the same way, is much easier to resolve. The boat must be mounted on her chocks or cradle in such a way that the waterline is exactly horizontal and she is plumbed into the vertical.

Chocking the boat to set her up level is not a difficult process, but it is worth spending some time to do it properly. An hour spent here ensuring that the levels are exactly right will make life a lot easier and the job a lot quicker as the work progresses. Being able to use a spirit level and plumb bob freely makes for fast accurate work. But when setting up the boat on her chocks ensure she is well secured so that as work is carried out and people trample around the hull she does not move out of the correct plumb position.

To ensure that the boat is level on her supports an open-ended water hose is used—preferably one that is transparent. The hose is first placed under the keel amidships and lined up on either

If the boat is not floating on her exact waterline, or parallel to it, the levels on board will be out of plumb.

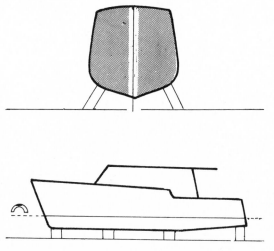

Using the plumb bob for thwartships levels and spirit level fore and aft makes light work of chocking her level.

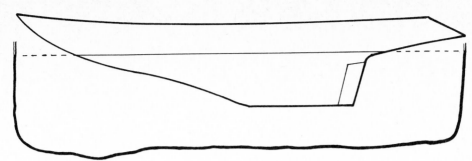

The water hose method of chocking the boat level.

side of the hull. Water is poured into the hose until it reaches the level of the scribed waterline on one side of the boat. If the boat is chocked level then the water level in the hose should also meet the scribed waterline on the other side of the boat. If not, the hull will need to be adjusted to port or starboard until the water levels in the hose align with the waterlines on either side.

The procedure is then repeated using the hose in a longitudinal direction under the keel from bow to stern. If adjustments to the trim are necessary they may upset the previously arranged transverse levels, so the whole procedure will need to be repeated until all levels have been checked and trimmed. When this has been achieved the hull is sitting dead level on her chocks.

With the boat levelled and secured on her chocks it is important to keep a check during the fitting out process to ensure that she does not move out of alignment. A plumb-bob hung over the bow and into a small bucket of water (to

dampen any swing) will immediately indicate if she has moved out of the vertical plane. Most shipwrights build base levels, both fore and aft and athwartships into the boat when she has been plumbed for use in working inside the boat and also to enable checks to be kept with the spirit level to ensure that she is constantly level.

Some hulls tend to move slightly during dry land storage, particularly those built of light material such as GRP. So that minor adjustments can be made without upsetting the chocking, small timber wedges, or adjustable

A plumb bob hung from the bow into a bucket of water ensures that any movement out of alignment is quickly spotted.

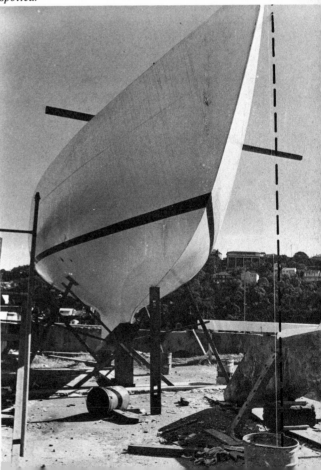

With the boat chocked level and well secured, and a good weatherproof cover over the hull, work can go ahead quickly and confidently.

If the boat is angled out of the horizontal on a hard, finding the levels can make fitting out a difficult task.

arms, may be fitted to the top of the chocks. If these are used they must be covered with canvas or some similar material to prevent scratching of the hull skin.

On an angled slipway

It sometimes happens, particularly on slipways, that the boat is lying with her bow up at an angle to the horizontal and there is no way she can be levelled to her waterline. This creates a big problem and the best solution is to try and avoid this situation at all costs. However, if it is unavoidable then the following procedure must be followed. (It is important to note that in a book for amateur shipwrights such as this the more complex methods of working are avoided for the sake of simplicity and to avoid confusion.

Thus the following explanation is reduced to as simple a format as possible.)

Firstly the boat must be checked to ensure that she is exactly upright on the cradle so that the athwartship levels are correct. Then, by means of a plumb bob, the angle between the true vertical and the verticals of the boat as she stands can be found. As the athwartships levels have been made horizontal, a straightedge or set-square placed at right angles to the plane of one of these, say the plane of the waterline, will represent the 'boat's vertical' as she stands. A plumb bob hung from the top of the set-square will show the angle between the two.

Now a piece of flat timber or plywood is cut in a right angled triangle format with the apex the vertical angle measured on the slipway. In order to obtain correct verticals when installing fittings such as bulkheads, the bulkhead is placed into roughly the exact position and the plumb bob hung from the centre of the top edge. The triangular piece of ply is then inserted between the top of the bulkhead and the plumb line, and the bulkhead adjusted until the angle between the plumb line and the bulkhead exactly matches that of the apex of the triangle.

There are, of course, many other more complex ways of determining levels in a boat. For the most part, however, these require not only expert shipwright knowledge but also the use of fairly specialised instruments. The methods described here are intended to be the simplest available for the inexperienced amateur shipwright with limited know-how and tools.

If the boat's waterline is actually parallel to the slipway, the angle of the slipway from the vertical may be simply applied to the bulkheads and other uprights.

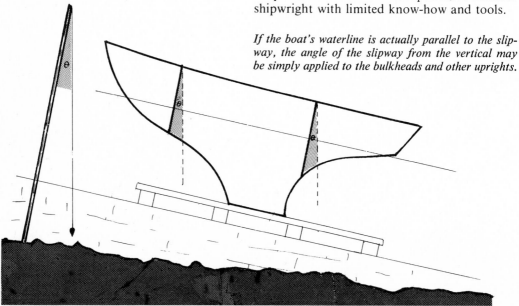

CHAPTER 4

Hull Fittings

BULKHEADS

BULKHEADS ARE PROBABLY the most important single structure in a boat's hull. They stiffen the tube shape of the hull to withstand both transverse and longitudinal stresses as well as counteracting the twisting action created by the yawing of the boat in following or quartering seas. Placed at intervals along the length of the hull they form a rigid structure capable of withstanding any strains the sea may impose.

In doing so, however, bulkheads divide the boat into a series of compartments which are not always compatible with comfortable interior accommodation. If the compartments are all virtually the same size you will have anomalies such as a bathroom as big as the main saloon, or an anchor locker as large as the motor compartment. So compromise is necessary in order to space the bulkheads to provide suitably sized compartments for comfortable living without prejudicing the structural strength of the hull.

There are other factors to be considered when fitting bulkheads. They may be used to compensate for areas such as cabin trunkways and hatches, where deck beams have been cut creating structural weaknesses. They may be used to provide structural strength where isolated areas of pressure exist, such as beneath the mast step. And they may, in some cases, be called upon to provide a watertight seal to prevent water getting into the hull if the skin is damaged.

It follows, then, that the first important step in placing bulkheads is to locate them where they will serve the required purpose both in terms of local areas and in the overall structure of the hull. Many boats have bulkheads already fitted during building. Or you may have the location of each bulkhead marked on the plans as required by the boat's designer. In both these cases the problem has been resolved, but if you have no fitted bulkheads and no plans, then you will need to sit down and carefully locate each bulkhead, bearing in mind the factors mentioned here.

Probably the best place to start is with the key bulkhead which, in the case of a yacht, will be the bulkhead that supports the mast, and in a motor yacht the bulkhead that separates the motor compartment from the rest of the boat. Since these bulkheads must be located in a specific position and cannot be anywhere else, there is no compromise with them

It is not always necessary to locate this bulkhead directly beneath the mast step. Indeed, many yachts either step their mast on the keel or provide a supporting spar beneath the mast step in lieu of the bulkhead. In these cases the bulkhead serves to close off the main saloon from the forward part of the boat and is not under such severe structural pressure as one supporting the mast. However, whether directly or indirectly, the main saloon bulkhead usually offers some support for the stresses of the mast via the cabin roof, and is a very important structural part of the boat.

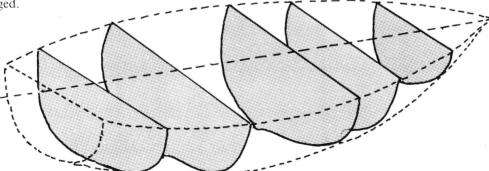

Bulkheads must be located in positions which allow conveniently sized compartments but which do not weaken the overall structure of the hull.

Carefully designed and shaped bulkheads can provide the required strength to the hull structure yet keep the interior open and comfortable for living purposes. Note the strong laminated capping around the aperture, giving added strength as well as pleasant appearance to the bulkhead.

When spacing bulkheads it is important to bear in mind that they are the most important part of the tube structure and thus must not be spaced too far apart. While it may be very pleasant to have a large main saloon, it will be pointless achieving this if, in the process, you weaken the hull. If bulkheads are widely spaced, some form of compensating structure must be fitted to reinforce the hull and this is both a difficult and often questionable exercise.

From the main bulkhead, whether it be beneath the mast or at the forward end of the motor compartment, the location of other bulkheads can be planned. Providing they are not too widely spaced, this becomes a matter of convenience in terms of interior accommodation. The location of heavy stress fittings on the deck, such as windlasses, may have a bearing, but other than this the location of each bulkhead will be determined by the size of the

A typical timber framework for a built bulkhead. Panelling can be fitted to one or both sides. Note how framework members are landed on structural hull members in order to spread the load.

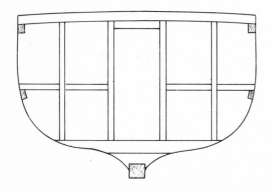

compartment it encloses.

Few pleasure craft fit watertight bulkheads, although some owners like a watertight 'collision' bulkhead right forward and a similar bulkhead closing off the lazarette, across the stern. Although the main intention of these originally may have been to prevent the main hull from flooding in the event of a collision—or pooping—which flooded the forward or after compartment, they are mostly used for stowing wet or dirty gear such as the anchor warp.

An anchor locker is standard in most craft and the sealed-off lazarette is quite a good idea, since it keeps the main bilges free of smelly water and the sort of dirty bits and pieces that tend to find their way into general purpose lockers. They can be self-draining as described on page 123 or fitted with a separate hand pump so that they can be cleaned and dried from time to time.

Built bulkheads

The simplest bulkhead is one cut from a single piece of plywood and fitted directly into the hull. If the deck has not been put on, this fitting is an easier task. But with a GRP hull and deck moulding the bulkheads should not be fixed before the deck, due to the flexibility of the two mouldings. They will both have to be flexed somewhat in order to accurately locate and fasten the hull/deck join, and if the bulkheads have been fitted first this will not be possible.

The framework will provide the basic structural form and the panelling can be of any type to suit the interior decor of the boat. The framework will need to be designed and built to take the structural stresses it will encounter, particularly where the bulkhead is located beneath a mast step or in some similar structurally important area. Usually a box framework is all that is required, of dimensions to suit the size of the boat and the stresses to be encountered. Such a framework makes the fitting of doorways easy and the sectioning of the bulkhead itself can be arranged to match the framework and conceal joins as much as possible. Obviously each join in the panelling must be landed on a part of the framework so that it can be correctly secured to make a solid homogeneous construction which will provide good structural strength.

Because the framework will bear the major stresses it is vitally important that the upright and horizontal members are correctly landed on and secured to structural members of the hull. In this way the stresses can be transmitted to the hull structure and not just to the skin. A vertical member of the framework simply landed on the bottom of the hull skin will create a 'hot spot' and penetrate the skin when the strains come onto it. Such verticals should be landed on floors or stringers while the horizontal members of the framework should be secured to stringers or landings across frames.

Bear in mind always that the hull structure must be bonded together as an integral whole if all parts are to bear an equal strain. Any member of the bulkhead structure not bonded into the whole to transmit its stresses throughout the boat will create a hot spot which will at least cause local damage and could at worst endanger the entire structure. It should require little ingenuity to devise landings which will disseminate all stresses throughout the hull structure. Jointing, with the joints glued and screwed, creates the best framework for this type of bulkhead.

With the framework in place the panels of the bulkhead can be readily fitted. The type of material used is not over important for although it should be strong enough to withstand any movement, the framework will absorb the greater stresses and transmit them to the hull. Where the decor of the cabin requires an attractive timber finish the choice can be made at this stage, although undoubtedly the most widely used material is plywood since it can be cut in large panels and the joins easily concealed. But narrow planks, attractively fitted, are suitable and can add character to the interior.

The question of panelling on both sides of the bulkhead framework is a personal one. Some boat owners prefer only to panel one side but, of course, much depends on the accommodation to be fitted to the reverse side. If a good finish is required both sides should be panelled. Again, this is something that offers scope for ingenuity. A bathroom will require laminex panelling or even tiling, in which case these materials can be used instead of the decorative timber finish used on the saloon side of the framework. Templates will be required to cut the panelling exactly to the required shapes.

The joins in the panelling can be concealed with beading or some similar decorative material and a timber trim or quad can be used round the circumference of the bulkhead to cover the join to the hull or deckhead and give the job a professional finish. Dimensions of materials

The framework of a cabin bulkhead on a motor yacht showing jointing of main members and cambered deckhead beam.

The same bulkhead from the other side showing panelling with window apertures cut and door in position.

used will, of course, vary according to the size of the boat.

One-piece bulkheads

If the deck is not in place a single-piece bulkhead is the easiest to install. A template must be cut to fit exactly and from it a single bulkhead cut from plywood and lowered into place. The thickness of the ply will be important and will obviously depend on the size and construction of the boat. As a rough guide, a yacht around 15 m overall length would need ply bulkheads of about 50 mm thickness.

Access through the bulkhead by way of a door can also be cut before it is placed in position. Bearing in mind that such an opening will reduce the strength of the bulkhead, the doorway should

Oval or elliptical doorways are the most suitable in terms of strength, but not always the most attractive. Combination of this type of access and standard doorways will usually cover most situations.

The bulkhead will often need to be fitted around hull members, such as the chine stringer and the side decking. A template is necessary both to locate these areas and also match the bulkhead to the curve of the hull.

be kept to a minimum. The elliptical shaped opening is most favoured as it allows a large area of uncut bulkhead both above and below the door, thus retaining much of the original strength, but where this is not suitable, such as in motor yachts, compensation in the form of structural framework may be necessary when cutting a larger doorway. Structural members such as those described for built bulkheads can be employed to strengthen the top and bottom of the doorway in cases such as this or in any areas where excess cutting of the bulkhead may lead to weakness. Bear in mind, again, that such members must not only be well secured to the bulkhead itself, but must be landed on and secured to structural parts of the hull.

Placing the bulkhead in position and securing it to create good structural strength can be done in a number of ways, depending mainly on the material of which the hull is constructed. In the case of a built timber boat the bulkhead should be secured at the hull side to a frame or similar vertical member and at the top and bottom to a deck beam and floor respectively. This may necessitate rebating the bulkhead to accommodate stringers and other structural members, a job which, if the template has been carefully cut, can be taken care of before the bulkhead is placed in position.

The bulkhead must always be secured at the top to a deck beam and to a floor at the bottom. If a rib does not happen to coincide with the bulkhead then a landing must be secured to the hull skin. The landing may be built from timber or the bulkhead may be bonded to the hull skin with fibreglass. Either way the bulkhead must be wholly secured to the shell of the boat at top, sides and bottom or it will not properly serve its structural purpose. Since timber bulkheads must be bolted or screwed to metal, hulls built of metal must have flanges or landings welded in place to secure the bulkheads if structural members are not already in the right location.

It goes without saying that the bulkhead must be fitted exactly plumb in the hull, a factor discussed on page 55 of this book together with the methods of achieving exact levels and verticals. This necessitates obtaining the exact location of the bulkhead before cutting the template and, as with all fitting-out work, much of the tedious work is involved with accurate preparation rather than the actual fitting.

Fibreglass hulls are probably the easiest to fit since bonding the bulkhead to the hull is a simple process and eliminates the need for landings and fastenings. The only danger, since the bulkhead is secured directly to the skin, is in creating hot spots where unevenness along the edge of the bulkhead will create uneven pressures on the GRP skin as the boat works. One way of avoiding this is to fit a thin layer of rubber or some flexible synthetic around the perimeter of the bulkhead prior to bonding in place.

The bonding-in of bulkheads, half-bulkheads and any major elements of interior furniture should be done so as to make a smooth transition from the narrow rigid area of the bonded-in piece to the larger and more flexible area of hull moulding. The first narrow strip of glassfibre should be followed by successively wider strips overlapping on both the hull and bulkhead surfaces. This is good practice for two reasons: first the narrow layers fill in the angle so that the wider ones put on later build up the tapered curve desirable for spreading localised stress; second, in the case of imperfect bonding of any layers, the others will have a chance to do the job. If the widest glassfibre strip is put on first, it is the only one in contact with the two pieces being joined, and any defect in that single layer means in effect total failure of the join.

Later in the job, the bulkhead can be finished off to suit the interior decor. Cut edges for the opening can be faced with wood or plastic edging, and any fibreglass bonding sanded and painted. If the glass strips have been neatly shaped and cut, and the work done tidily, the join will look acceptable, though generally it will be concealed by furniture. It is worth protecting the bulkhead surface with heavy paper until final finishing.

The structural function of the bulkheads in maintaining the vessel's shape means that they are one of the first items to be fitted to a bare hull, and must be strongly and securely fixed. The same can be said also for any floors, stringers or beams —the bones of the boat—and before any linings or interior fittings can be considered these must be in position. Moulded liners normally take this fact into account, and these and other types are dealt with on page 159.

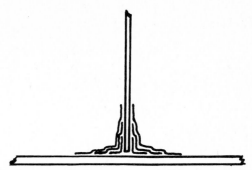

Bonding-in with glass, as for a bulkhead. Note that the first layers applied are narrow, and that each successive layer is in direct contact with the parts to be joined.

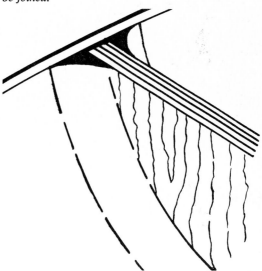

Tapering the GRP bond makes a neat finish to the fastening of the bulkhead as well as providing a strong fixture.

Where a hull is to be decked in timber, rather than with a moulding, the bulkheads may be fitted before the decking. Here a three-piece bulkhead has been bonded in with good wide GRP fillets.

FLOORS

The nautical floor is a reinforcing member in the bottom of a boat whose nearest household equivalent might be the beam. In a sailing boat with a ballast keel the weight of the keel subjects the skin of the boat to considerable stress which will tend to distort the shape of the hull. To counteract this the localised stress at the keel bolts must be evenly distributed into the structure, via members attached to that structure and also to the keel proper, the backbone of the boat.

As an identifiable component of the structure, the floor is most clearly seen in the hull of a heavily ballasted, deep-draft sailing cruiser of timber construction. There it sits athwart the keel, is probably bored for one of the keel bolts, and may be carried several feet out onto the topside planking. In steel and ferrocement construction, where the skin and framing are more substantial, its presence may be less obvious, and it is often a short steel brace between frames. But when we come to the moulded fibreglass hull, more than likely it has no floors or frames, although since a GRP laminate is certainly more homogenous than a skin of timber it is more effective in distributing stress.

GRP sailing hulls may be roughly divided between those with a deep moulded keel and those with a bolted-on external fin keel. In the former the ballast will often be cast to fit snugly within the keel moulding, and the moulding itself will be beefed up with additional laminates, perhaps rovings, to support it. But in addition there should also be fibreglass across the top of the

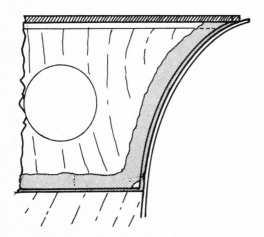

GRP yachts distort less than their timber ancestors, but a web floor in way of a ballast keel provides useful stiffening, as well as a basis for a cockpit sole.

keel casting of at least 6 oz/sq. ft, and carried a minimum of 6 in. up the sides of the keel moulding. In this way the ballast is secured, while the laminate forms a moulded U-shaped floor to maintain the shape of the hull. Within a deep hull web frames of marine ply may be added for further stiffening, as shown in the sketch, and they will also form a base for the cabin sole. Their large area in contact with the hull also more effectively distributes the loads placed on the sole, whereas if simple bearers are used their ends will need to be landed on a stringer bonded along the bilge.

Boats with a bolted-on keel need a strong matrix bonded in the shell, as a mounting for the keel bolts and to distribute the high localised stress which they present. This matrix, normally of high density polyester foam, can only be correctly incorporated during the original moulding process, and it should therefore be an integral part of the hull as supplied by the manufacturer. Foam frames will carry the stress from the immediate keel area out into the topsides, and there will be a heavy pressure pad in way of the keel on which to pull down the bolts.

Within the bottom of a motor boat hull the stress situation is clearly somewhat different from that in a sailing boat. The degree of strength will largely depend upon whether the boat is to be used at planing or displacement speeds, and in the latter case there may be no need for structural floors as such. More common are short bulkheads to the level of the cabin or cockpit sole, and while these give the hull skin a measure of extra rigidity, their prime function is to accept the sole and weight from above.

The bottom of a planing powerboat is normally stiffened fore and aft with stringers and/ or spray rails, and athwartships with short floors or bulkheads. In addition to the stiffening fore and aft, normally included during original moulding, there may also be a riser, or landing, bonded to the topside to give an all-round location and support for the sole.

The location of the short floors in general tends to be governed by the layout of the engine installation and accommodation. In boats of 30 ft. and less headroom is always at a premium, and it is not uncommon for the 'sole' of the central companionway to be the bottom of the boat. But like a sailing boat, a power boat should have a bilge, and here it is normal to take the main cabin bulkhead down to the hull skin in such a way as to completely seal off the engine space from the accommodation. The bulkhead thus forms an all-round stiffener within the hull, and where a forecabin bulkhead is similarly carried the full depth of the boat, there may be no stiffening other than the stringers and keel.

Aft of a motor boat's main bulkhead will often be the engine space, or with a centre cockpit it may well be amidships, but it is here under the engine that short floors will be of most use in dealing with the motor's torque and vibration. They should be linked with the bearers to form a matrix uniting the engine with the boat, a subject more fully discussed in Chapter 7.

One last point when installing floors is to leave provision for bilge water. Many motor cruisers confine this to the engine compartment, where a stern gland may leak, but a seagoing yacht may ship water other than through her bottom, and for this a bilge chamber should be provided beneath the after cabin from which she can be pumped clear. The line of the keel will usually allow water to drain aft, and so that it is not impeded limber holes must be provided in the bottom of the frames or floors.

CABIN SOLE

At this point the cabin sole can be cut and placed into position on the floors. The centre panels should be screwed but not glued in case it is necessary to remove them at some later date. Good firm planks or plywood, in the order of 20 mm minimum thickness, should be used to avoid warping, and they should be closely fitted with a finger hole at each end to facilitate lifting.

The actual makeup of the sole will vary with the individual boat since it must be cut to fit the shape of the hull and to accommodate any fittings which pass through to the floors. A mast stepped on the keel is one such fitting, as are motor casings and toilet mounts. Providing the interior of the hull is well decked, as it were, and one section can be removed for bilge access, the laying of the cabin sole is merely an exercise in your own ingenuity. The tighter and lower the sole is fitted the more space there will be in the cabin area.

Probably the most common system is to totally deck-in the sole right across the top of the floors, leaving only a central area between two fore and aft members open as an inspection area. Covers which match the surrounding sole are then fitted so that they can be lifted in sections for inspection of the bilge. These sections should be landed on the floors at whatever spacing is required so that access can be gained to bilge pumps, tank hoses or similar fittings located in the bilge area.

The basic arrangement of floors, deck beams and sole in a round bilge yacht. Access to the bilge is attained by removing central planks in the sole.

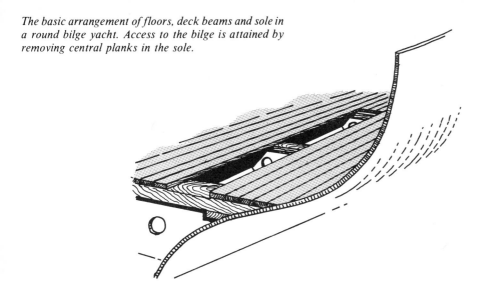

DECK BEAMS

While deck beams are really a part of the hull structure, and therefore not usually part of the fitting out process, some hulls, particularly those of moulded fibreglass, come without a deck. In any case, fitting out the interior of the boat is always easier if the hull is open, so many boat builders now leave the deck until the last when most of the major interior fitting out has been completed. For this reason, we shall include decking in as part of the fitting out process.

Of first importance in constructing a deck are the deck beams. These are the cross members which hold the sides of the hull apart as well as supporting the deck and its various fittings. They are an important part of the structural makeup of the hull and therefore must not only be strong in themselves, but well secured to the rest of the boat's structure. The landing to which the beams are secured at each side of the boat is a special longitudinal member, one of the most important in the hull structure, and generally known in small craft by the descriptive name of *beam shelf*.

The purpose of this longitudinal member is twofold. In running from stem to stern it provides a landing for the deck and at the same time provides one of the major fore and aft stiffening members which prevents the hull from bending when hogged or sagged on a wave. This member is an integral part of the hull structure and must be considered to be already in place before fitting out commences. Without it there would be no point to which the frames (in a timber hull) could be attached and in the case of fibreglass the hull skin would have nothing to hold it in shape. Beam shelves are usually laminated or made from a heavy piece of timber scarfed to provide full length strengthening from its attachment at the stem post right aft to a similar attachment at the transom.

The deck beams themselves are also often laminated, since this is not only one of the easiest methods of forming the curved shape required for the camber of the deck, but also provides the

Deck beams rebated into the bonded beam shelf of a GRP hull. But the beams should have been set with their widths vertical to correctly support the side deck.

necessary strength with minimum dimensions. This is an important factor since space inside the boat is at a premium and downward-projecting deck beams can reduce the headroom considerably. The beams may also be cut from timber baulks, in which case the curved shape can be obtained by cutting to shape. Where relatively lightweight beams are required, and also to form the ends of deck openings such as hatchways and cabin areas, this method of cutting a solid beam from one piece of timber is often employed.

In the case of steel and ferro-cement craft—and sometimes in other types of boats—steel angle frames are bent and welded into a framework onto which the deck can be laid. This, however, is uncommon in timber and fibreglass boats since laminated deck beams are often cheaper and easier to fit and offer a more attractive finish.

The technique for laminating is described on

Cross section of a typical boat hull in way of deck beam and shelf, showing major structural members.

Laid deck

Margin board

Rubbing strake

Deck beam

Beam shelf joint

Ply or GRP underlay

Beam shelf

Hull

page 36. A mould is made onto which the deck beams can be laid up and glued. Since the camber of the deck as well as the length of the beams will vary from stem to stern, individual moulds will need to be cut from templates for each beam. This may seem a somewhat arduous process, but often one mould shaped from a large piece of timber can be adjusted quite simply to form the shape of following beams once the first has been taken off. The shape of the beams can be taken from the plan if one is available, or will need to be obtained by fitting templates to each beam position in the hull and carefully shaping to the required curve.

Since flat decks are unheard of other than in very small craft, all deck beams will have some curve, at least on the top edge, in order to form the camber of the deck. The dimensions of the beams will naturally vary according to the size of the boat and the stresses likely to be placed on the deck. Certain beams, such as those at the

A strong steel deck structure made up principally from deck beams and diagonal straps. The latter add considerable strength to the normal deck structure.

forward and after end of deck openings, need to be especially strong. The same applies to beams onto which are secured heavily stressed fittings such as a windlass, samson post, mast step or mast partners.

Whatever the dimensions used, and whether they are obtained from the boat's plans or assessed on the job, it is important to remember that the deck structure is not just a means of making the boat watertight. It is also a vitally important part of the boat's structural makeup and undersized beams would create a weak link which may not show up until the boat is working

in heavy sea conditions. It is therefore always better to err on the safe side and make the deck beams too large rather than too small.

The best timber for deck beams is laminated spruce, which is both light and strong. However, most easily worked timbers, particularly pines, are suitable.

The beam ends can be landed on the shelf directly, or rebated, to make a snug fit. The shelf

Laminated deck beams (aft) *and a cut deck beam* (forward) *make up this heavily cambered section of foredeck. Either system is suitable, but laminations are more practical.*

should not be rebated or it may be weakened, although it is not uncommon practice in some yards to lightly rebate both shelf and beam. In order to carry the camber of the deck out flush to the hull skin it may be necessary to plane down the top of the beam shelf to flush with the deck beam. Gluing and through bolting with stainless steel bolts is the best system of securing deck beams to the shelf.

It goes without saying that all deck beams must be plumbed at right angles to the fore and aft centreline of the hull. Where the foredeck and other large areas are formed, fore and aft members are jointed into the beams to lock the whole structure into a solid unit.

BEAM KNEES

The wracking action of the hull places tremendous strain on the joint between the deck beam and shelf, and some kind of support is necessary to prevent movement which would break it apart. This is usually achieved by a beam knee which, in effect, fills the corner between the beam and the side of the hull. Beam knees may be constructed simply from a triangular piece of plywood or metal, secured along one edge to the deck beam and down the other to a frame or rib.

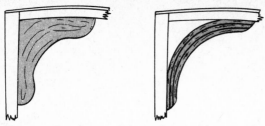

Two popular forms of beam knee with attractive appearance—grown knee and laminated knee.

However, since they often intrude into the cabin, knees can be made more attractive by using laminated or 'grown' timber. The laminated knees can easily be made up over a mould, but grown knees must be cut from a special piece of timber where the grain of the wood follows the curve of the knee. Without doubt the grown knees are the most attractive where the interior of the boat is to be stylishly finished with wood panelling or similar surfaces, but the easiest method, outside of the basic plywood triangle, is to form laminated knees (around a mould) which can be easily secured into position against the beam and the hull, and look most attractive when finished with a clear varnish.

Normally, particularly in timber craft, the knee is attached to the hull via a frame. In fibreglass hulls, where there are few if any frames, it will be necessary to distribute the stresses which will be carried by the knee across an area of the hull skin to prevent the formation of a hot spot. A layer of foam or some similar material must be placed between the knee and the hull skin, and the GRP bond tapered from the point of contact to distribute the load, as described for securing bulkheads into position.

Fibreglass knees can be formed around tubes of paper or shaped timber inserts as described on page 48. In this case the knees can be kept quite small and the load distributed more evenly across the hull skin. If it is easier they may even be formed *in situ*.

CARLINES

In order to complete the structural shell of the boat the deck beams and the deck should completely cover the upper surface. In practice this would make access to the hull very difficult so deck openings must be made to accommodate hatches and the deckhouse or cabin trunk. Where small hatches are concerned they may often be fitted between two beams, but where large hatches, and in particular where the cabin trunkway is fitted, many deck beams must be cut to allow sufficient space. In the case of a yacht, this may be restricted to relatively small areas, particularly in reverse sheer and high topside hulls, where most of the accommodation is below the main deck and only a small coachhouse is provided. But where there is a large coachhouse, and particularly on motor yachts where large cabin areas are involved, the deck beams must be cut for some considerable distance along the length of the deck to allow this accommodation area to be fitted.

When these beams are removed, compensation must be made so that the structural strength of the decking is not reduced, and the short beam sections that remain not made ineffective. In order to compensate for the transverse strength of the missing beams, the first and last beams are reinforced considerably, often to the extent of having a bulkhead placed against

Where deck beams are cut compensation must be made in the form of carlines (fore and aft) and bulkheads or heavy beams (thwartships), or the structural framework of the hull will be weakened.

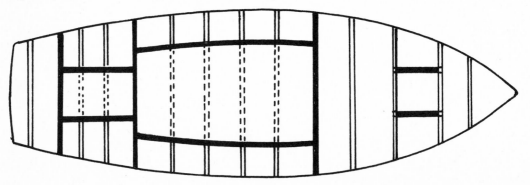

them, thus ensuring adequate strength to overcome the weakness of the deck opening.

To accommodate the cut ends of the deck beams and to form the sides of the coachhouse or cabin trunk, heavy fore and aft members are fitted into place which resemble in many ways the deck shelf on either side of the hull. These are termed *carlines* and are in effect a type of hatch coaming or longitudinal structural member into which the shortened deck beams are rebated. The carlines terminate in the reinforced deck beams or bulkheads at the forward and after end of the deck opening.

An interesting timber framework that may perhaps best be used to illustrate what not to do! The carlines should be of greater section for the size of cabin opening, while the side deck beams should be set with their widths vertical, and their housings must not cut across the beam shelf.

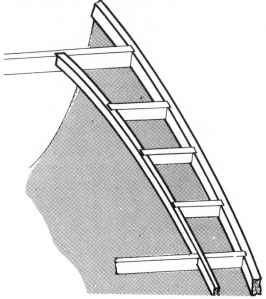

The correct framing for a side deck, with a carline laid between two full-width beams and deck beams set vertically, notched into housings in the carline and beamshelf.

Thus, despite the fact that a large area of deck including many of the deck beams has been cut away, compensation in both transverse and longitudinal directions is provided. At the same time support is given to the cut deck beams. Carlines are generally cut from one baulk of timber since they are usually straight or have only a little fore and aft bend, but they must have good depth in order to provide longitudinal strength. Where small hatches are concerned, carlines are merely filler pieces between two deck beams forming the hatch opening.

Where the carlines are very long, or where considerable bend is involved, they can be laminated as described on page 36. Indeed, where the deck area of any boat involves bends in one or more directions, laminating will be found to be the best method to use.

DECKS

The deck preserves the watertight integrity of the ship, and needs to be strong, light and waterproof. In a steel boat it will usually be made of light-gauge plate laid over a suitable framework of beams, and in the great majority of fibreglass boats it is a GRP moulding. But for the home builder the most popular choice is undoubtedly marine plywood. Today, the handsome teak laid deck is also almost invariably laid over a base of sheet ply, steel or GRP, while ply also lends itself to being sheathed with fibreglass, Cascover or the traditional canvas, as well as a number of proprietary coverings.

One of the major factors in favour of plywood as a decking material is the fact that large areas can be cut and fitted as one piece. Not only does this eliminate a great deal of work but it ensures a completely watertight deck no matter how severe a workload the boat may have to endure. And since one of the greatest problems with decks is keeping them watertight, this is indeed an asset. More often than not, other forms of decking which may be more attractive to the eye use plywood as an underlay to compensate for their own lack of watertightness.

A plywood deck can be laid on a hull of any construction and while the general trend is to keep deck and hull of similar material, particularly where fibreglass and metals are concerned, the ease of fitting and the versatility of plywood makes it prominent as a deck material for almost any craft, particularly home-

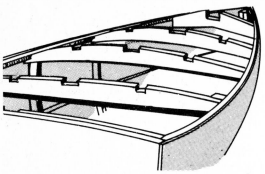

It may be necessary to rebate deck beams to carry fore and aft bearers in order to provide the deck with a firm structural base.

built or home-fitted boats. Its laminated strength adds to the structural tube form of the hull that is so vital if a boat is to be structurally sound under all sea conditions, and its cost is competitive when compared with other materials.

Of first importance, of course, is the selection of the right plywood. While top quality, treated marine grade plywood should be used for any fittings on a boat, one can get away with slightly lower grades when fitting interior furniture and fittings which will not come in direct contact with water or heavy use. But since a deck is immersed for much of its working life, and has to withstand stresses and wear and tear that will rarely be encountered by other areas, only the top grade plywood can be used if problems at a later stage are to be avoided.

There are, naturally, some disadvantages in using plywood for decking. One is the thinness of the laminates. In heavy working use, and also from exposure to all weathers, the top veneer can be quickly worn through or damaged; while this will not affect the structural strength of the material it will nevertheless look most unsightly.

By covering the plywood with a more durable material such as fibreglass or treated canvas this problem can usually be avoided.

Assuming that the carlines, the deck beams and bearers have been fitted as described earlier, they must now all be faired off to take the plywood deck flush onto their upper surfaces. Good contact between the structural members and the deck makes for a very strong whole structure and since the deck is a vital part of the hull construction, strength is important if wracking and similar problems are to be avoided.

The fairing-off process is, as much as anything, a case of trial and error. Because of the camber of the deck it is not an easy job and may require a number of attempts before a flush seating for the deck sheet is obtained. The shelf must be slightly bevelled to match the camber of the deck beams as the deck is carried right out to the hull skin. Inter-costal pieces such as bearers must be similarly faired, as also must the carlines. Even the deck beams themselves may need slight planing to match the camber and sheer.

When the section of decking to be fitted has been initially cut it can be lightly nailed into position on either shelf and then the fitting of beams and bearers examined from the inside of the hull. Bad fitting can usually be spotted immediately, but if the interior is getting dark due to the placement of the deck, a torch held on the opposite side of a deck beam will show up any gaps between the top surface of the beam and the decking. The deck is then removed, the errors rectified and the whole process repeated until a first class flush fit is obtained.

Ply sheets must be cut to butt on structural members in order to make the joins waterproof and firm. Where deck beams or bearers are not available, intercostal members must be fitted on which to land the butt join.

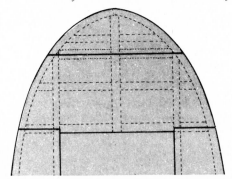

The plywood panels should be tacked lightly in place until all fairing off has been completed, then glued and screwed onto the beam and bearers.

To prevent possible damage to the actual ply sheet to be fitted, a template of a lighter gauge piece of ply may be used as a substitute. While this may seem a somewhat extravagant way of going about the process, the plywood template can always be used for other templates or interior fittings at a later stage. To ensure that fitting of the deck is absolutely correct and to avoid the possibility of spoiling a heavy piece of plywood, the lighter section may be used not only to fair-off the structural work, but also as the final template. In this case the decking job is done virtually to completion point with the light gauge plywood tacked down with nails before it is removed and the final heavy deck plywood cut from its shape.

When the final deck piece is cut an overlap of at least 5 mm on the gunwale should be allowed to permit planing back to a flush fit at the topsides. This is the vulnerable point if watertightness between deck and hull is to be ensured. The slightest error in cutting and the entire sheet of plywood may be rendered useless, for while it is always easy to plane back an overlap, there is no way of building up an undercut section. This is particularly the case at bow and stern areas where the flare of the hull will necessitate a certain amount of bevelling at the edge of the deck.

By far and away the most popular method securing a plywood deck into place is with glue and screws. The decking must first be exactly aligned in a 'dry run' where one corner (or the 'eyes' of the bow) is exactly aligned and the plywood drilled. A nail holds this corner in position while the centreline is aligned and the location of fastenings marked with a pencil. Great care is needed at this point since any misalignment may result in wastage of the whole decking sheet.

Selection of the right drill is most important, since the fastenings will need to be countersunk, and the screws should be either brass or monel. The holes are carefully drilled as described on page 30. Then the glue is prepared, the whole area swept clean of drilling dust or planing shavings, and the glue applied to both deck and framework surfaces.

Screwing should be commenced on the centreline and worked out towards the sheerstrake. The fastenings should be drawn up hard and should be countersunk unless the deck is to be later covered with fibreglass or some other protective material. Even so, it is good practice to countersink as the job looks neater for it. If the top surface is to be left uncovered, the countersunk holes must be plugged with dowels, but in the event of covering—unless it is a transparent covering—some form of plastic filling will suffice.

The decking is laid in sections, the sizes of which are determined principally by the convenience of working and the size and shape of the areas being decked. On medium and small craft the foredeck can usually be covered with one sheet, but large craft will require the wider deck spaces to be covered in sections. This is no problem and the plywood can be butt-edged (scarfing is almost impossible *in situ*) providing the joins land on a beam or bearer.

With the deck firmly screwed and glued into position, the trimming process can begin. As the entire deck was cut with a few millimetres overlap all around the boat's gunwale and

A plywood deck glued and screwed in place, ready for painting or covering.

Nothing looks more attractive than laid decks. But not only are they difficult to lay, they are vulnerable to leakage problems unless laid on an underlay of plywood or some similar material.

around the hatches and deck openings, these edges should now be planed back flush with the surrounding surfaces to complete the job. The fitting of covering pieces such as coamings, toe rails and sheet capping is described elsewhere.

Fitting a laid deck

Nothing looks more attractive than a laid deck. No matter what the age, design or construction of the boat, laid decks add the touch of class that lifts her above the common herd of plywood, canvas, fibreglass or metal decks. But—as always—there is a drawback, in that laid decks are the most difficult of all to fit. Even so, for the boat owner with patience and time, the rewards of the beautifully laid timber more than justify the effort.

Another drawback with laid decks is their tendency to leak, particularly as they age. Modern caulking glues and compounds have reduced this tendency but after weathering in hot sun or being subjected to hard working in a seaway, even the best laid decks tend to suffer. For this reason the best procedure is to first lay a plywood deck to achieve watertightness, then to overlay with a laid deck to gain the appearance.

The plywood is laid as described earlier. The laid deck can follow a number of patterns as illustrated, probably the most popular for yachts being that in which the planks are bent to follow the curve of the hull and butt into the *kingplank* down the centreline of the boat. This is a relatively easy method to lay on large craft but becomes difficult with small yachts and motor cruisers because the sharper curve at the bow requires hard bending of the planks. In such

cases one uses planks which are virtually straight and are notched into the *margin plank*, or *scupper board* as it is sometimes called.

In all cases the planks must be shaped at the ends and fitted carefully to ensure not only an even pattern but also a good fit, particularly where they notch into the kingplank or margin plank. The planks should be fairly narrow and rift sawn with the grain running as nearly vertically through the planks as possible. This ensures that the decks wear evenly and there is less chance of splintering.

As with all fitting-out procedures, a dry run should be the first step to ensure that the planks fit closely and evenly. A light rebate in the upper corner of the plank is the best way of forming a seam, then the planks can lie close together at their bottom edges, forming a homogeneous second layer over the ply deck with marine glue or sealant between as a bedding and adhesive. One can lay the deck and then run a router along the seams, or else rebate the planks first; practice varies as to whether the rebate should be in a V-form or a simple rectangular rebate. These arguments developed in the days when laid decks were rarely underlaid with ply and therefore the tightness of the seam determined the watertightness of the deck. With the ply underlay these problems are eliminated and the seam is more for appearance than for waterproofing.

With the planks cut and prepared the kingplank and margin plank must be fitted. This is probably the trickiest part of the exercise since it almost resembles a jigsaw puzzle and fitting the notched part flush and accurately takes a great deal of time and patience. The best

The most popular system of laid decks with each plank butting into the kingplank.

procedure is to secure the kingplank and margin plank in place, having previously cut them from templates made during the dry run, then to shape the ends of the planks to fit as they fall in place. Whatever the system, it will not be easy and involves a lot of trial and error but the ultimate result will be well worth the painstaking effort. Working from the kingplank outwards is the best procedure.

Fastening the deck planks can be done by 'secret' nailing, or screws drilled and driven from the underside of the plywood thus eliminating the problem of dowelling the deck. As with the plywood, the margin plank can be overcut by a millimetre or two to allow for any inconsistencies around the gunwale of the boat and then planed back, together with the ply flush with the topsides. After caulking, the final job is sanding with a heavy industrial sander to achieve an even, smooth surface.

Caulking

It is almost impossible to caulk a deck to complete watertightness over a long period of time. Despite the advent of synthetic caulking compounds replacing the old tar and pitch, obtaining completely watertight seams is next to impossible over any great length of time. The shrinkage and expansion of the timber planks in varying conditions of sun, rain and seawater will eventually loosen even the best bonding material.

However, caulking still has its place in terms of appearance and the dark seams between the planks are half the attractiveness of a laid deck. Although the decking is embedded in marine glue, and the plywood provides a more watertight and rigid base than the old planked decks, in the long term it is still well worth excluding water as much as possible, to prevent rot and softening around fastenings and under deck fittings. Properly applied synthetic caulking adheres well and is flexible enough to expand and contract with the seams.

Originally the seams were packed with oakum or cotton which was then sealed with pitch or some other composition. Nowadays the packing can be eliminated altogether and the seams simply filled with an appropriate composition. Indeed, so sophisticated has this process become that one may now even lay deck seams in the colour of one's choice!

In the days of the old windjammers there used

The kingplank must be shaped to fit around deck fittings. Since these may be of an awkward shape, templates will be necessary to ensure a flush fit and good connection with the planks.

The deck is totally laid and fastened before caulking and finishing are commenced. Note how kingplanks have been placed to accommodate cabin structure; also note the relatively small margin plank on this craft.

The deck laid and ready for finishing. The dowels and kingplank must be planed back flush and the seams cleaned out prior to caulking.

to be a jingle which described the lot of apprentice seamen—

'Six days shalt thou labour, and do all thou art able,
On the seventh holystone the deck and scrub the cable.'

And while it is debatable that in this day and age apprentices turn out on Sunday mornings to holystone the decks, nevertheless holystone is still considered to be the best treatment for laid decks, on Sunday or any other day. A big block of sandstone, rubbed up and down the decks with a strong detergent solution to help remove grease and oil, will bring up the timber to a pristine brightness that will shade even the most ambitious soap powder advertisement.

Holystone should be used wet to bring up a slurry on the deck rather like that obtained on brightwork when rubbing back with wet and dry sandpaper. This slurry, plus the action of the detergent, removes dirt and grease, skims off any dirty surfaces and when washed away leaves the deck sparkling clean. It should be first done when the newly laid deck has had time to cure.

Laying a planked deck

A planked deck is, of course, similar in many respects to a laid deck, the main difference being that the laid deck is a very classy piece of workmanship intended to add to the appearance of the boat and, as a result, uses fine timbers well prepared and artistically designed. The planked deck, by contrast, uses wider timbers of less sophisticated material intended to be covered and therefore simply laid straight down without any pretentions to artistic appearance. Ordinary cheaper timbers such as oregon may be used,

Planked decks are laid fore and aft with no curve or kingplank. The only shaping is with the margin plank and the surrounds of deck fittings. Since these decks are invariably finished with some kind of covering, relatively inexpensive planks can be used.

although care must be taken to prevent the possibility of rot underneath the covering. Certainly the high quality appearance timbers such as teak or mahogany would not be used.

The planks are simply laid in the most convenient form, usually fore and aft, and sawn to flush with the margin plank. There is no need for a kingplank and although it is always wise to countersink the fastenings they may be plugged with plastic filler rather than the more attractive dowels.

The covering may be fibreglass or one of the proprietary brands of synthetic coverings or simply the old fashioned canvas which is still a popular material for this purpose. Where synthetics are used they will need to be opaque in order to cover the roughness of the planking beneath. A non-skid finish is essential and can be obtained by applying non-skid deck paint or by sprinkling fine sand from a sugar shaker over a coat of wet deck paint, finishing off with another coat.

Covering with canvas

Apart from its appearance and waterproof qualities, one of the greatest advantages of a canvas deck is the fact that it can be laid on almost any surface. Fairly rough-laid plank decks are frequently used as a cheap, easy method of decking, using the canvas covering to give it an attractive and watertight finish. Where

A canvas-covered deck not only looks good but is very waterproof if correctly laid. Careful fitting around deck openings and proper treatment with paint are the secrets.

fibreglass and other synthetic coverings require virtually virgin timber before they will take successfully, a canvas deck can be laid over any timber, no matter how old, salt-encrusted or dirty.

Of first importance is the canvas to be used. It should be of fairly heavy grade, around 20 ounces per square foot, to withstand the wear and tear it will encounter. It should be of good quality, preferably new, and washed in warm water to remove any size or similar treatment that might affect the finish. After washing, the canvas should be stretched in all directions as much as possible with the aim of having no stretch marks or wrinkles in the final appearance.

Treatment of the deck before laying the canvas is simple—it merely has to be painted. Undoubtedly the best treatment is to cover the deck with white or red lead, although these preparations take a while to dry, but their waterproofing and anti-rot qualities make it well worth the extra time and trouble.

Before the paint is thoroughly dry the canvas—pre-cut to shape with a good overlap on all edges—is laid over it. If possible it should be tacked into place with copper nails, starting with a line down the centre of the deck. However, this may mar the final appearance of the deck and, provided it is not too large an area, tacking can be confined solely to the outer edges which can later be covered. At all events the laying commences at the centreline and, whether tacked or not, pressure is applied, smoothing the canvas down onto red or white lead from the centre and working out towards the edges to remove all

To make corners watertight, the canvas must be turned over and tacked with copper nails, then covered with beading when the job is finished.

bubbles and wrinkles. A good method is to stretch the canvas fore and aft, tack it into position and then stretch in athwartships, gradually removing all blemishes.

Care will need to be taken when laying round obstructions such as deck fittings, hatches and cabin trunkways as watertightness is important in these areas. Allowing even the slightest seepage into the timber joins in these corners can cause pockets of rot at a later date and the canvas must be so laid that it prevents any such seepage. The system normally used is to fold the edge of the canvas up along the side of the fitting and cover it with a length of quad timber or a batten. Liberal use of a sealant or caulking putty in these difficult areas will help make them watertight.

When the canvas has been satisfactorily stretched and tacked down the surplus can be cut away and the tacked areas covered with battens

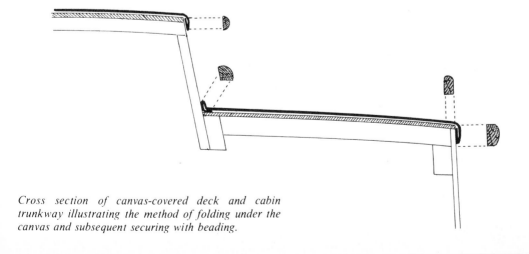

Cross section of canvas-covered deck and cabin trunkway illustrating the method of folding under the canvas and subsequent securing with beading.

or, along the gunwale, by the toe rail. Wherever possible deck fittings should not be installed until the canvas has been laid and given time to cure. The fewer the breaks in the canvas the more watertight the deck will be. Winches, stanchions, sheeting tracks and similar fittings can be left until last, and the canvas should be cut only for deck openings such as hatches and cabin trunkways.

Once laid the canvas should be given time to cure, particularly if red or white lead has been used beneath it. Then it can be painted with a primer, undercoat and top coats as with any other paint job. The finish, of course, should be a non-skid deck paint.

Sheathing with fibreglass

There are many proprietary brands of deck surfacing which use a resin base, and to lay these successfully the manufacturer's instructions must be followed carefully. But there is no reason why ordinary GRP cannot be used for it provides a very durable and watertight deck covering. The glass fibre offering the best finish for this job is the woven cloth that looks something like a loosely woven linen.

The condition of the deck onto which the fibreglass is to be laid is all important. Unless the timber is completely and absolutely dry and clean there is every likelihood of the surface lifting at some later date. Obviously the best condition is for the timber to be in virgin condition. Once it has been painted or wetted, particularly with salt water, it is very difficult indeed to get it to a condition of cleanliness that will ensure a good bond for the fibreglass. Consistent scrubbing with warm fresh water will help but then it is just as important to ensure that the resultant dampness is thoroughly dried out as the resin will lift equally from damp timber as from dirty or greasy surfaces. Nevertheless one

After curing the GRP must be sanded back to even out undulations and rough areas. The surface should be finished with non-skid deck paint.

still sees a number of sheathed decks where the GRP has lifted, and this is often due to the earlier belief that polyester resin is also an adhesive. It is, but not a very good one, and to obtain good adhesion a bonding agent must first be applied to the wood, before the resin.

Before this, however, the other essential job in preparation is to cut and trim the cloth to accurately fit each section of the deck. Once the resin has been applied and curing is under way there will be little enough time to move it into the right position, and less still for any trimming.

Assuming that a woven cloth has been chosen for the job, a further reason for getting it accurately cut to size is the need for a decent surface finish on the completed deck. Cured polyester resin is extremely hard, and while it can be smoothed down with a power sander life is much easier if the job can be neatly done at the start. The power sander will also flush off bumps and voids, but it is also likely to grind away the glass cloth and rather nullify one's efforts.

A light scuffing of the timber with a sander will assist in providing a good key, or the area can be lightly scored with a sharp knife. Clean up any sawdust and then cover the whole area with the bonding primer in accordance with the maker's instructions. While that is drying, mix up a manageable quantity of resin and catalyst (usually about a litre), again in strict accordance with the maker's instructions.

With the pre-cut panels of cloth laid out, the resin may now be applied, starting from the centre of the area and working outwards. Lay one edge of the cloth in position, and then smoothly put down the rest of the panel. A stiff old paintbrush is useful for dabbing out any voids, and for ensuring an overall even pressure it's difficult to beat a stiff sponge paint roller. Make particularly certain that where there are any corners or angles the cloth is firmly pressed in; work quickly and neatly. Successive panels should overlap by at least an inch, and when completely covered the sheathed deck should be given another two coats of resin. More recently, epoxy resin has been preferred for deck sheathing, and for the small extra cost it offers a much stronger finish.

Sheathing metal decks

Steel and aluminium decks can be covered (sheathed) with timber quite successfully. Indeed, the appearance of these decks can be considerably enhanced by laid timber. The method used is similar to that described for fitting a laid deck on a plywood underlay with an intermediate layer of marine glue or sealant as a flexible, waterproof bedding for the top layer. It is vital to prevent corrosion of the metal deck, an area that is out of sight and where water cannot drain away as it can from an exposed surface. Special care should be taken around deck fittings, any through-fastenings, and at the edges of the sheathing.

Screw fastenings from beneath the metal deck may be used, but the most common method is to bolt the deck from the top down through the metal. The bolts are countersunk into the timber planks and set in a watertight compound of caulking putty or sealant, then plugged with dowels. Since these bolts provide a weak link in the watertight pattern of the decking a great deal of attention should be paid to ensuring that both the drilled holes and the bolts are a close fit and that the dowel and bolt head are well embedded in sealant.

A similarly treated washer and nut beneath the metal deck will add to the watertightness of the fastening.

An important factor with metal decks, particularly in aluminium, is to ensure that the fastenings and fittings are all of similar specification. If not, electrolytic corrosion may occur. The normal marine grade aluminium specification number is N8.

MAST SUPPORTS

Since the mast, rigging and sails of a yacht are its power unit, they are subject to the enormous pressures and stresses that are associated with any power source. Imagine, for example, the thrust stresses that are placed on the mountings of a big diesel motor powering a 10 or 15 tonne motor yacht. By the same token, similar stresses will be encountered on a sailboat of the same size being pushed through the water at the same speed and most of these stresses will be around the mast and rigging.

When a big diesel motor is installed in a motor yacht its mountings are so arranged that it spreads the load through much of the boat's structure, avoiding the possibility of hot spots. The same applies to a yacht, and when mast and rigging are fitted the sailing stresses must be spread as much as possible throughout the hull structure. Where the motor mountings transmit

The enormous stresses that are placed on a mast under load can be seen from this picture. The mast must be firmly stepped so that the stresses are dissipated through the hull structure or both boat and mast will be damaged.

these stresses to the motor yacht hull, the mast step and chain plates are the principal areas where sailing stresses are transmitted to a yacht's hull.

When a mast is under load it is in compression, which means that tremendous stresses are directed down the mast itself and thus into the mast step, through which they are directed into the hull. This obviously places a huge load on the point where the mast step is located, a load which must be spread as much as possible throughout the hull structure or the stresses may drive the mast right through the hull. Since many modern yachts have their masts stepped on deck, it follows that the deck or cabin top beneath the mast step must be well supported and strengthened, not only to prevent it collapsing, but to transmit the stresses down through the hull as evenly as possible. Before fitting a mast the structural area beneath the mast step must be carefully designed and built or damage will result when the mast is under load.

Stepping on the keel

Fewer masts are stepped on the keel nowadays for two main reasons: firstly, having a mast running down through the middle of the cabin cuts down on useful accommodation space and is cumbersome and, secondly, the hole where the mast penetrates the cabin roof is often difficult to keep completely watertight. Outside these disadvantages, stepping a mast on the keel is structurally good since this part of the boat's hull is structurally more suited to take the downward stresses of the mast under load and distribute them to the hull.

The support given to the mast by the cabin roof structure is also an advantage and makes for a firmer mast stepping. However, the convenience of an uncluttered cabin seems to be more popular and generally speaking the majority of mast steps are located on deck or on the cabin top, rather than on the keel, particularly on smaller yachts.

Stepping a mast on the keel is usually a simpler structural matter than stepping it on deck, and in all but the smallest timber boats there will be a hog or keelson fastened on top of the keel as an

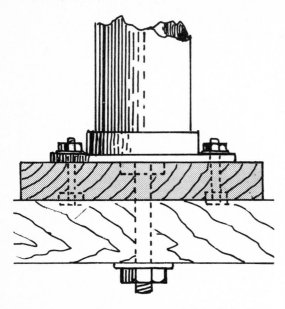

A simple type of mast step intended for light loads. The step under the socket should be made longer and thicker for greater rigidity and load-spreading. The bolts are essential to prevent movement.

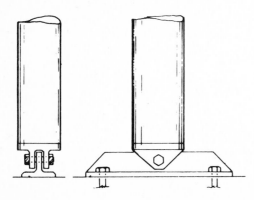

T-section mast step, bolted to the cabin top. As so much load comes on the single bolt, this arrangement is only suitable for smaller boats of say 35 ft or less.

attachment for the frames and planking. This member is thus connected to the rest of the ship's structure, and is therefore an ideal base for the mast step. The step itself is normally a separate piece of timber fastened to the hog, with a slot to accept a large tenon cut in the mast heel.

While these will be the arrangements in a timber boat, where a hull is built of metal or GRP the same structural considerations will need to be borne in mind: that the thrust of the mast is directly transmitted to the keel, and from there into the framework of the ship. In a GRP boat this may well be via the matrix bonded into the hull to support a ballast keel, or alternatively short floors may be bonded in way of the mast to which a step is then fastened. This latter method has the advantage of apparent simplicity, but in larger craft the floors will need to be tied to bonded-in frames or bulkheads so that the stresses on the step and floors are adequately distributed into the hull. For aluminium masts there are a variety of fabricated metal steps.

Mast collar

When the mast is stepped on the keel it penetrates the cabin roof or the deck via an area known as the *collar*. This serves a twofold purpose in giving support to the mast and in keeping the area watertight when the deck is awash. Because the mast moves when the rig is under load, making this aperture watertight is not easy. Plastic collars now available can often

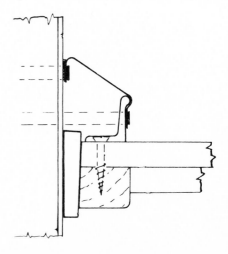

An aluminium mast through a wooden deck, showing the mast coat attached to a flange, and wedges. It is vital that the opening in the deck is stiffened on all sides.

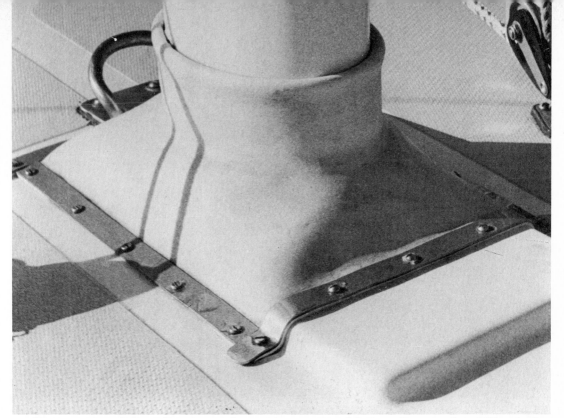

A plastic mast coat held in place by stainless steel straps. Although a neat job, water and salt will lie in the groove at the top of the coat and eventually cause *corrosion of the mast. Tape or a shaped fillet of sealant could have prevented this.*

be secured quite tightly, yet they are flexible enough to allow a certain amount of movement, or canvas collars can be secured in place to effect a similar result, providing care is taken with detail when fitting.

The first step in making a mast collar is to shape a series of small wedges into a circle which can be hammered home in the space between the mast wall and the perimeter of the hole in the deck. This hole is usually cut to a larger diameter than the mast section to allow for tuning. Once the mast is in position the wedges are then driven home to hold it firm. It is possible to obtain a rubber fitting which will sometimes do the same job, much depending on the size and shape of the mast. Many aluminium masts are pear-shaped or oval while sometimes timber masts are round or even rectangular in section. If a bought fitting is not available to make a firm collar around the mast the wedges can usually be shaped.

Once well secured, the collar is made watertight by covering it with a sleeve of canvas, rubber or plastic which is tapered as nearly as possible to fit to the mast and lap over the collar. The tighter the fit the better the chance of eliminating leaks, and with this in mind the covering is usually secured around the mast and again around the deck outside the collar. A stainless steel ring similar to a hose clip may be used at the mast and the base of the collar may be secured to the cabin roof by pop rivets or, in the case of timber decks, by small copper tacks. Again, it may be possible to purchase a stainless steel ring or similar fitting which will drop over the collar and secure to the deck, thus holding the watertight cover well into position. No matter how this is done the collar must be firm and yet provide a waterproof seal even with the movement which is inevitable when the mast is under load.

Stepping on the deck

The most important difference between stepping a mast on the keel and on the deck or cabin top is the structural system used to take the load when the mast is under compression. In the case of the keel-stepped mast the floors, already in position, are used to distribute the stresses. But cabin or deck beams are not sufficiently strong in their own right to withstand such stresses and structural compensation must be made in order to transmit the load without placing too great a strain on the deck beams.

There are two principal methods of achieving this. The simplest is to support the mast from directly beneath with a pillar stepped on the floors. This has the effect of transmitting the load directly to the floors and thence into the hull structure just as though the mast itself were stepped on the keel. However, this defeats one of the purposes of having the mast stepped on the deck, inasmuch as a pillar in the middle of the accommodation area is little better than a mast and just as inconvenient. The second method involves the use of built structural members directly beneath the mast step which carry the load out to the side of the hull rather than directly down to the keel. These may take the form of steel girders, heavy timber members or a bulkhead, any of which if correctly fitted is suitable. At the sides of the hull these stresses are transferred to the frames or the beam shelf and spread throughout the entire hull structure.

Basically, this amounts to reinforcing the cabin roof or deck in such a way that the load of the compressed mast is carried outwards to the hull sides. If the mast is stepped on top of the cabin there is the added problem of transmitting the load through the cabin sides and then across the side-decks to the beam shelf, thus involving quite heavy reinforcement in a number of different directions. For this reason steel girders are usually the most suitable, since their dimensions can be kept relatively small and thus not intrude into the cabin space over much. The girder can be shaped to fit the contours of the cabin top and sides as well as the side decking and can be bolted into the beam shelf quite simply. As a general rule two angle girders or a U-frame are used, although this will depend on each individual boat and trial and error will be necessary to obtain the best cabin reinforcing without reducing the headroom or creating an unsightly steel girder. The problem is less acute where the mast is stepped on deck rather than the cabin top, as the steel girder is simply flushed underneath the deck, running from side to side to all intents and purposes like another deck beam.

Probably the easiest and best system is to place a bulkhead directly beneath the mast step as a

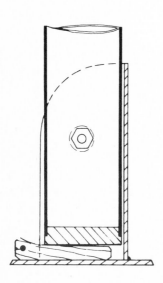

A mast stepped in a tabernacle will place a heavy load on the pivot bolt, and the holes made for it in the mast wall will tend to ovalize in time. This hardwood wedge transfers most of the load to the deck.

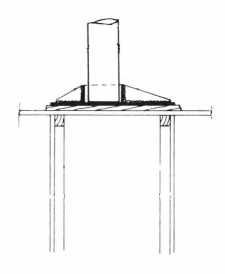

A mast step designed for rigidity and to spread load between supports which are not directly under the mast, in this case the deck beams, pillars under them, and two structural bulkheads. Because the step is made up from heavy thick sides welded to a long baseplate, and on a hardwood pad, it is tremendously strong and rigid.

The support for the mast can never be too strong. Here the pillar beneath the deck is supplemented by steel deck beams on either side which transmit some of the load of the mast across the boat as well as into the keel.

Although pillar supports tend to intrude into cabin accommodation space, they can often be disguised or utilised as part of the furniture.

reinforcement. The bulkhead acts as a good structural unit, distributing the stresses not only to the side of the boat but also down each side of the hull and into the keel, and it does not look unsightly. In order not to weaken the bulkhead in a direct line below the mast, the door opening should be offset to one side. If this is not possible for some reason then the opening must be reinforced at top and bottom to spread the downward pressures across the width of the bulkhead.

The location of the mast step has much to do with the choice of support. If you are lucky and the mast step is in a position immediately above a planned bulkhead there is no problem, but if a special bulkhead has to be fitted to support the mast it may not be a convenient location and may upset the plans for the general layout of the accommodation area. In this case one of the alternative methods must be employed.

It sometimes happens that the mast step falls between two bulkheads. If these bulkheads are reasonably close together—as with a bathroom, for example—a U-channel girder run between both bulkheads will provide an ideal mast support and spread the load between the two. This is a common practice when the mast step is also of a U-girder type, allowing adjustment of the foot of the mast in a fore and aft direction.

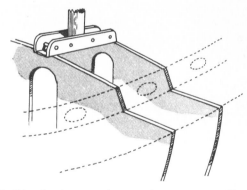

A bulkhead makes a good support for a mast step. Where two bulkheads are close together the load can be spread across them by means of a reinforced mast step or channel bar.

CHAINPLATES

Chainplates are one of the most important fittings on a yacht since they are the medium through which much of the power of the sails is transmitted to the hull.

Because they are designed principally to secure the rigging holding up the mast, they are likely to come under enormous stresses as the power of the sails creates a load on the mast which in turn is transmitted to the hull through the rigging and

75

chainplates. Thus, the chainplates must not simply be a location point for the bottom of the rigging, but must be well-anchored, well-stressed fittings which will not pull out of the hull when under load, nor create hot spots or uneven patches of stress in transferring the load from the rigging to the hull.

There are numerous ways of securing chainplates into the hull and it would be impossible to deal with all of them in a book of this type. However, for the most part they can be divided into two categories—chainplates secured to the hull skin and chainplates secured through the deck or cabin top. The former is the more common and probably the best type of chainplate, but on some modern racing yachts, particularly those carrying large headsails, it is preferable to locate the chainplates inboard of the gunwale through the deck or cabin top in order to allow the headsail to be sheeted close.

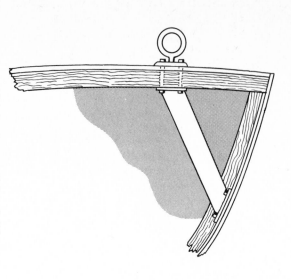

Basic arrangement for an inboard or through-deck chainplate. The smaller the angle of the internal plate to the hull, the more direct the stresses are applied.

Through-deck chainplates

Since the load from the mast, sails and rigging must eventually be transferred into the hull, the location of the chainplates anywhere other than on the hull skin must be a compromise and, in effect, a transit point between the rigging and the hull sides. Thus the only real difference in the structural makeup of chainplates mounted in from the side of the boat is the means of transferring the load from the rigging terminal to the side of the hull. At this latter point the stresses will be transferred through the hull in exactly the same way as though the chainplates were located at the gunwale. In short, locating the chainplates inboard requires additional structural work between the chainplates at the hull side, transmitting the stresses through the hull, and the terminal.

It would be quite impossible, for example, to construct a chainplate simply by securing it through the deck. Unless secured through a structural member which will transfer the stresses out to the side of the hull, the chainplate would simply pull out of the deck when under load. There is a tendency for some cheaply constructed boats to eliminate the need for this additional structural work by strengthening the deck in the area of the chainplate terminal. This is asking for trouble since, even though the area in the vicinity of the chainplate may be reinforced sufficiently, unless this reinforcing is carried out to the hull itself, a weak point must be created which will eventually carry away when

the rigging is under load. In other words, while the terminal of the chainplate may remain secured in the deck, the bond between deck and hull may be severely weakened or pull apart when the rig comes under load.

Basically, then, the terminal chainplate inboard from the gunwale requires two stages through which the load can be transferred to the hull. The first is some means of reinforcing the deck to prevent the terminal pulling out, and the second is to transfer the stress from this point across the deck and into the hull structure. This latter can be achieved in a number of ways, the most common of which is to secure the chainplate to a deck beam. The beam acts both as a reinforcing for the chainplate terminal, and also transfers the stresses via the beam shelf and beam knee. The only drawback is that the deck beams must be in the right location for the chainplates, which is not often the case. However, it requires only a little ingenuity to create some structural filler piece between two beams, if they are not too widely spaced, onto which the chainplate terminal may be secured. If this is done, it is important to remember that the stresses must be evenly and firmly transmitted to the deck beams or structural problems will arise with both the chainplate and the deck above it.

Where there is no convenient deck beam it will be necessary to build a suitable structure to meet these two requirements. Assuming that the chainplate fitting is already in place on the hull side, then the stresses can be transmitted by a plate or welded triangle of 1 cm stainless steel strap secured to the underside of the deck between the chainplate and the rigging terminal. The outboard side of the structure must be firmly welded or bolted to the chainplate structure to disseminate the stresses through the hull, and the whole unit fastened securely into position rather like a large beam knee.

This structure is preferable to a simple strap across the deck and down the hull side, since the hypotenuse of the triangular section will offer a more direct transmission of the upward stresses on the rigging to the chainplate. The only drawback with this type of structure is the fact that it intrudes somewhat into the interior of the boat. However, fitting chainplates inboard from the gunwale is a compromise and the intrusion into the cabin space must be accepted as part of the compromise.

Gunwale chainplates

By far the most common system, this involves fitting chainplates to the side of the hull with the terminals as an integral part of the structure. Since the basic chainplate structure is required no matter where the terminals are located, it follows that much of the work described above is

A chainplate fabricated from stainless steel strap and tube. If the hull is timber, the vertical straps must land on frames and the horizontal tube flush up beneath the beam shelf.

eliminated when the stresses of the rigging at their terminal ends can be transmitted directly into the hull. Often the entire chainplate structure is built as one unit and fitted against the side of the hull with the terminals pushed up through the deck. Particularly is this a good system where fibreglass or metal boats are concerned. It can also be used with timber hulls providing the structural members of the hull are suitably located.

The stresses on the chainplates are principally upward when the load on the mast stresses the rigging. However, there are also forward and backward stresses, particularly on chainplates situated abaft or ahead of the mast respectively. Allowance must be made in fitting the chainplate structure to the hull to disseminate these stresses so that hot spots are not created or undue stress put on any hull member which is not adequately reinforced.

This can be quite a problem with fibreglass hulls where there are few structural members to which the chainplates can be secured. In this case the chainplates themselves become the structural members, disseminating the stresses across a large area of the hull skin. A good arrangement is a framework made of 1 cm stainless steel strap in a squared arrangement whereby the terminals create deep vertical structural members and the fore and aft cross pieces act as miniature stringers. With this structure the upward stress on the chainplate terminal is transmitted deep into the hull, while any other stresses are disseminated through the cross pieces. The depth to which this structure runs down the hull side should be not less than one metre beneath the deck, and preferably more if space and cost permit. The fore and aft dimensions will be controlled by the location of the chainplate terminals which, in turn, depend on the placement of the shrouds.

In constructing this chainplate framework, it is important to locate the top crosspiece close under the deck. This enables it to resist upward stresses on the chainplates, and if possible it should be butted hard up under the deck or the beam shelf. Some shipwrights prefer to use an angle iron or piece of stainless piping for this top cross piece to offer greater resistance to the deck or beam shelf and thus less chance of the unit being pulled out. However, these are matters of personal preference, and providing the chainplate structure is of sufficient size to spread the load well across the hull skin or structural

In GRP hulls the whole unit is firmly glassed to the hull tight up under the deck. The stainless steel tube prevents any upward movement while the rest of the fabricated structure disseminates the stresses through the hull skin to which it is firmly bonded with GRP.

The chainplates will need to be firmly held in place while the GRP cures. A close fit at all points is essential to avoid hot spots.

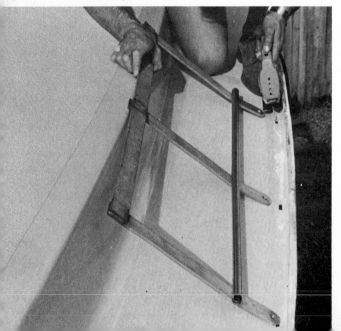

members to which it is attached, and is well secured into position, it should serve its purpose adequately. The dimensions mentioned here are for average medium-sized yachts and can be increased or decreased to suit individual craft.

Fastening the chainplates into position will depend on their location and the type of hull involved. With timber hulls, bolting is the most common method, while welding is obviously preferable with steel and aluminium. Ferrocement boats may adopt either welding or bolting, depending on the structure to which the chainplate is to be secured, while almost invariably in fibreglass hulls the entire chainplate unit is thoroughly glassed into place to form a solid bond with the hull skin.

To obtain a flush fit it is often necessary to bend the chainplate unit to match the curves of the hull sides. This is not always easy, and it may be necessary to make some adjustment to the framework of the unit to fit an individual hull. By using a little ingenuity and lots of G-clamps, you can usually flush the chainplates reasonably close to the hull skin or the structural members to which they must be secured. As is the case with all matters related to fitting out the interior, the use of templates in the early stages may avoid unnecessary cutting or waste and reduce the amount of work involved.

The location of the chainplates will be governed by the rigging plan and measurements can be made on deck for the exact position of the terminals. A hole closely matching the dimensions of the stainless steel strap should be made from the deck downwards and the whole unit pushed up from beneath so that the terminals are protruding the required amount above the deck and the top crosspiece is snugged hard up against the deck or beam shelf. The unit must then be held in place until sufficient fastenings have been attached to prevent any movement when the remainder are secured. If the unit is being glassed into position G-clamps or some temporary scaffolding-type arrangement may be necessary to hold the framework unit in position until the resin has cured. The pierced deck in way of the terminals must be well sealed with some flexible sealant to allow the movement which will occur as loads are placed on the chainplates, yet retain a watertight seal. Chainplates are one of the most

The holes cut through the deck to accommodate the chainplate terminals must be matched closely and well glassed or they will leak when under load.

vulnerable points for leakage because of this movement when under load and considerable attention should be paid to making them watertight.

BALLAST KEELS

While a form of ballast is sometimes required in a motor yacht to adjust her trim or settle her down to her designed waterline, this is only a minor operation and generally it can be assumed that ballast is not part of the makeup of a motor boat. A yacht, however, requires considerable ballast to counteract the pressure of the wind in the sails and give her good stability. Since it is an integral part of the boat's design the ballast, in terms of both location and weight, will have been predetermined by the designer and is therefore often fitted when the hull is built. However, it is becoming fairly common, particularly with fibreglass moulded construction, to sell the moulded hull without fitted ballast and to leave the fitting to a later stage.

Ballast keels come in many different shapes and sizes. The most basic form, sometimes seen on small racing yachts, is a moulded cast iron fin, aerodynamically shaped to place the weight of the ballast low yet reduce the resistance of the water to a minimum. Such fin keels are usually bolted directly to the flat bottom of the boat and fitting is a simple process of alignment, drilling, bolting and sealing according to the directions of the designer or according to the plan.

More common among larger yachts is the system of securing the ballast either externally or internally to a deep keel which is already built as an integral part of the hull. Since the main aim is

Lead ingots are a handy type of internal ballast as they enable the boat to be trimmed easily by moving individual ingots. Once correctly ballasted the keel must be sealed over to prevent the ingots moving.

to keep the centre of gravity of the ballast as low down the keel as possible, external ballast is usually applied at the bottom of the built keel, while internal ballast is dropped down into the built keel and sealed into position.

External ballast
This usually comes in the form of a moulded block of either lead or cast iron which has been shaped to fit snugly to the bottom of the built keel on the boat. The ballast is equipped with bolts which match holes drilled in the built keel and enable it to be bolted securely in place. Cast iron ballast is not easy for the amateur to mould and other systems, such as concrete, are rarely suitable even when cast iron chips or disc ballast is incorporated. Lead ballast, however, can be moulded with relative ease providing you have the patience.

Casting a lead keel
A plug must be made of the ballast and carefully shaped so that it matches exactly the smooth aerofoil shape of the deep keel. There are a number of materials that can be used for this, of which balsa is probably the easiest to work. However, a little ingenuity may come up with some better material depending on the size and the shape of the ballast. Once the plug is faired off to match the built keel a mould can be made, and once again a number of materials are suitable for this.

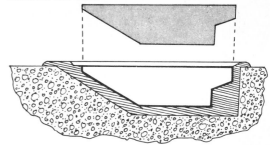

Casting lead ballast in a ground pit. The lead must be poured in one run and keel bolts inserted before it solidifies.

Probably the simplest method of making a mould, from an amateur's point of view, is to dig a small pit in the garden and fill it with moulding sand. The plug is inserted into the sand which is then tamped down hard all around it so that when the plug is removed an exact replica in the shape of a female mould is left. The molten lead is poured into this mould and the keel bolts inserted well into the surface before the lead has

The cast keel ready to be fastened under the hull. It is often easier to lift the boat onto the ballast than vice versa.

time to harden. The bolts should have been previously measured and cut to suit the directions on the plan and should be of stainless steel with hexagonal heads which are on the lower end inserted well into the moulded lead.

When the lead has set and cooled—give it a day or two—it can be lifted from the sand pit and shaped to fit the bottom of the keel before being bolted into position. As often as not, the weight of the ballast makes it simpler to lift the boat onto the keel rather than lift the keel up to the boat, but this will vary from boat to boat and should not create too many problems whichever way it is done.

With the ballast bolted into position, the cleaning up and fairing off process now begins, using chisels and surform plane, and finishing with a power sander to obtain a good flush fit with the built keel. A common practice with many boatbuilders is to then sheath the entire keel area with a coat of fibreglass or some patent GRP finish such as Dynel. This not only adds an additional seal to the joint between the ballast and the keel, but provides a protective coating to the entire area against moisture or attack by marine growth. Fillers and sealants can be used to ensure that any cavities between the top of the ballast and the deep keel are filled and made watertight and the join between them flushed to a point where it can hardly be distinguished.

Internal ballast

As with external ballast, there are a number of different ways of placing internal ballast in the hull. If the boat is not fitted with a deep keel, the ballast ingots may be simply laid along the keelson on the frames, or on a length of timber on top of them, and secured in place. External ballast is

commonly lowered into the hollow built keel and sealed in position so that it cannot move.

Ballast comes in a number of forms, including iron ingots, concrete blocks and cast iron chips, but without doubt the most popular is lead in the form of ingots or, preferably, lead shot. Apart from its greater density, and thus lower centre of gravity, lead is less liable to corrosion than cast iron and, at least in the form of lead shot, much easier to stow low in the built keel.

The built keel section should be sufficiently reinforced to take the ballast. As a rule this is part of the moulding process with fibreglass yachts; with timber yachts the deep keel is an integral part of the hull structure and the frames curve down into it until their structural work is taken over by the floors. More often than not, if the ballast is not fitted, floors will have been eliminated and will need to be fitted at a later date. Suffice it to say at this stage that generally it can be accepted that the hull should be sufficiently strengthened to take the ballast without need for strengthening members to be added before lowering the ballast in place.

It might be worth checking with your builder, particularly in the case of a fibreglass moulded

Loading the ballast into the keel. Ensure that the construction of the bilge/keel area is sufficiently strong to take the weight, and avoid resting ingots on the hull skin.

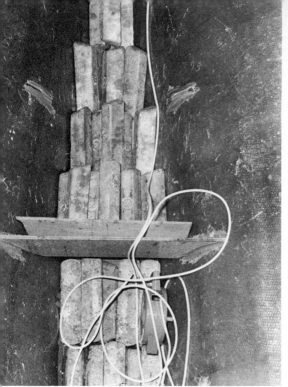

The ingots must be stowed neatly and air gaps reduced as much as possible so that the centre of gravity is placed as low as possible. Glassed timber 'floors' hold the ballast in place temporarily. Note distribution of ingots to create correct trim.

hull, to ensure that distortion or undue stress will not be placed on the built keel part of the hull when the ballast is lowered into position. If so, his advice on how to strengthen these areas will need to be followed. Web framed floors are usually the answer.

As mentioned, lead shot is the most suitable form of ballast since it not only resists corrosion but stows itself compactly in the built keel and, in so doing, keeps the centre of gravity of the ballast much lower than would be the case with ingots. The shot should be poured into the keel together with a light mixture of polyester resin or, as some boatbuilders prefer, concrete. This latter is an obvious saving in cost, but its efficiency as compared with resin is questionable. When all the ballast has been placed and tamped down into position before the resin has had time to cure, it should be sealed off by a heavy layer of GRP across the top which is tapered upwards to the sides of the hull.

Ingots, whether they be of lead, iron, concrete or any other material, and also other forms of ballast such as steel pressings and chippings, will need to be juggled into position to eliminate as much air space between them as possible and thus keep the centre of gravity down low. This is not easy, and may take a lot of time and patience since ingots are not light and juggling them around in the difficult confines of a built keel will lead to bruised fingers and skinned knuckles. However, it is imperative to keep the weight low down and this means juggling the ballast is essential. Often the amount of ballast necessary would appear impossible to fit, and the top of the ballast may come well up into the bilge area of the hull. But providing the ingots are well stowed, jammed in to prevent movement and sealed with resin, they should all settle firmly into the area specified by the designer.

The advantages of lead shot as ballast can be easily seen at this stage. Filling the air gaps around the ballast is a matter of personal preference, some boat builders preferring to leave the air spaces between the ingots unfilled, others using a mixture of concrete, resin or potch or some similar material. Obviously, filling the air spaces with any type of material adds extra ballast weight, albeit fairly small. It also prevents the possibility of water getting in and corroding iron ballast.

The only reasonable argument against filling the air spaces would be in making it difficult to remove the ballast at some future stage, a viable argument in racing yachts where adjustment of ballast may be necessary to improve performance. However, in general use, it is best to ensure that the ballast does not move, even when the boat is in a heavy seaway.

Before sealing off the ballast it is as well to check the actual trim while afloat, since the weight calculations for the hull or the ballasting may not be exactly right, and may even have

When the boat has been trimmed and ballasted correctly the temporary retaining pieces are removed and the ballast sealed into position with cement or GRP.

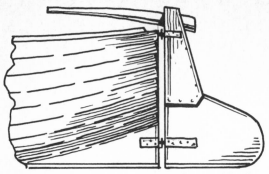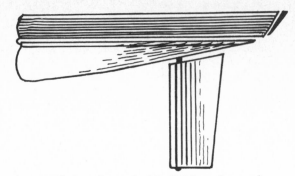

Two basic rudder forms: a transom hung rudder, here with a small skeg forward of it (left), and a spade rudder that is 'balanced' to a small degree and lacks a skeg (right).

upset the trim badly. Although trim can often be adjusted later by using tanks or internal ballast, it is as well to start with the ballast in the correct position and the boat in correct trim. Shifting the ballast after it has been sealed in can be a very difficult task.

RUDDERS

Like so many things concerned with boats, rudders come in a number of shapes and sizes— so many shapes and sizes, in fact, that it would be impossible to describe in detail here a specific method of fitting a rudder which would apply to all craft. Motor yachts, because of the close proximity of the propeller throwing a rapid flow of water across the rudder blade, need totally different rudders to those fitted to sailing craft, where the flow over the rudder is dependent on the speed of the hull through the water.

Even from one craft to another, particularly with yachts, there can be tremendous variations in the shape of the rudder blade and the means by which it is hung. Long-keeled yachts usually have the rudder hung by pintles from the trailing edge of the keel, using a long, narrow blade often set quite considerably out of the vertical. Fast fin-keeled yachts, by contrast, are more likely to be designed with spade rudders considerably aft of the keel, supported by the rudder stock and bearings and in some cases by a skeg also.

These are the two extremes in rudder construction and between them lie a host of different types of rudders—some suspended from the transom, some flushed into a skeg, some pivoted from the forward end of the blade, some pivoted at a point along the blade, some with shaped, aerofoil blades, some with square, flat blades. Much depends on the shape of the hull

and the relation between the hull and the keel, for one basic factor is true of the fitting of all rudders—they must be located in a clear flow of water to be effective.

The chances are that your rudder will either have been supplied with the hull, and needs only to be fitted according to directions, or the plan of the yacht will indicate dimensions to which the rudder must be made and subsequently fitted. In both cases, there is little that can be added in a book such as this, for so individual are rudders that only the rudder designed specifically for your boat is the one that should be fitted. The description of fitting a rudder that follows here is intended for cases where, for some obscure reason, the dimensions of the designed rudder

A sailboat rudder is often at the after end of the keel or deadwood where a heel fitting provides good support and also some protection. Above, a watertight trunk carries bearings for the rudder shaft.

are not available and you have to do the best you can. Even then, the choice of size, shape and type of rudder will still be your responsibility for no book could really specify a basic rudder to suit a broad range of hulls.

There are two main types of rudder: the hung type attached at the leading edge by pintles and gudgeons, and the spade rudder. There are also numerous combined forms, where support is given both by fittings on the leading edge or heel and from a rudder stock and its bearings in the hull. A 'balanced' rudder is one in which the axis of rotation is aft of the leading edge, for more effective steering, usually on power craft. 'Aspect ratio' refers to the ratio of the height to the fore-and-aft width of the blade under water. All of these parameters are designed according to the hull form and construction, water flow, prop wash, speed range, etc. of the boat.

Hung rudders

As described above, the blade of this type of rudder is usually fairly long and thin and, although sometimes aerodynamically shaped, is more often flat or only partially shaped. In the case of trailerable or shallow draft craft, it is usually hinged at some point so that the blade can kick up when the boat grounds. In this case, the rudder is invariably hung on the transom, and the design follows that for centreboard sailing dinghies where the upper part of the rudder is secured to the transom on gudgeons and pintles and the lower half pivots from it. This type of rudder is essential where, in order to get a good bite on the water, the rudder blade is deeper than the keel.

Deep draft yachts, particularly the older type with long keels, often use a hung rudder which is attached to the trailing edge of the keel and runs from beneath the counter to a bearing on the bottom of the keel. These rudders are even longer and thinner than the transom-hung variety and may be shaped to flush with the sides of the keel, or may simply be a flat blade with hangings attached where required. The thrust of the rudder is taken by heavy metal straps bolted through the blade, which help to reinforce it against twisting as well as transmitting thrust to the hull via the hangings.

Usually one or two gudgeons are located down the leading edge of the rudder to match with pintles secured to the trailing edge of the keel. Most of the weight of the rudder in its static state is taken by the bearing at the bottom known as

the bearing pintle. Here the situation is usually reversed and the pintle is attached to the foot of the rudder while the gudgeon is an extension of the foot of the keel. This type of rudder is often angled out of the vertical and thus requires a great deal of care in fitting to ensure that there is even loading on each pintle and gudgeon. The dimensions for the rudder blade as well as for all rudder fittings will, of course, be dependent on the size of the boat and can be taken from the plans.

The construction of this type of rudder, particularly if it is flat, is probably best done with timber planks or, if dimensions permit, a large sheet of marine ply. The rudder blade must be cut and shaped as required and the edges rounded off as much as possible to make for an even flow of water. The trailing edge of the rudder should always, if possible, be tapered almost to a point throughout its entire length. Planks of hardwood

A common form of transom hung rudder used on modern craft. Note the way in which the skeg blends into the rudder shape. Skeg must be heavily reinforced to take the load on the bearing pintle when in use.

can be used providing they are carefully butted together and glued with a waterproof glue while the straps of the gudgeons are located so as to supplement the construction of the blade and transmit stresses across its surface. Most of the stress when the rudder is under load comes on the trailing edge and for this reason the pintle straps should be carried right out to the rear plank.

A fibreglass coating will add to the overall strength of the unit as well as providing a waterproof coating. Where the rudder is required to be shaped to an aerofoil section in order to flush with the keel, construction can be of timber, or preferably of fibreglass foam, as described for balanced rudders. In this case a basic framework, in which the stainless steel pintle straps are joined together by a vertical strap, can be fitted inside the fibreglass blade leaving a smooth unbroken surface.

Spade Rudders

Spade rudders are independent of the keel and take the name from their general oblong shape. They are built around a stock, which takes the stresses of the boat's movement through the water and of turning. The rudder bearings transmit the thrust from the rudder to the hull and also support and brace the stock. Because a spade rudder is unsupported at the lower end it can be very highly stressed indeed, especially in heavy seas and by high speed use. A skeg ahead of and extending part way down the rudder allows further support to be given to the blade, bracing it against bending and the effects of the boat being thrown sideways. It also may save the rudder, or part of it, if an obstruction is hit.

The blade is usually of aerofoil section to create a smooth flow of water and may be secured to the stock either at the leading edge or some way along the length of the blade. In the latter case, it is more correctly called a balanced rudder since part of the blade is forward and part aft of the rudder stock.

There are many methods of shaping the rudder blade and securing it to the framework, the most common of which are to use timber (in the form of two 'cheeks') or a fibreglass casing which fits around the stainless steel framework, which in turn is welded to the rudder stock. Since there are no pintles or gudgeons involved in this type of rudder, the stock and the framework can be made separately into a very strong unit with the surface panels of timber or fibreglass bolted on later.

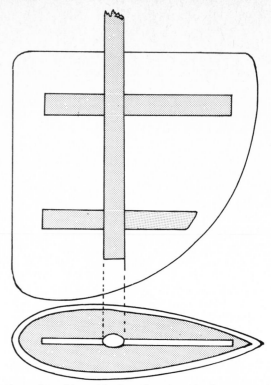

A spade rudder with shaped timber cheeks mounted on a cruciform metal frame, the complete assembly sheathed in fibreglass.

Once again, much depends on the size of the craft, but ¼" x 1½" stainless steel strap should be sufficient for the framework of most average rudders. Bearing in mind that considerable stress will come on these straps when the rudder is turned, it may be necessary to increase the thickness according to the length of the rudder blade. The balanced type of rudder with the stock more centrally located offers a better arrangement since the load is distributed more evenly across the pivot point of the stock and therefore the straps are shorter. Since the framework is vitally important in terms of structural strength it may be as well to have it made up by a professional welder since failure of a weld when the rudder is under stress could quite easily mean the collapse of the entire rudder.

With the basic structural unit made up as described and welded to the rudder stock, the covering panels can be fitted. Two shaped panels fitted one either side of the unit and bolted directly through holes in the straps can be made from timber. These two cheeks should be glued together and bolted to the stainless steel framework with the bolts countersunk and filled to flush the outer surface of the rudder blade and allow a smooth flow of water.

Making the outer casing of the rudder blade from fibreglass is a popular method of constructing this piece of equipment. The timber cheek method described previously can be adopted, making up the core from balsa, foam, or similar material which can be shaped to form the rudder. It is important, however, when constructing a rudder in this way to ensure that the core material is sufficiently strong to transfer the stresses on the fibreglass casing to the stainless steel structural framework.

Normal sandwich GRP materials are not suitable unless the framework is adjusted so that it is in direct contact with the fibreglass outer casing or in some other way fabricated to directly absorb the load and prevent the filler or core material coming under strain. This usually means shaping the framework of the rudder in stainless steel strap so that the fibreglass casing is attached to it rather than using just a central framework which relies on the core for structural strength. Solid GRP tends to be too heavy but if separate cheeks are moulded and bonded to the framework, literally anything can be used for the core. The actual shape of the rudder can be controlled by the moulding or, if hand built, by the shape of the core. Moulding the rudder offers the best results but since this involves a plug and then a mould, it is both expensive and time consuming.

Other rudder arrangements

One of the most popular arrangements for modern yachts is a hung rudder supported by a bearing pintle at the heel, with a bearing around the stock where it penetrates the hull. This is, in effect, a combination of hung and balanced rudders and is a simple and efficient method of fitting the rudder.

The stock is located in a gland at the hull skin and sits in a bearing pintle attached to the trailing edge of the keel or skeg. The stock is fitted to the leading edge of the rudder blade and is welded to a framework similar to that described for a balanced rudder. The blade is usually aerofoil in shape and again constructed similarly to a spade rudder.

The only area that must be carefully strengthened with this type of rudder is the heel of the skeg or keel where the bearing pintle is attached. Since almost the entire weight of the rudder is acting on this point, the pintle must be strong and the point of attachment reinforced to take the thrust of the rudder and any additional strain placed on it in use, for instance when the boat goes aground or dries out and takes the bottom in harbour.

STEERING GEAR

Rudder trunk

In case of failure of the rudder stock itself, or of the gland where it passes into the hull, a very dangerous leak is likely in an area that may be difficult to reach and repair. A trunk sealed to the hull shell at the lower end and the deck or cockpit sole at the top, so that even if it is full of water the integrity of the hull is maintained, is the traditional safeguard. It has proved its worth in recent cases of rudder failure. Although a gland is a useful first line of defence against water coming in, either the installation in the hull or the packing have been known to fail. The bearing or bearings for the stock should not be regarded as watertight seals; their function is to take the rudder thrust and support the stock.

Wire and pulley system

The system comprises two separate units—the steering wheel and the rudder—connected by a system of wires and pulleys which transmit helm movements from the wheel to the rudder. The steering wheel is geared to a drum or linkage system from which wires are run through a system of pulleys to the vicinity of the rudder. On the rudder stock a quadrant provides the terminal for the wires. The quadrant may be, as its name denotes, a quarter of a circle or, as is often the case, a larger sector.

Helm movements on the steering wheel are transmitted via the wire and pulley system to the quadrant which, in turn, moves the rudder stock and thus operates the rudder. The rudder stock penetrates the hull through a watertight gland located beneath the quadrant. This also acts as a bearing in some cases and certainly as part of the rudder securing arrangement.

Most steering systems are supplied as a complete unit or as two separate units—the steering wheel and associated gear and the quadrant with pulley and wire system. Either way, fitting the steering gear means, to a great extent, following manufacturer's directions. The

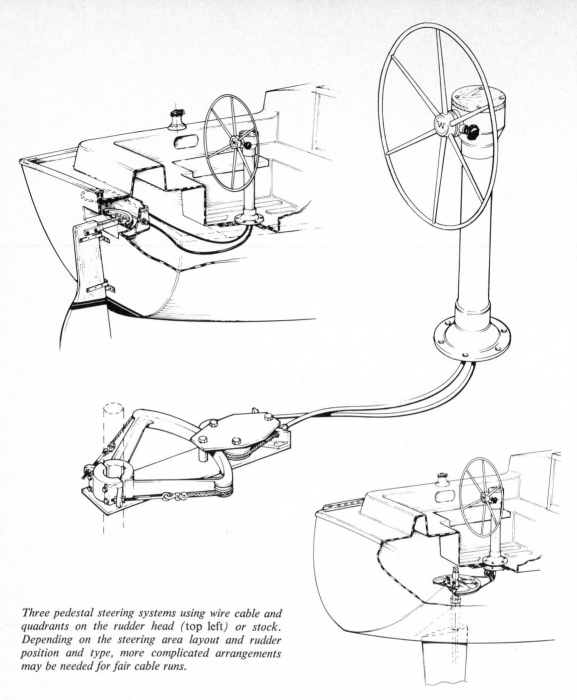

*Three pedestal steering systems using wire cable and quadrants on the rudder head (*top left*) or stock. Depending on the steering area layout and rudder position and type, more complicated arrangements may be needed for fair cable runs.*

obvious first step is to ensure that the equipment is of the correct dimensions and shape for the boat. Where, in the case of a power boat, the wheel is mounted on a dashboard it will be necessary to ensure that the structure of the dash is sufficiently strong to take fairly rigorous stresses when using the wheel in a seaway. It is somewhat disconcerting to find, when you need the steering gear most, that the wheel comes away in your hand or the dashboard structure starts to crack up under the strain.

If the wheel is pedestal mounted, as is the case with many yachts, then the basic fastenings at the foot of the pedestal must be well secured. The best method would be that described for stress fittings on page 99. A body falling violently against the pedestal, or exceptionally heavy use of the steering wheel, could place considerable

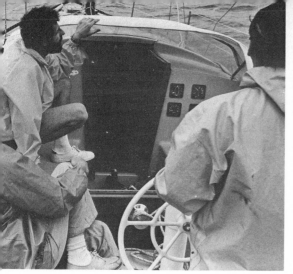

The wheel must be mounted in a position that gives clear visibility all round. Power boat steering positions are usually offset to one side; most yachts steer from a central position.

strain on these fastenings so they must be secure and correctly braced. It may be necessary to strengthen the area around the steering wheel using one of the methods for stiffening described on page 47.

It goes without saying that some thought must be given to the location of the wheel so that visibility is good from the helm position and the wheel or pedestal does not clutter up the cockpit or intrude on working space. The actual location of the wheel on the centreline of the boat is not important, and indeed most power craft have the wheel offset to one side or another. More important is that it is structurally sound.

The wire and pulley system transmitting the wheel movements to the quadrant is a fairly simple arrangement, but must nevertheless be well secured, for failure of the wire due to incorrect installation or to one of the pulleys coming loose, will render the whole steering system useless. The pulleys must be securely fastened as described for stress fittings although the actual method used will vary according to the equipment supplied. The wire passing around a pulley should do so at the maximum angle possible since acute angles place a lot of strain on the pulley and shorten the life of the wire considerably.

The exact type of pulleys and wire will vary from system to system, but in all cases secure fastening with ease of movement are the keynote to successful steering installation. It may be necessary in some cases to make up metal brackets to assist the wire system around difficult

corners but this is far too individual to deal with here and must be assessed in each case as the installation progresses. A little ingenuity will usually resolve most problems since, as mentioned, the basic principle of installing steering gear is to reduce stresses as much as possible and attain an easy, positive action throughout the whole system.

The wire, when secured to its terminals on the quadrant, must be tuned up tight to reduce any slackness. Usually turnbuckles or similar equipment are provided for this purpose. Likewise, the quadrant must be well secured to the rudder shaft and keyed to ensure that under stress there will be no slipping or take-up.

In some larger craft the wire and pulleys are replaced by a system of rods and linkage. This makes for a more rigid, positive steering system but is very expensive and difficult to install.

The installation of the rudder is described on page 82 but it is important at this point to emphasise the correct fitting of the *rudder gland*. This not only acts as a support (or bearing) for the shaft, but also provides the waterproof seal between the inside and outside of the hull. This only applies to balanced rudders, of course, since transom-hung rudders have the attachment of the steering equipment above the waterline.

As a rule, the rudder gland, like the stern gland, is purchased as a complete unit and fitted into the hull. The method used will vary according to the type of gland involved, but it is obviously necessary to ensure that the bond between hull and rudder gland is watertight and structurally strong since considerable stresses will be placed on it when steering in a seaway.

In the case of timber, fibreglass and ferro-

The rudder gland not only makes a watertight seal in the hull but also acts as a support for the shaft.

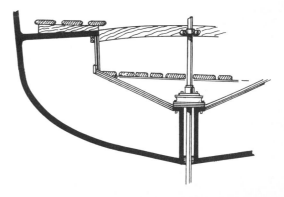

cement boats it may be necessary to reinforce the area with stiffeners of some description, and as a general rule a steel gland bracket welded to the hull skin will serve the purpose on a steel boat. Much will depend on the location of the gland, particularly where other structural members are concerned, as all stresses should be spread throughout as much of the hull as possible. If the gland can be braced between two stringers or floors, the load is well spread. Failing this, inter-costal members or local reinforcing may be necessary.

Single cable steering is widely used in small power craft. Note the gradual curve of the cable below the wheel— severe curves make the system difficult to use.

A rudder shaft showing the gland where it passes through the hull, but without a trunk. This gland and the bearing at the upper end are both acting to support the shaft and are under stress.

Single cable steering (Teleflex Morse)

A modern development of the wire and pulley system uses a single cable without pulleys, but with an inner moving cable secured at the rudder end to a rigid arm. Movements of the wheel are transmitted via the inner cable to the rigid arm which in turn moves the rudder stock via a tiller or quadrant. Installation of this system is much easier since it does away with much of the fastening of pulleys, the only requirement being that the cable is not bent through too acute an angle. Something in the vicinity of a curve with a 25 cm radius is considered to be the minimum bend.

This system, known through a variety of trade names, is one of the most popular systems in use for small craft. Ease of installation and modest maintenance requirements make it ideal for runabouts and power craft up to about 30 ft., over which the rudder loads dictate a cable and quadrant system.

In fitting this system, the principal requirement is the firm attachment of the outer cable. Along the length it may be secured by fairly light fastenings, but at each end, and in particular at the rigid end, it must be through bolted to the hull structure as it will come under considerable stresses when the steering gear is in use.

Hydraulic steering gear

Yet another system, and one which is popular with larger craft, is the hydraulic steering system. Here the pulleys and cables of previous systems are replaced by hydraulic pipes—usually copper or high pressure rubber—filled with oil. The operation of the rudder is not unlike that of the brakes on a car in that any movement of the

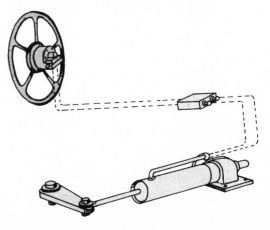

Basic features of a hydraulic steering system as described in the text.

steering wheel is transmitted via the pipes to the rudder. Twin pipes are necessary to gain movement in both directions, and a master cylinder in which a piston moves and in turn moves the rudder stock via a tiller, operates the rudder end of the system. A pump is sometimes employed to activate the pressure in the pipes at the wheel end although, as with all steering gear, much depends on the individual brand as to the exact method of operation.

Installation is simple as a rule since there are no areas of great stress in the hydraulic system other than at the rudder end. The piston unit must be well mounted since it has the task of thrusting the rudder stock to one side or the other, and through bolting will be necessary. With the hydraulic lines, a more important factor is the need to make gradual curves around bends and not create sharp corners or kinks.

Emergency steering gear

Since the steering gear is one of the more important control factors on a boat, many owners like to have standby equipment in case of failure of the main steering gear. Obviously, the type and design of emergency gear will depend on the design of the main gear. There will be little problem, for example, in replacing a broken tiller, but by contrast, emergency equipment for a hydraulic steering system could be quite involved.

Assuming that the boat has a remote control steering system—i.e. anything but direct tiller attachment to the rudder—an emergency unit can be made up without much effort. It must attach directly to the rudder stock and therefore the two requirements necessary before making up such gear are: access to the rudder stock, and the head of the stock must be machined to take an emergency tiller.

Access is easy, since it only involves cutting a hole in line with the rudder head and fitting a watertight cover so that it is closed when not in use. Machining the head of the stock will probably involve lifting out the entire rudder unit, so this is best done before the rudder is fitted. A square or hexagonal head can be welded onto or ground from the head of the stock.

A matching tiller must be made to fit onto the head of the stock, and this is where it will be necessary to adopt individual techniques to suit individual boats. If, for example, there is room in front of the rudder stock to operate a standard, horizontal type of tiller, this is the one to use. But

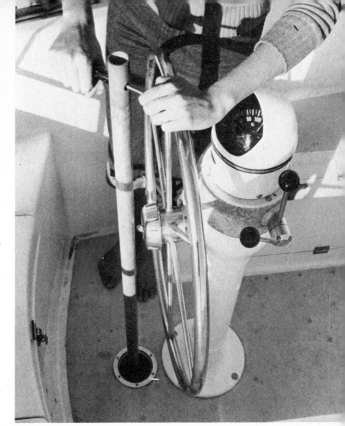

An emergency steering tiller of the type described in the text. The lower end of the pipe is machined to fit onto the head of the rudder stock.

this is not usually the case—mostly, access to the rudder head is through a deck and thus the tiller must be of a design that can be operated vertically.

A good type of emergency tiller to suit these conditions can be made up from a piece of galvanised water pipe a metre or so in length, with a nut or similar piece of metal to match the head of the rudder stock welded at one end. The tiller can then be lowered through the deck to fit directly onto the stock, and a cross-arm fitted to the top of the pipe to provide the necessary fulcrum to operate the unit.

This design has the advantages of requiring only a small hole in the deck for access to the rudder, and if the cross-arm is made portable, the whole unit can be folded down and easily stowed away. Stainless steel pipe is obviously preferable to galvanised steel, but is very expensive.

RUBBING STRAKE

As its name denotes, the rubbing strake is designed principally as a protective fender around the outside of the hull. It may be made of timber or heavy duty rubber or plastic, the latter being used widely on small craft. Timber is more widely used on large craft by virtue of its appearance, and also because of the difficulty of obtaining and fitting large sections of rubber. Where timber is used, the rubbing strake can be made quite decorative and can also hide blemishes or unattractive joins in the hull construction such as the bonding between deck and hull mouldings in fibreglass craft.

Timber rubbing strake
Teak is the ideal timber because it is tough, withstands heavy knocks, and yet looks attractive in either varnished or natural states. The dimensions of the rubbing strake will obviously depend on the size of the boat and whether or not the rubbing strake is to serve any purpose other than its basic one of protecting the hull. If, for example, it is to cover the bonding between the deck and hull mouldings of a GRP boat, it will need to be wide enough to incorporate the bonding and yet allow room for through bolting. Similarly, if it is to be decorative, its depth will depend on the design to which it is to be shaped.

The width of the timber from the hull to its outer edge is perhaps the most important dimension, since this has to serve the purpose of providing good protection to the hull and yet not appearing unsightly. Here again, much will depend on the individual boat, since power boats used as work boats which will be coming alongside jetties or other craft consistently will need a heavy rubbing strake in contrast to the relatively light gauge timber that can be used on a yacht which is kept principally on a mooring. By the same token, too light a section will be liable to crack or even shatter on severe impact, while too heavy a section will be very difficult to fit round the curve of the hull in one piece.

Where a relatively light section timber can be used, such as in small to medium-sized yachts, single section teak is usually the best. Larger sections will need to be steamed—a tricky process—or laminated. (The processes of both steaming and laminating are described in detail on page 36.) Except when laminated, the rubbing strake will rarely be available in one single length and scarfing will be necessary. Scarfing methods are described on page 41. In most cases, the flat inboard side of the rubbing strake will be flush against the hull while the outside corners will be rounded off. Once again, this will depend on individual requirements, particularly where the rubbing strake is to be decorative.

When the timber has been shaped, laminated or steamed and checked against the hull, it is ready to be fastened in position. Fastening should commence at the bow where the rubbing strake will usually start a little way aft from the stem post. There is no point in attempting the difficult business of taking the rubbing strake around the stem since the overhang of the rake will render it useless as a fender. Much the same applies to motor yachts with flared bows, since again the gunwale will be outside the rubbing

Severe bends in the rubbing strake will require steaming or laminating or there will be a risk of either splitting the timber or failing to flush the strake correctly to the hull.

A timber rubbing strake used to cover the hull to deck join on a GRP boat. Such coverings help to strengthen the join and make it watertight while at the same time adding to the boat's appearance.

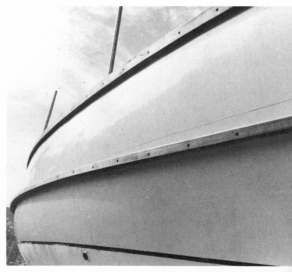

strake—unless of course the strake is fitted at deck level—and will not be protected.

The location of the rubbing strake (apart from any decorative aspect) is where it will be of most practical use. It is always a good idea to leave the strake slightly longer than necessary when commencing to fasten it in place so that any errors in fitting may be taken up. Scarfing, where necessary, must be done before it is curved round and fixed to the hull. Through bolting is the only satisfactory fastening, and bolts should be spaced not less than 20 cm apart along the length of the strake.

Drill the rubbing strake after carefully checking the hull to ensure that the through bolting does not conflict with any item or fitting inside the hull skin. This is particularly important in timber hulls where a hole drilled in way of a beam knee, for example, will make it difficult to secure a nut in the inboard end. Some moulded fibreglass hulls are secured to the deck mould with rivets, and a check should be made to see that the planned bolt hole does not coincide with one of these rivets. At the bow the strake should be drilled to take two bolts within about 6-10 cms of each other, as initially much of the bending stress will come on these fastenings when pulling the timber strake into the hull.

It is not good practice to drill the hull before fitting the strake as curves along the topsides may cause errors in alignment as the strake is drawn up tight. A mastic compound or sealant should be placed between the strake and the hull and also in the bolt holes to ensure watertightness. The boltheads must, of course, be countersunk, and if the finished strake is to be varnished or, in the case of teak, left *au naturel*, dowel plugs will be needed to fill the countersunk hole.

G clamps hold the rubbing strake tight to the hull while bolts are drilled and fastened. Note the pads under clamps to prevent damage to the surface of the timber.

When the two forward bolts are secured—with particular attention paid to load spreading under the nuts—see fastenings page 26—the strake can be bent around the hull by any number of means, such as G clamps or, if these are not practical, a rope passed round the hull well aft and tensioned with a spanish windlass. The location of the rubbing strake and the shape of the hull will determine the type of equipment used to pull the timber tight before each hole is drilled. Unless this is done very carefully, misalignment will occur, and the rubbing strake will not fit flush to the hull.

The procedure is repeated with each bolt hole until the final fastenings near the transom are drawn up tight. The overhanging piece of rubbing strake is then flushed off or shaped to the transom, as required. The whole procedure is then repeated on the opposite side of the boat until both rubbing strakes are in place, when any excess sealant can be wiped off and finishing treatment applied.

Because the rubbing strake is likely to come in for fairly heavy stresses under impact, the through bolting must be given close attention inside the hull. If, as may be the case with timber

With GRP hulls, load-spreading pads or a specially fitted stringer glassed into place is essential to distribute the stress of the rubbing strake along the hull.

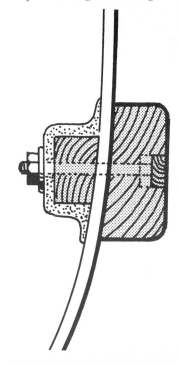

or metal craft, a stringer or deck shelf lies in way of the rubbing strake, it will provide the ideal landing for the bolts. In other cases, particularly with GRP hulls, solid, load-spreading pads must be used. A timber stringer running the length of the hull and matching the rubbing strake on the inside makes for an excellent landing in a GRP hull and distributes the load well throughout the hull structure. In many cases, for the sake of appearance, as well as to prevent fastenings coming undone, this stringer may be glassed over or covered with some form of internal liner.

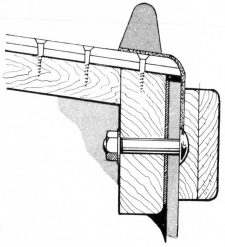

The beam shelf or any similar structural member makes an ideal fastening point for the rubbing strake if it is conveniently located. Timber hulls usually have stringers or frames in a suitable position even if the beam shelf cannot be used.

Rubber rubbing strake

Rubber or some of the high-strength synthetics are often used as rubbing strakes for relatively small craft. The section of material is usually hollow and so designed that bolt or rivet heads can be concealed within the outer surface, thus improving the appearance and preventing the possibility of damage either to the bolt heads or to other craft lying alongside. The procedure for fastening the rubber in place is similar to that described earlier for timber rubbing strakes, although there is generally less need for heavy bolts and pads on the inside of the hull since much of the impact is absorbed by the rubber. When measurements have been carefully made for placement of bolts, the rubber should be secured at the forward end and then stretched hard before each hole is drilled through the rubber and the hull—at the same time. Failure to

A stainless steel strap used in preference to washers, as a load-spreading pad under the bolt heads, will prevent synthetic rubbing strakes from sagging between fastenings as they become stretched with use.

stretch the rubber hard will result in sagging between fastenings at a later date.

While the pads on the inside of the boat need not be as elaborate as for a timber rubbing strake, they should still be adequate to prevent stresses which may damage the inside of the hull surface or allow the fastening to be pulled out. In addition, a large washer must be placed under the bolt head against the inside of the rubber to prevent the bolt head from being pulled through the rubber when under load. A sealant should be placed in each bolt hole and a firm synthetic glue used to bond the inside of the rubber to the hull. A stainless steel strap running the length of the boat between the bolt heads and rubber will eliminate the need for washers and prevent sagging between each bolt.

The open ends of the rubbing strake at the bow should be capped with special fittings which should also be fitted where the rubbing strake terminates near the transom unless, as is often the case, it is taken right round the boat. Since the flexibility of rubber or synthetic material allows it to be bent round reasonably acute corners, it is quite easy to fit an all-round rubbing strake.

TANKS

There are a number of problems associated with fitting tanks, not least of which is the question of weight distribution. Since neither water nor fuel is of light weight when carried in quantity, tanks located in the wrong place can quickly upset the

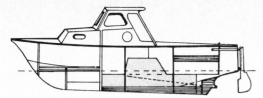

Placement of tanks in the hull must be planned carefully if the boat is to trim correctly and not become tender or stiff when the tanks are filled or empty.

trim of the boat and impair her performance. Placing all the weight down low can cause her to be 'stiff' and move with a jerky, uncomfortable action in a seaway, which will strain every fibre of her construction. By the same token, too much weight too high will make her 'tender' and cause her to be unstable. Weight forward or aft will cause her to ride bow up or bow down respectively, making her hard to handle and even dangerous in a difficult sea.

For this reason the tanks should be located according to the designer's plan. His calculations will have taken into consideration the location and size of the tanks and their effect on the trim of the boat when full or empty. If a plan is not available then you will have a real problem, but undoubtedly the basic formula to work on—primitive though it may be—is to keep the weight down low in preference to high up and as centrally located as possible. In a yacht this indicates the keel and in fact most tanks are fitted in or near the keel area. But in a motor yacht with relatively small keel space the problem is not an easy one. Wing tanks on either side of the motor are a popular position for the fuel storage providing they do not upset the boat's stability.

Another problem is the material from which the tanks are to be constructed. Without doubt the advent of synthetic and rubber tanks which, like heavy duty balloons, fill up and fit into any space is one of the greatest innovations of recent times. But these are usually restricted to fairly small sizes and while ideal for yachts with small auxiliary motors are not suited to motor yachts with long range and high fuel consumption. Stainless steel is an excellent material for fuel and water tanks but is very expensive. Mild steel and galvanised steel can also be used. Brass is not recommended for fuels as it tends to build up a sludge residue.

Most popular in modern craft where fitted tanks are required are fibreglass tanks which can be built to fit each individual boat without too much expense and which, if correctly constructed, can be of good size. This material can create problems with water tanks—great care

must be taken in mixing the resin or the water may become contaminated when the tank is filled. Whatever the material used to build the tanks they must be properly constructed since all but small tanks can create stability problems, particularly when the fluid has a 'free surface'—i.e. the tank is not completely filled and the liquid can slosh from side to side. This should be prevented in tanks of 20 litre capacity or more by fitting internal baffles.

Baffles divide the tank into compartments but allow the liquid to flow easily from compartment to compartment, usually by means of staggered partitions or large holes.

Construction

Since both fuel and water tanks must usually be fitted into tight or awkward corners of the hull they must often be specially made. In the case of motor yachts with wing tanks on either side of the hull it may be possible to purchase a ready-made tank which will fit without too much hassle. But the complex curves of a yacht's keel will create a lot of problems in making a tank to fit. In many cases of this type, the hull itself is closed in to form a tank. Indeed, the keel area makes an excellent tank simply by closing in the top and dividing the tank into compartments. Big ships carry most of their fuel and water in their double bottom tanks which, in effect, are the sealed off bottom of the ship.

The following may help in the planning and construction of tanks.

1 cu. ft holds 6.25 Imp. gal., 7.5 US gal. or 28.1 L.

1 cu. ft of fresh water weighs 62.5 lbs; of petrol or diesel fuel about 46 lbs.

Petrol or diesel weighs about 7.2–7.5 lb/Imp. gal., 6–6.25 lbs/US gal., 0.72–0.75 kg/L.

10 Imp. gal. = 12 US gal. = 4.55 L = 1.6 cu. ft.

1 L = 0.22 Imp. gal. or 0.26 US gal.

1 US gal. = 0.83 Imp. gal. = 3.78 L = 0.13 cu. ft.

Allow 1 gal./person/day fresh water consumption.

14 gauge mild steel plate is quite suitable for water tanks, galvanised inside and out, and cement-washing the inside of the tank will inhibit corrosion.

Marine grade stainless steel is also suitable;
Filler pipes should be not less than 1½" (38 mm) diameter;
Outlet pipes for water—PVC tube;
Outlet pipes for fuel—seamless copper or a copper/nickel alloy such as Monel.

Wing tanks

This is a term generally given to fuel tanks carried on each side of the boat and attached to the hull. They must be strategically placed not to upset the trim of the boat as they are often raised well off the floors to gravity-feed the motor. An important point in fitting wing tanks is that they should be connected by a levelling pipe so that as fuel is used from one tank it can be levelled with the opposite tank, thus preventing any upset to the thwartships trim of the boat. A tap fitted to this line under each tank will allow the tanks to be levelled when necessary but will shut off the levelling line when not required. This is quite

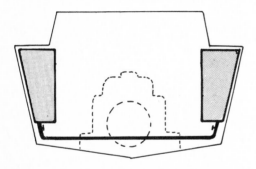

Layout of wing tanks in a diesel motor yacht. Note the connecting fuel line and stop cocks to prevent inadvertent flow of fuel from one tank to another.

important, since an open line between the tanks will create a constant surge of fuel between the tanks as the boat rolls.

There is an additional small pipe attached to a diesel tank, known as a *spill return*, which carries the leftover diesel fuel from the engine back into the tank. This pipe enters the top of the tank.

Fibreglass tanks

There are three commonly used methods of making GRP tanks. The first is integral with the hull, closing off a section to form the tank, and generally restricted to GRP hulls. For safety reasons, this is confined to diesel fuel only, and where petrol (gasoline) is employed the second and more common method is necessary. Here the tank is moulded separately and

installed in the hull in much the same way as any other tank, and it should be sited as far as reasonably possible from a petrol engine. The third method involves making up the separate sides of the tank in GRP, and bonding them together *in situ*. This may be necessary for reasons of access, but in fitting out a new hull a little planning should obviate such a problem.

Whichever method is used, it is most important to employ the correct resin and to ensure that it is very fully cured. It must have a good resistance to salt water, to the fuel that is being used, and to alcohol and lubricating oil. It should also be fire-retardant, and if not a fire-retardant composition should be added. The proofing of the interior of the tank against penetration by fuel relies on a thick resin coating, and after completing the laminate the interior should be completely coated and allowed to cure for a period of at least one month.

Hull tanks

When the hull itself is used as part of the tank construction, the surface of the GRP hull skin will probably need treatment before it is closed in. This is an ideal method of utilising awkward corners of the hull, particularly yacht keels and bilge areas, but because the gelcoat in the layup of the hull will be on the exterior surface, the chances are that the interior surface will not have been treated at all, or at most only with some

Forming a tank in the cavity of a yacht keel is a popular practice. Here the GRP hull skin is to be treated and the top closed in. The baffles are already in place.

kind of sealer. To ensure that there is no reaction with the chemicals in the fuel and to prevent the possibility of water absorption into the GRP, it is a wise precaution to thoroughly line the area of the hull skin to be used as a tank.

This can be done with gelcoat brushed on or with one of the other patent sealers. Gelcoat is probably best since it will offer good adhesion to the other sides and top of the tank to be bonded later. The inner hull surface should be thoroughly cleaned by scrubbing with carbon tetrachloride or a strong detergent solution to ensure that no grease or dirt is remaining, and then the surface thoroughly dried before the gelcoat is brushed on evenly, thickly and in one direction. This ensures a good, even coat which must be worked into all corners and cavities. It is particularly important to ensure that the gelcoat covers the surface adequately or stray glass fibres may break off at a later date and be drawn into the fuel or water system and cause problems.

The fitting of sides and top to the tank will vary from boat to boat and according to the section of the hull that is involved. Although heavy weights are best kept out of the ends of the hull, if necessary tanks can be under the forward bunks, though not right in the bow. (Aft and bow spaces are better used for stowing bulky but light gear.) Either lockers or tanks make a good platform on which bunks can be built, and side tanks in the centre section often form part of the base for furniture.

The keel area of a yacht beneath the cabin sole is an obvious place for tanks, and because of their usefulness in trimming the hull wing tanks on either side and fore and aft tanks at bow and stern are useful in any craft. The convenience of sealing off the awkward spaces in a GRP hull (which need specially shaped and fitted tanks in craft of other constructions) makes the fitting out job considerably simpler.

The sides and tops of the tanks can be made outside the hull, either from flat sheets of GRP stiffened to take the pressures, or from timber, particularly plywood, which has been well sheathed with a layer of GRP and then sealed with gelcoat resin. The stiffness is particularly important where large surface areas are concerned since the sloshing of free-surface liquid in a tank can place enormous strain on any part of its construction but particularly will tend to buckle the surface.

Ply around 10 mm thick is the lightest gauge which can withstand such pressures without

further reinforcement. Bonding of the edges and corners of the tank to ensure that they are completely sound and watertight can be done using woven fibreglass tape on both the inside and the outside, thoroughly saturated with normal resin and finished with a layer of gelcoat resin. A good-sized inspection hatch will enable the last joint in position to be sealed on the inside.

A large tank only partly filled will have a large surface area of liquid which will slosh around as the boat moves in a seaway. This can create considerable stresses on the tank itself as well as upsetting the stability of the boat, therefore any tank of large area must be divided into smaller compartments by means of baffles. These are simply partitions bonded transversely (in the case of a long tank, also longitudinally) across the full width of the tank. The idea is not to divide the tank into separate compartments so much as to break up the movement of any fluid, thus the baffles have large holes in them allowing free flow of the fluid from one compartment to another while at the same time preventing a sudden rush.

The baffles can be constructed of lighter gauge plywood than that used for the sides, completely sealed with GRP and a layer of gelcoat and well bonded to the sides of the tank. The baffles must be in place before the top of the tank is bonded in place. The top edges of the baffles do not need to be bonded to the top of the tank, provided they are well secured along other edges. Apart from breaking up the free-surface effect of the fluid in the tank the baffles, when properly constructed, can add greatly to its strength.

Moulded tanks

Where tanks are to be built separately and placed in the boat in a completed state, the best procedure is to mould them and allow them to cure well prior to fitting in place. Since the inside is to be the smooth side a male mould can be used for laying up the tank and the lid bonded later. The male mould can be constructed of any material, even another old tank if it is of a suitable size, providing the finish of the mould is smooth and the corners are rounded. Laying up is quite simple and should be done as described on page 19, not forgetting the need for structural reinforcing or bracing of the tank sides.

Wing tanks in a motor yacht are typical of the sort of practical use for this type of tank, and

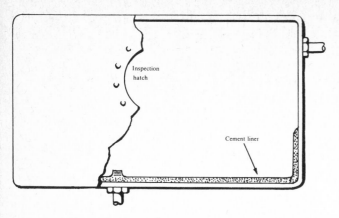

An interior liner of cement wash will help destroy the taste of GRP that is often detected in water from a newly moulded tank. The drawing illustrates the makeup of a typical water tank for small boat use. Baffles may be added, depending on the actual size of the tank.

reinforcing will be essential as the sides of the tank may well be more than one metre high and several metres long. Where the tank is to be fitted into an awkward corner, a great deal of care will be needed to ensure that the mould, allowing for the additional thickness of the tank sides, is the right shape. Trial and error is often the only way when working in difficult corners such as these.

The wall thickness of the GRP should be at least 5 mm for a 40 gal. tank, 6.5 mm up to 80 gal., and 7.5 mm above that. Inspection hatches and inlet and outlet pipes should be incorporated in the moulding, and the best way to ensure that they are fuelproof is to base them on a nut plate. The localised pressure under the flange of a bolt or union will tend to crush the laminate and thus allow a leak, and a nut plate accepts this pressure and forms a good joint. The plate should be of sufficient diameter to permit secure bonding to the wall of the tank, while presenting a clean metal face on which to make the joint. It should be of the same metal as the union or inspection hatch. The laying-up procedure is described on page 19.

When the main body of the tank has been removed from the mould, the top can be bonded in position by means of woven tape inside and outside, and finished with a surface layer of gelcoat resin. This can be done through the inspection hatch after the lid has been sealed on. Where special fittings are required to secure the tank in place brackets or tangs can also be moulded into the construction of the tank, preferably to one of the stiffeners.

Built GRP tanks

Where, for some reason, moulded tanks are not suitable, a GRP tank can be built in place by the simple method of laying up each side of the tank separately then bonding it into position in the boat. Obviously this is restricted mainly to box-shape tanks, and is much more difficult where awkward corners are involved. The separate sides can be constructed of plywood sheathed with GRP or of straight GRP construction, in which case some form of reinforcement or stiffening will be necessary. The face of each side, the ends, top and bottom which are to face inwards must be sealed with gelcoat resin. Similarly, lead-off points such as inlet and outlet pipes and inspection hatches may be incorporated as part of the construction process. Where a curved side is involved, the GRP will need to be laid up on a similarly curved mould or special laminated timber used as the core.

Fitting the tank into place then consists solely of sealing all edges together with glass tape thoroughly impregnated with resin and sealed on the inside with a layer of gelcoat resin. The same principle of using baffles to break up large-volume tanks and stiffening large surface areas applies as it does to other forms of tank construction. The curing process must also be carried out for the same period of time whether the tank is designed for fuel or water.

Installation

The system of bonded-in nut plates already mentioned will facilitate the connection of fuel pipe unions and the neck for the filler pipe, and while this method is preferable for inspection hatches also, where there is no pressure on the hatch (as at the top of a tank) the arrangement shown in the sketch may be used.

When filled with fuel, a 50 Imp. gal. tank may weigh about 450 lbs, and in a planing powerboat at speed it may exhibit a desire to move around:

Forming the inspection port by glassing bolts into position under the tank top. A heavy gasket provides a seal. A hard rigid flange under the bolt heads and all around the opening will make a better base on which to tighten down the cover, however.

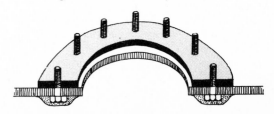

clearly it must be properly secured. And while a diesel tank may normally be below deck, a petrol tank should be either in an open cockpit or in a separate sealed compartment tight against leaks and vapour getting below.

The supports for the tank must be strong enough to support the bottom of the full tank, plus the shock loads imposed when the boat is under way. Additionally, there must be no chance of abrasion occurring between the tank and its mountings, and it is useful if the entire outside surface of the tank is ventilated. Metal straps are a popular and effective way of fixing tanks, and here some soft rubber or other non-abrasive must be interposed between the tank and the straps.

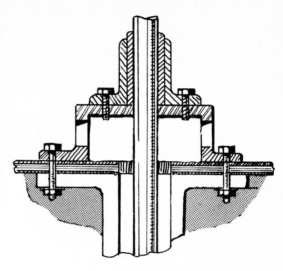

Construction of a complex skin fitting, designed to carry a shaft and thus provide a bearing as well as a waterproof seal.

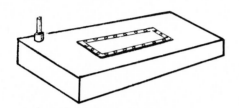

Inspection hatches need not be round ports; square or oblong hatch covers offer easier access to the compartments in the tank but must be well secured to avoid leakage when under pressure.

SKIN FITTINGS

Wherever a hole is drilled through the hull a weakness is created and weaknesses, whether in the hull or anywhere else, cannot be tolerated as they may cause problems when the boat is under stress. Unfortunately it is usually necessary to pierce the hull to fit seawater intake and discharge points for various service functions on board. The weakness thus created must be strengthened and secured by a skin fitting so that risk of structural damage or flooding is minimised.

Skin fittings are required for equipment such as propeller shafts, depth sounders and log impellers. These are specialised pieces of equipment which usually have custom-made skin fittings designed to strengthen and make watertight the hole in the hull through which they pass. Normal water intakes and discharges for equipment such as motor cooling, toilets, galleys and pumps will require a standard skin fitting where they pass through the hull. Whether these fittings are above or below the waterline, the weakness they create in the hull must be compensated for in terms of strength and watertightness.

These skin fittings can usually be purchased as ready-made units. They come in a range of sizes, shapes and designs but basically are constructed of strong plastic or metal (usually bronze) tube which allows the water to pass through the hull and are attached to a (usually) circular plate or flange which forms a strong and watertight seal flush with the hull. The skin fitting should be equipped with a seacock on the inside so that the whole unit can be sealed off in the event of a leak somewhere in the piping system.

The seacock is important even though the skin fitting may be above the waterline, for when the boat heels or rolls in a seaway the fitting will be immersed and water will flood into the hull unless it is closed off with a seacock. Particularly is this important on board yachts where they.may be heeled to one side for some period of time. It is not unknown for the crew of a yacht to find the cabin half full of water due to a simple water intake, such as a toilet or sink discharge, being immersed for some period of time without the stopcock being closed.

Seacocks are usually gate valves, or stopcocks turning through 90°. Flap valves on the outside of the hull are not satisfactory as these can easily seize or function improperly, allowing water into

A typical small skin fitting with valve attached, widely used for boats of all sizes.

The outside of the skin fitting must be neat, smooth and watertight. Many fittings below the waterline are countersunk into the skin so that turbulence, as the boat moves through the water, is reduced to a minimum.

the hull. A valve which can be opened and shut manually is the most suitable.

Much of the secret of success in making skin fittings watertight lies in the seal between the flange and the hull. The hole in the hull skin should fit as tight as possible around the tube of the fitting to ensure good watertightness and reduce the chance of the fitting working in the hole when the hull is under stress. Care in cutting and shaping the hole and in carefully filing out to get an exact fit will ensure trouble-free operation when the boat is in use.

Similarly, the outboard flange of the fitting must be flushed neatly against the hull. It is always a good practice to have a dry run to ensure that everything is lined up both inside and outside the hull before fastening it into position. If the flange is secured to the hull by bolts, exact alignment of the holes in the flange and the hull can be made during the dry run. Many modern fittings utilise the intake pipe itself as a threaded fastening onto which a threaded plate on the inside, or a nut, is tightened down onto a heavy backing pad, usually of wood. A solid pad is needed to maintain axial alignment, give a good seal area on the thread, and make a rigid base against which to tighten the nut.

With everything aligned, the skin fitting is removed, and the surfaces of both the hull and the fitting coated with a thick sealant. Now the fitting is worked back into place and fastened into position by whatever means is provided. The sealant should be squeezed into bolt holes as well as the main hole and liberally applied round both the outside and the inside of the hull so that when the fitting is screwed up tight the sealant will be squeezed into every nook and cranny, thus ensuring watertightness. Some shipwrights like to seal over the whole interior section of the skin fitting with fibreglass to ensure that it is watertight, and skin fittings are provided with rubber or similar washers for much the same reason. Whatever the method, the ultimate aim is to ensure that the skin fitting is rigidly bolted into place and is absolutely watertight.

TOWING RING

Trailer boats require an eye bolt set into the stem to which the winch wire can be attached. When retrieving the boat from the water enormous strains are placed on this eye bolt—indeed, one could safely say that the entire weight of the boat is at some point virtually hung on this fitting.

The fine angle of the bow plus the curve of the forefoot often make it difficult to fit a metal plate under the nut and it may be necessary to shape or bend the plate so that it fits snugly. Special care must be taken to ensure that hot spots are not created when fitting this plate and it should be so designed as to spread the load evenly into the nearest structural members. Particularly is this the case with fibreglass boats where it is not unheard of for incorrectly secured eye bolts to pull the stem off!

Because of the difficulty of fitting load-spreading pads in the eye of the bow, GRP hulls may have a solid GRP section filled in to take the stress of the towing ring. U bolts or ring bolts are suitable providing they are well secured.

CHAPTER 5

Deck Fittings

STRESS FITTINGS

MANY DECK FITTINGS must be designed to withstand heavy loads. Particularly is this the case with yachts where much of the running rigging is keyed to deck fittings such as sheet blocks and tracks which, when in use, must withstand considerable stresses. These fittings must not only be well designed and specially constructed to withstand stress, but must also be secured to the deck in such a way that the load is spread over the deck structure as much as possible and not concentrated on one area to create a hot spot.

In Chapter 3 I discussed means of spreading loads across the structure of the hull and of strengthening areas where fittings are secured to weak structural surfaces. The same principles exactly apply to deck fittings and the procedure for strengthening weak areas and spreading the load is similar to that used on any other part of the hull. Much will depend, of course, on the structure of the deck in the vicinity of the fitting and of the material from which the deck is made. A steel plate deck, for example, may be sufficiently strong for many of the deck fittings to be simply welded into place. A fibreglass deck, by contrast, will need considerable strengthening in the area of the fitting because of the flexibility of the synthetic material and the general lack of structural members.

The basic approach to securing deck fittings which will come under stress is to fasten them, wherever possible, through a major structural member such as a deck beam or shelf. If this is not possible, the load must be spread across as large an area of the deck as possible, or preferably to the nearest structural members. With timber decks, this is fairly simple, since if a deck beam is not located in a convenient position an inter-costal member can be fitted between the two adjacent beams, or a strongback type of beam secured across them to take the fastenings. Imagination and ingenuity can do much to locate deck fittings so that the load is readily spread and hot spots are avoided. Because of the framework type of structure used to support wooden decks,

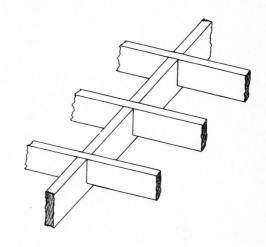

Intercostal bearers can be fitted singly between two deck beams or across a number of beams, depending on the type of fitting to be secured through it. The intercostal must be rebated to take the beams. The beams must not be rebated or they may be weakened.

it is rare to have large areas without a deck beam or some other structural member in the right position to support a fitting.

Fibreglass decks present the greatest problems, since structural members are frequently lacking over quite considerable areas. The two basic methods of reinforcing a fibreglass deck in the area of a fitting are to use a large pad of timber or metal—the latter is preferable for fittings which come under stress—to spread the load to adjacent structural members or, if that is not possible, over a large surface area of the deck. The pad may or may not be glassed in but should have its edges chamfered and corners rounded to prevent hot spots being formed around the perimeter. Stainless steel plate or plywood are most commonly used.

Although a ferro-cement deck also needs load-spreading pads if there is no structural member in the vicinity of a fitting, in this case the pad is usually of lighter gauge and sometimes smaller than one used for fibreglass in a similar position. The structure of the ferro-cement deck is in itself a good load-spreading medium.

The makeup of a ferro-cement hull is excellent for load spreading and does not have the problems of GRP where stress fittings are concerned.

Metal decks may need reinforcing between the structural members, but this will depend on the size of the unsupported area, the gauge of the metal and the amount of stress to be placed on the fitting. As already mentioned, sometimes merely welding the fitting to the deck is sufficient; in other cases structural reinforcing beneath the deck may be necessary to spread the load to adjacent structural members.

One type of deck construction which requires special attention is the GRP sandwich formation using outer and inner sheathings of fibreglass and a core of balsa, foam, or some similar material. Although the basic format of pad or other load-spreading device as described for fibreglass decks is used with sandwich construction, it must be augmented by the use of compression tubes or some similar device to prevent the weak inner core being crushed, and thus collapsing the deck, when the fastenings are drawn up tight.

The compression tubes must be cut to the exact thickness of the deck so that when drawn up tight, the nuts and bolt head are flush against the load-spreading pads, yet are not creating any compression on the deck. It is still necessary to use load-spreading plates, otherwise the GRP surface will be damaged or a hot spot created. The compression tubes or spacers, as they are sometimes called, only relieve the compression stresses; all other stresses must be distributed through the deck as much as possible.

Another method of preventing damage to a sandwich deck is to replace the sandwich construction in the area of the fitting by a solid, non-compressible substance such as solid fibreglass or timber. Normal bolting is then used,

and the nuts drawn up tight in the usual way. The important factor, of course, is to ensure that the load is well distributed by the solid insert and no weakness occurs where it joins the rest of the deck. To achieve this a stainless steel pad placed beneath the fitting should extend beyond the perimeters of the solid insert thus transferring the stresses well out to the surrounding sandwich deck.

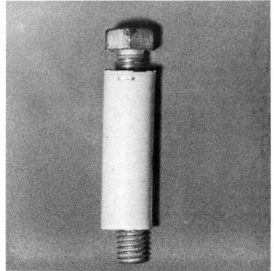

One method of preventing damage to sandwich construction is to place compression tubes between the head of the bolt and the load-spreading plate to prevent the deck being compressed when the fastening is drawn up tight.

Cleats

One of the most typical of deck fittings which encounter heavy stresses in use and which require the type of stress fitting described earlier, is the cleat.

There is a great variety of cleats, ranging from the traditional *horn* cleat through to the more modern *jam* and *Clam* cleats. Some are used for securing halyards and sheets, some for mooring ropes and even, on smaller craft, for mooring chains. Some may be attached to masts or bulkheads, but most are fitted to the deck or some area close to the deck such as cockpit coamings. Whatever the type, every cleat will come under severe stress when in use since its purpose is to secure a rope and more often than not the rope will carry a load.

This puts the cleat into the category of a stress fitting and requires it to be securely fastened, always with through bolts and a means of load distribution on the under side of the deck. Pads or load-spreading plates will be necessary beneath the cleat unless it is bolted through a structural member such as a deck beam. The use of screws or other light fastenings is out of the question.

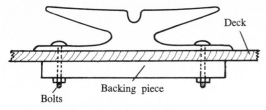

Basic method of fastening a cleat where a structural member is not conveniently located.

To prevent leaking the cleat should be set in a thick layer of sealant before bolting up tight and it is a good idea to place a layer of sealant between the base plate and the deckhead as well as in the bolt holes. When the fitting is bolted up tight the sealant will then be squeezed out to fill every cavity and make a good watertight seal. The excess can be wiped away or left until it has hardened and trimmed with a knife. It is important when locating cleats to align them as nearly as possible with the direction of the load. This offers better strength when under load, as the stresses are longitudinally arranged on the cleat and its fastenings, along the length of the baseplate.

Winches
Sheet and halyard winches are among the most heavily stressed of deck fittings, and for this reason they must be securely fastened with the appropriate load-spreading backing pads. In addition, it is worth giving a thought to the structural stiffness of the deck or coaming to which the winch will be attached, and whether that too can contribute to the general security of the fitting. For instance, headsail winches are commonly fastened to the moulded cockpit coaming of a GRP deck, which apart from being handy for the crew is also a nice top-hat section with excellent inherent stiffness. The load on a winch is also often predominantly in shear, and so, as much as the backing pad, strong and snugly fitting bolts are also important.

Elsewhere on the boat there may not be mountings as ideally shaped as the cockpit coaming, and perhaps the winch may have to be sited off the immediate deck to obtain a fair lead.

If the base is in the correct position, the winch is merely bolted through the deck or coaming to some load-spreading medium underneath. On small craft, the winch's handle can sometimes foul the liferails, as seen here, and this should be checked before determining the position of the winch.

In cases such as this a small platform or mounting bracket may have to be made, along the lines shown in the sketch overleaf. On the subject of lead angles between the sheet and winch, it is worth mentioning that the load on the sheet may be well over a ton. An unfair lead will chafe the rope and promote riding turns, or worse, damaged fingers.

Perhaps the most frequent call for a separate platform for a winch is at the mast, where most sailing boats over 25 ft. now require a halyard winch. The walls of an aluminium mast are relatively thin, and almost certainly round or oval in form, such that a mounting plate is necessary to secure the winch and give a fair purchase on the halyard. Such plates are a normal part of a mast manufacturer's range of fittings, and will have accurately pressed feet which fit snugly on the mast section. The area of the feet is made sufficient for an adequate number of rivets or screws, and in this way the localised loads on the winch mounting bolts are safely carried by the mast.

The simplest form of winch mounting which is easily adjustable to angle the winch in the required direction is a metal bracket in the form of an inverted U which is bolted through the deck or cockpit coaming. Adjustment to the height of the bracket and the angle of the base enables the winch to be tilted in almost any direction. Providing it is made of sufficiently strong gauge metal—preferably stainless steel—and is properly fastened through the deck, this type of bracket should withstand any stresses which will come on the winch in use.

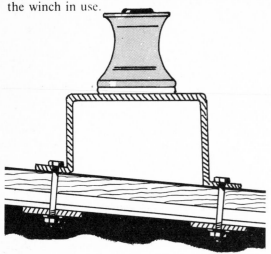

A simple arrangement for levelling a winch on a cambered deck, or angling a winch to align with the lead of the rope.

Where this type of winch mounting is used on timber, ferro-cement or fibreglass boats, it must be through bolted with an appropriate load-spreading plate or structural member on the underside of the deck. Bonding, even with GRP, is not sufficiently strong. Steel craft will most likely have the bracket welded directly to the deck which, providing the deck is structurally strong enough, is sufficient. The methods of fastening and the type of plates to be used will vary according to the location of the winch.

It sometimes happens that a winch needs to be mounted in an unusual position, such as on a pedestal, but these situations are much too individual to deal with in a book such as this. Suffice it to say that providing the mounting itself is sufficiently strong and is correctly fastened through the deck, there is no reason why a winch cannot be mounted anywhere that it is required.

Sheet winches are usually located on or near the cockpit coaming. If the coaming is not sufficiently strong or suitably constructed then it may need to be built up to provide a suitable

A winch needs to be sited to provide a fair lead and a good purchase on the line it serves. These examples also prompt the observation that it is only a winch, not a stowage for a sheet!

base. The base may be constructed from a U-plate as described earlier, or shaped from a solid timber block. The aesthetics of blending the base into the general line of the coaming must be taken into consideration for nothing is worse than a hotch-potch of mountings which not only appear unsightly, but also stub toes and create other problems in use. Once again, where no suitable base is provided, it becomes a matter of ingenuity to adapt each individual location.

One of the most difficult locations in which to mount a winch is on the side of the mast. Apart from the need to drill, and thus weaken the mast wall, there are other problems associated with mast-mounted halyard winches such as corrosion, compression and reinforcement. Mounting and fastening winches on a mast is dealt with in detail later in this book.

There is a school of thought which favours the use of tapped bolts for mast fittings where through bolting is not possible. Much depends on the fitting and the load it will carry. Only light gauge winches can be mounted this way, and then only on relatively small craft. Halyard winches do not come in for the enormous stresses that are placed on sheet winches and it is sometimes possible to use tapped bolts for halyard winches mounted on the mast—but only if the preferable system of through bolting is quite impossible.

STEMHEAD FITTING

The *stemhead* fitting, or *bow plate* as it is also known, comprises a number of fittings which may sometimes be individual, but are more commonly combined into one large fitting. It may include the forestay chain plate, the mooring roller, fairleads, the base for pulpit stanchions and may also, in some cases, be fitted with a mooring cleat or bollard. Stemhead fittings are almost invariably constructed of stainless steel and shaped to fit the bow of the boat. For this reason, they are very individual and it is usually better to purchase the correct fitting for your boat than attempt to adapt or build your own.

Where a one-off design has to be fabricated for a particular boat, however, wrought iron or plough steel makes an equally strong fitting which after welding is heavily galvanised.

The major upward strain on a stemhead fitting will normally be the jibstay, and to anchor this a tang may be incorporated in the fitting and carried down the stem on the hull. Where the stay is secured a short distance inboard of the stem on a deck plate, a rigging screw (turnbuckle) is usually fitted between the underside of the plate and an eyebolt in the stem to similarly transfer the load.

The major downward strain on the stemhead is usually from the anchor cable, and where a shallow draft boat veers about at her anchor this can be considerable. The fitting therefore needs to incorporate a decent sized deck plate with adequate bolts so that it may be securely fastened through the deck. We have dealt with the subject of backing pads to spread the load; while the pyramid form of the bow will assist with this, a metal pad must be fitted, or alternatively a timber pad at least one inch thick.

The subject of the anchor cable raises the question of the best material for the bow roller. Nylon, Tufnol, mild steel and stainless steel are all frequently used, but where there is anchor chain only the last is hard wearing and corrosion-free. Bronze was at one time often seen in this application, occasionally for the complete stemhead fitting, but today its use is unfortunately rather rare.

A look around any marina will show that the stemhead fitting has often allowed its designer full rein for his creative art, and some examples are shown here. The more complex varieties are invariably found aboard fibreglass craft where the simplicity of the bow moulding permits a more elaborate design, and in boats of steel, ferro or timber construction the presence of a stempost and other structural components will usually dictate something simpler.

FAIRLEADS

A fairlead can be subjected to great stresses which mostly create pressure down onto the fitting or in a fore and aft direction rather than upwards. Indeed, many fairleads are open at the top so that no upward pressure can be placed on them, their purpose being solely to provide a guide for mooring ropes or chain and also to reduce wear on the vulnerable edges of the deck.

For this reason fastening of the fairlead is fairly simple and is usually achieved by through bolting. Two good bolts secured through some structural member beneath the deck is the usual practice. There may be stresses placed on the fastenings by transverse pressures when the boat rides awkwardly on the mooring or is pushed sideways by wind or tide. These can place a lot of strain on the fairlead so it is important that the fastenings are well secured inside the hull.

In the case of timber boats the fairleads may be bolted through the deck and a beam or plate beneath. Ideally they should be fastened through the beam shelf, and if conveniently placed this will eliminate the need for a plate under the deck. Where a suitable structural member is not located directly beneath the fairlead an intercostal beam or an under-deck plate or pad will usually suffice.

Fairleads are usually welded into position on a steel deck but ferro-cement decks will need the through-bolting system used for timber with a pad or plate on the underside. Fibreglass decks

likewise need a strengthening piece beneath the fitting—this can take the form of a thickened glass section or a timber or metal pad. Washers should be used between the pad and the nuts and a waterproof sealant placed beneath the fairlead before bolting up tight.

The location of the fairlead is important since one of its main functions is to prevent undue wear or chafe where a rope or chain runs over the gunwale. The fairlead should be placed into the approximate position and trial and error with a piece of rope used to determine the best location to offer protection to the deck. Particularly is this important with bow fairleads, since the movement of the boat on her mooring cable can create different angles and cause different pressures on the fitting. At all times the fairlead must hold the cable clear of the hull and deck. If it fails to do so then a larger fitting or a different location is indicated.

A roller or similar fitting placed over the bow is the best system for mooring cables. Not only does the roller offer friction-free movement of the cable, but it also holds it well clear of the stem with less likelihood of the boat riding up onto the chain and causing chafe damage. As a rule these roller fairleads are incorporated as part of the stem head fitting described earlier.

Where a conventional fairlead does not prevent chafe or wear no matter how it is fitted a stainless steel plate will need to be bolted onto the deck around the 'mouth' of the fairlead. This often occurs where, because of structural problems, the fairlead cannot be located right on the edge of the deck. The space between the fairlead itself and the gunwale must be protected. The plate may be screwed in place since it will receive only downward pressures, although light bolts will prevent the possibility of the whole fitting being ripped out of the deck if a rope catches under a corner. Stainless steel plate must be used for this fitting and it will need to be carefully cut and shaped to fit the surface it protects. A template will provide the best guide for this work.

BULLSEYES

Bullseyes serve much the same purpose as fairleads—guiding a rope—and are even constructed in much the same way, the only difference being that the bullseye is closed at the top while a fairlead is usually open. Bullseyes are mostly equipped with U-bolt fastenings

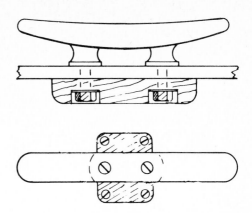

Bullseyes are used to guide ropes and are not heavily stressed as a general rule. However they should be through bolted against the possibility of unexpected strain which might pull them out of the deck.

and generally speaking are secured in the same way as fairleads. However, because they completely enclose the rope they are liable to more severe upwards strains than the open-topped fairlead and thus require a very secure fastening. Where possible bolting should be through a structural member or heavy inter-costal member, but failing this a good sized plate or timber pad will be necessary.

EYEBOLTS

Eyebolts are usually used for heavy work such as deck fastenings for rigging or purchases and while somewhat similar to fairleads or ringbolts, they are of much heavier dimensions. For this reason they must be fastened through a strong structural member or a very solid under-deck plate. Even where the bolt pierces a structural member, a plate is necessary to distribute the considerable stresses around the nut. A good sized washer will do in some cases but where the fastening is made through the deck a stainless steel plate of good dimensions will be necessary.

Heavy gauge plates are ideal for this sort of fitting, although where really high stresses can be expected, angle iron might be necessary. Once again the main problems are with timber, fibreglass and concrete, but even steel decks may need structural support for eye bolts that come under great strain or there will be a tendency to

buckle the deck plate. A piece of angle iron welded to the underside of the deck will take care of this problem.

Only one hole needs to be drilled since the eye-bolt, as its name denotes, is a single bolt with an eye or ring as part of its structure. Hence, all the stresses are at one point rather than spread through two or more fastenings as is the case with most other fittings.

SHEETING TRACKS

These fittings are usually some form of metal rail secured through the decks or toe rail to provide an adjustable location for headsail sheeting blocks. Since these blocks create the angle between the powerful sheet winch and the sail itself, enormous strains are transmitted to the hull through the sheeting track when the headsails, particularly big genoas, are full of wind. It follows, then, that this is most definitely a stress fitting and as such must be very well secured to the main structure of the deck.

The choice of track is a personal one and there is a variety of different sections to suit different boats or different sheeting mechanisms. However, no matter what the construction of the track, it must be securely through bolted into the main structure of the deck. If the track is to be mounted on the gunwale then some structural member of the hull such as the beam shelf will probably provide the ideal strength member for this.

Where the track is set onto the deck, usually inboard of the gunwale, then it will need to be secured through the deck beams. If these are too widely spaced—as is usually the case—or are insufficient, as so often happens with fibreglass, then pads of steel plate or heavy plywood will need to be placed beneath the deck to spread the load. Inter-costal members are also a common method of taking the stresses from the sheeting track, and it is not uncommon to use aluminium or steel angle irons as inter-costal members. These inter-costals must be snugged up to the underside of the deck and not simply laid across the beams, since the upward pressure would distort or break them when the track is under load.

The number of bolts required will probably be predetermined by the drilling of the track, and this also, of course, will dictate their location. Since this may not always fit with the location of deck beams and similar structural members, the system of using a pad beneath the track is probably the most common one. Certainly it is ideal for fibreglass decks where beams are widely spaced or not fitted. Steel decks may not need reinforcing, the track can be welded in some cases directly to the deck plating, providing it is of sufficient strength. Should it tend to buckle, reinforcing will be needed in the form of a welded angle iron beneath the deck.

The exact location of the tracks must be

Tracks or travellers with unsupported spans must be reinforced to cope with the considerable stresses that will be placed on the fitting.

worked out before if the deck plan is not available. In many cases the tracks are angled across the deck rather than following the line of the gunwale and in many craft, particularly high-performance yachts, several short lengths of track are staggered at different locations along the deck to suit different sized headsails. Since there is only one sheeting position for each sail if it is to be correctly set, then obviously the location of the sheeting tracks is of vital importance. If the deck plan is not available then the sailmaker who made the sails should be called in to check where the sheeting tracks should be located in order to get the best out of his sails.

Self-tacking jibs and mainsails are usually sheeted to a track running athwartships across the deck or cabin top. Once again the location of these must be indicated on the boat's deck plan or trial and error experiments carried out to find the best location for the tracks to be secured. They must be fastened just as strongly as headsail tracks since the stresses on them may be just as severe. In the case of a mainsail track where it crosses the cockpit, it may be unsecured for part of its span and therefore the fastening at either end must be extra strong.

Since in all cases the centre of pressure is movable, the track must be firmly secured along its entire length where this is possible. Heavy duty tracks will assist in spreading the load but the fastenings are the most vital part of this fitting since through them the stresses are transferred into the hull's structure. In addition to secure fastening, since they penetrate the deck they must also be made well waterproof by liberal use of a flexible sealant.

A typical deck-fastened sheeting track for the headsail of a medium-sized cruising yacht. Some tracks are curved; others are in short, staggered lengths to suit different headsails. Some boat owners use the toe rail and shackle the sheet blocks through one of the 'scuppers'.

Ready-made handrails are available in a variety of designs and materials and are easily bolted into place on the cabin roof.

HANDRAILS

Handrails come in many shapes and sizes and are made of a number of different materials, and in purchasing a handrail for your boat you will need to match aesthetic appearance with the location and usefulness of the fitting.

Stainless steel, chrome or aluminium handrails come complete and need only to be through bolted as for any deck fitting. Make sure that there is a good back-up under the cabin roof to spread the load.

Handrails should never be screwed as under load they may pull out, and in doing so cause the loss of a person overboard. These rails, although they need to look good to enhance the appearance of the boat, are stress fittings and must be firmly secured to the boat's structure.

Probably the most popular type of handrail, particularly with yachtsmen, is made from timber. Teak is the favourite material. Handrails of this type are low in profile and, when varnished, add tremendously to the appearance of the boat. They are easy to construct although they can be purchased complete and ready to fit into position. A simple small boat handrail is quite simple to make to virtually any size. 20-25 mm thick teak is suitable for most sized craft providing it is good clear timber with no weaknesses.

A template should be cut and placed in position on the cabin roof to determine the appearance of the finished product. It is also a good idea, if possible, to match up the fastening locations along the rail with cabin roof beams. This ensures the best possible fastening and avoids the need for plates or pads beneath the cabin roof.

The template is then transferred to a plank or section of teak or other hardwood and the hand rails cut out using a jig saw. There will be a fair amount of shaping to be done, depending on how round you require the hand grip part to be, but with 25 mm thick material, just a general rounding off of the corners and the ends is sufficient. This, obviously, will depend on your ability as a shipwright and the finished appearance you require.

Bolts must be used to secure the hand rails in position and where possible these should be secured through a cabin roof beam. Failing that, an inter-costal member or a metal or timber pad must be used to spread the load at the nut. The bolt itself must be countersunk and a dowel used to plug the head and provide a smooth, unbroken timber appearance. It is important to ensure that the grain of the dowel runs with that of the hand rails. The bolt hole and surrounding areas must be waterproofed with a coating of sealant and the dowel glued into position. The whole unit should then be finished off by smoothing away the dowel, firstly with a chisel—taking care not to split or groove the dowel—and then hand sanding. Some boat owners prefer their teak hand rails to be left raw but oiling with linseed oil or a coat of good varnish will enhance

Teak handrails are easy to make and attractive, providing they merge with the boat's profile. After through bolting, the fastenings are concealed beneath dowels which are flushed off and sanded back to merge with the surrounding timber.

their appearance considerably and is the type of finish most commonly adopted.

As with all timber work, the finish makes the product and time spent sanding initially and between coats of varnish will pay dividends in the final appearance. I have found that a varnishing procedure will give the ultimate result although there is nothing to say that synthetic varnishes do not equal the more traditional oil varnishes in terms of appearance and lasting qualities.

PULPITS AND LIFERAILS

The principle of pulpit and liferails is to surround the boat with a circle of safety. For this reason the first step in setting about the job is to ensure that the rails, stanchions and pulpit are of sufficiently strong gauge. It is quite pointless taking the time and effort to fit the circle of safety if, as soon as it is required, it collapses under the weight of the person using it. Many boatowners go to great pains to fit a beautiful pulpit and liferails, but neglect to check that they are of sufficient strength.

Surrounding the boat with a circle of safety means using liferails and stanchions of adequate dimensions and fastening them to the boat correctly so that they can withstand heavy stresses.

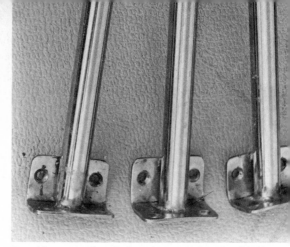

Stanchions must be of adequate strength and welded to base plates which are correctly designed to fit the scuppers where they will be fastened.

Stanchions

The strength of these fittings depends mainly on the gauge of the metal piping used and its diameter. A basis on which to work is that if galvanised iron or stainless steel piping is used it should be of not less than 25 mm diameter. Assuming that the stanchions will be of average height (say 70-80 cm), this will give them sufficient strength and rigidity to withstand the weight of a body thrown against them. Stainless steel fittings can be of slightly lighter gauge as also can monel.

Another strength factor lies in the way in

Extra rigidity can be obtained by welding a bracket to help support the base of the stanchion. Note the shape of the base plate, designed to gain all possible strength from the area in which is it bolted.

which the piping is secured to the base plate. Particularly is this important with stanchions which have no intermediate support. The base plate must be sufficiently wide and of sufficient gauge to be bolted firmly through the deck and likewise withstand the impact of a body against the upright of the stanchion. Using galvanised steel as an example, the gauge of the base plate should be in the region of 3 mm and the dimensions not less than 10 cm x 10 cm. Stainless steel plates may be of fractionally lighter gauge.

The pipe for the upright must be welded to the base plate, although where removable stanchions are required a deep socket can be welded to the plate to accommodate the stanchion. A really good weld may eliminate the need for bracket support at the base of the stanchion, but if there is any doubt about the ability of the weld to hold the upright solidly in position a triangular corner bracket should be welded to add support to the stanchion. In extreme cases it may be necessary to weld a full height angular support to the stanchion. This sometimes occurs at gangways and similar areas of great use.

The stanchions, when completed, must be capped, usually with a wood dowel, or sealed at the top in some other way to prevent water getting down inside the pipe. In case it does get in—and somehow it usually does—a small hole should be drilled at the base of the stanchion just above the base plate to allow for drainage. Holes must be drilled through the stanchion to accommodate the flexible life rails, and if possible these holes should be sleeved to reduce wear and tear on the wire. Plastic covered stainless steel wire is a popular choice for liferails.

Pulpit and pushpit

The pulpit and pushpit should be constructed from the same gauge piping as the stanchions. There is a wide variety of formats for both pulpits and pushpits; obviously much will depend on the individual craft and on the personal choice of the owner. The only criterion is that they have adequate strength. Since many people sit on the pulpit, particularly when changing headsails, and passengers invariably sit on the pushpit, it goes without saying that these must be rigid and well constructed. Similarly the base plates must be well built and firmly welded to give the whole unit a solid firmness that will withstand even heavy knocks.

Pulpits, pushpits and stanchions must, wherever possible, be bolted through a beam or beam shelf. Bolting through the deck is not sufficient and screwing is quite useless. The moment a heavy strain comes on the stanchion the screws will tear out or a section of the deck will come away. If it is not possible to bolt through some structural member—which may be the case with fibreglass decks—then a large pad, preferably of steel but failing that of heavy plywood, must be fitted on the underside of the deck to spread the load and offer a firm base.

Setting up the stanchions and pulpit is relatively easy. When located in their right position—say not more than 2 m apart in the case of stanchions—the deck can be marked and drilled taking care, as mentioned, to ensure that

Pulpits, or bow rails as they are sometimes called, can be purchased as a complete unit, in a number of fancy designs. Whatever the shape or material used, the rails must be firmly fastened through the deck or their purpose will be negated.

Whatever the method of fastening the pulpit, it must be well secured. This part of the safety equipment comes in for great stresses in use.

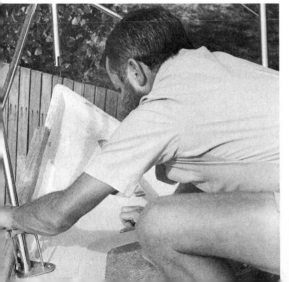

the bolts will go through a structural member or load-spreading pad. To ensure watertightness a synthetic sealant should be used between the base plate and the deck and also in the bolt holes. Always be liberal with sealing compounds under stanchions as watertightness of the deck is very important.

With the stanchions, pulpit and pushpit in position, the liferails can be measured and cut. They should be fitted with swaged eyes at each end and secured at the forward end by a turnbuckle (or lanyard) to allow tensioning, and at the after end by a pelican clip so that they can be released quickly and effortlessly. This is important on yachts since, when running free, the mainsheet or spinnaker gear may drag across the rails creating chafe and damaging both rails and gear. It is also necessary at gangway openings although often in this case just the short section of rail at the gangway is fitted with clips to enable quick release when passengers are boarding.

The whole unit of pulpits and rails should be tightened up when in use as nothing is more likely to cause a man overboard situation than loose, sloppy liferails. Providing the pipe fittings have been well constructed and firmly bolted and the liferails tensioned, the boat should be surrounded by an adequate circle of safety.

If children are carried aboard regularly, or if the boat is an ocean-going craft, the efficiency of the liferails can be increased by securing to them a wide mesh net set between the top rails and the deck. Alternatively, a light line woven between

top rail and the deck will help catch things which might otherwise blow overboard. A canvas dodger laced round the after pulpit and for some distance along the rails on either side provides good shelter for the cockpit area.

HATCH COVERS

There are two basic forms of hatch covers used widely on board boats—the drop-on type which may or may not be hinged, and the sliding hatch cover which is mostly used over companionways on all types of craft. The difference between them is self-evident—the drop-on type is removed from its supporting coaming by lifting either directly upwards or on a hinge, whereas the sliding hatch runs along rails or similar guide fittings and is simply pushed to open the hatchway.

This is hardly the place to go into the advantages and disadvantages of each type. It is sufficient to say that the sliding type of hatch cover is found most useful for hatches which come in for a lot of use and particularly where stairways or companion ladders are involved, but this advantage is offset by the fact that the drop-on type is more secure and less liable to damage or leaking when the boat is at sea. As with many fittings on boats, hatch covers are therefore a compromise, but it would be safe to say that the drop-on hatch cover should be used wherever possible in preference to a sliding hatch, the latter in general use being confined solely to access to the cabin areas.

Drop-on hatch cover
This can be constructed of almost any material. It is a simple box-like cover rather like the lid of a biscuit tin and therefore easily constructed. In the case of metal boats a welded hatch cover is the easiest thing in the world to make, and indeed

The best method of tensioning the liferails is to fit turn buckles or rigging screws at one end. A cheaper method, but equally effective, is to use a lanyard at the pulpit terminal.

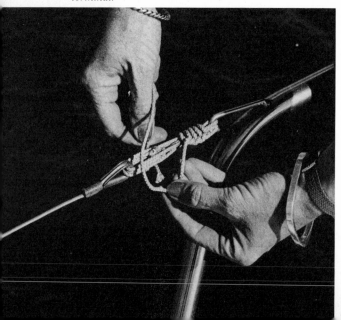

Hatch covers can be purchased as a complete unit and simply bolted into place. Aluminium or stainless steel may be used for the coaming and cover, with tinted armoured glass or Perspex to allow light below decks.

they are the ideal medium for practising your welding skills since they are easily replaced or rebuilt if the practice does not turn out to be perfect! Similarly, moulded fibreglass hatches, as described later, involve simple basic moulding procedures and even the more complicated construction of a box-frame timber hatch cover is unlikely to stretch the abilities of the average handyman.

Probably the most common types of hatch covers are either timber or moulded fibreglass since these can be fitted to any type of boat. It goes without saying that before a hatch cover can be built the hatch coaming must be in place as it is from this coaming that the dimensions of the hatch will be taken.

To obtain the curve in the hatch cover the top may need to be laminated over a mould.

Timber hatch covers

A softwood framework with ply panelling is the most common and simplest method of constructing a built timber hatch cover. Depending on the size of the opening, it may be necessary to reinforce the hatch cover, but small hatches may use the strength of the plywood laminate at the top plus the curve of the inbuilt camber to give sufficient strength without further reinforcement. The dimensions must be precise, since the finished hatch cover should fit snugly over the coaming and therefore the interior dimensions of the hatch cover sides should be only fractionally

A basic timber hatch cover is easily made from softwood framing with ply top. The secret of a good watertight cover is a snug fit to the coaming. Hatch covers which will be stood on may require strengthening.

greater than the outside dimensions of the coaming. A tight fit is essential to ensure watertightness as well as good structural strength. A sloppy fitting hatch is liable to damage easily when walked upon, to say nothing of flying open every time a gust of wind gets under it.

The dimensions of the timber involved will vary according to the size of the hatch cover. Since the whole unit may come in for some fairly heavy loads as crew tramp over the top, the sides should be not less than 25 mm thick and the bigger the hatch, the heavier, proportionately,

the timber used. The forward and after ends of the hatch should be curved to create a cambered surface on the top, which adds considerable strength to the whole construction. The amount of curve will depend mainly on the thickness of the ply to be used on the top panel, since heavy gauge ply will be difficult to bend over too sharp a curve.

The four corners should be jointed with either dovetail or mortice and tenon joints and if the hatch cover is of some size, or the surface ply panel of light gauge, a support beam, matching forward and after ends, will need to be jointed transversely across the centre of the framework. If a very large hatch is involved more transverse, and even some longitudinal, members may be necessary. Jointing is described on page 37.

To ensure a flush fit with the sides the top panel should be cut slightly larger than required and planed back after it has been bent and secured in place. Screwing and glueing will

A curved top is very strong and needs only the supporting framework of the hatch unless it is likely to come under heavy stress, in which case bearers must be fitted inside the framework.

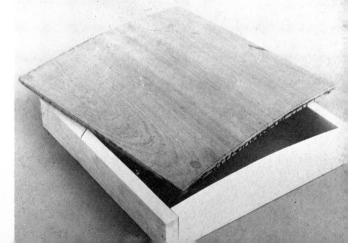

ensure a good fastening and this should be left for a day or two before planing back to ensure the glue has cured properly. The thickest possible plywood should be used in order to make the hatch cover as solid as possible.

Finishing is principally a question of filling or dowelling the countersunk screws, planing off the edges to flush with the sides and covering the ends of the plywood with half-round or similar trim. Paint or varnish is then used to add the final touches.

Fibreglass hatch covers

It is possible to build up a hatch cover by using a male mould and laying up GRP over the top of it, but as a general rule the finish in this case is not entirely satisfactory, and most hatch covers are moulded in a female mould. This means that a mould must be constructed first—usually of GRP also—from an original hatch cover or a made-up plug. The plug can be built from almost any material but the dimensions must be carefully measured to ensure a flush fit around the coamings when the moulded hatch is secured in place. This means that the dimensions of the mould must be slightly larger all round than the dimensions of the coamings and the GRP built up in the mould to the exact thickness required to make if fit flush over the coamings.

Construction of the mould and preparation for moulding are described on page 21. An important factor to remember is to round off the

Moulded GRP hatches can be made in all shapes and sizes. Here the drop-on forward hatch (with clear skylight) and sliding companionway hatch are neatly moulded to enhance the appearance of the boat.

corners where possible as this not only makes for better laying up in the mould, but also produces a stronger finish.

The laying up of the hatch cover is no different to moulding any similar fitting in GRP and is described in detail on page 16. However, because of the flexibility of the finished moulding and the fact that considerable weight may at times be placed on the top of the hatch cover, reinforcing will be necessary in all but the very smallest of hatch covers. There are a number of ways in which this reinforcing can be applied, most of which are described elsewhere in this book. The use of stiffeners as described on page 47, or of foam, end-grain balsa or similar sandwich-type fibreglass construction, is fairly common and the most suitable system can be adopted. The edges of the hatch can be finished with an aluminium trim pop-riveted in place and if the cover is to double as a skylight, the top can be left without gel coat as described on page 115.

Securing the hatch cover in place, as mentioned earlier, is more a question of personal preference than anything else. Hinges are not over popular as they tend to break or be easily strained so that the hatch does not fit closely, which inevitably leads to leaking. Some boat owners prefer to trim the inside edge of the hatch combing with a rubber seal to ensure that it is watertight and this is a particularly good idea when hinges are employed.

Probably the best, if not the most convenient, way of securing a hatch cover so that it is sound and completely watertight is to use 'strongback'. This is an old method still widely used in which a beam or heavy section of hardwood is placed across the underside of the hatch coaming and a long threaded bolt passed through it from the hatch cover. The head of this bolt may be secured into the underside of the hatch cover or passed through a hole drilled in the top panel. While the latter case is probably the most suitable, care must be taken to ensure that the hole is watertight and that the head of the bolt is low and perhaps even slightly countersunk to flush it as nearly as possible with the surface of the hatch cover. A butterfly nut provides the tension which draws the strongback up under the hatch coaming and pulls the hatch cover tight down on the rubber seal.

The bolt should be marine grade stainless steel, and a washer should be fitted between the butterfly nut and the strongback. Releasing the pressure even slightly will enable the strongback

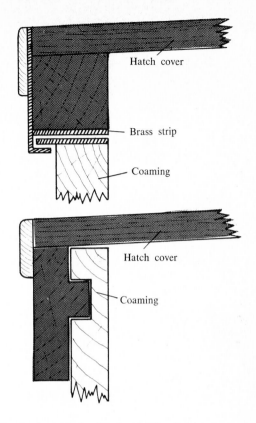

Hatch cover

Brass strip

Coaming

Hatch cover

Coaming

Two basic methods of fitting a sliding hatch to its tracks.

The simplest form of sliding hatch is a normal drop-on hatch adapted to run on rails.

to be swung to one side and the hatch cover to be removed quite easily. Where hatch covers of this type are used it is a wise precaution to attach them to the underside of the coaming with a light safety line, as an unsecured hatch can quickly blow over the side.

Sliding hatch

There must be literally hundreds of different ways of securing a sliding hatch into position. There are so many variables—GRP, timber, metal or even ferro-cement—that most home-made sliding hatches will differ one from the other as a matter of course. Then apart from the material concerned, the shape, size and individual requirements of the hatchway will create different needs and thus different types.

As a result, in a book of this kind I can offer only two basic forms of sliding hatch. They are widely used but will probably have to be adapted to suit individual requirements. Working to these basic designs, however, adjustment is fairly simple and should not tax your ingenuity too much! Most sliding hatches, unless they come as part of the boat kit, will probably be made of timber as this is not only the easiest material to work, but also looks nice even on GRP, metal or ferro-cement boats. Probably the next most popular sliding hatch is one moulded from

fibreglass, but this requires more work than a timber hatch since a mould must first be made up, and often the plug for the mould is almost as much work as making the hatch.

The construction of the hatch cover itself is similar to that described for a drop-on hatch cover. The basic difference is that allowances will have to be made at each side for it to run on some kind of rail. In the case of a timber hatch the best method is to build the hatch cover to exact dimensions to overlap the coaming and then rebate it to fit the fore and aft coamings which are capped by a metal slide rail. As a general rule these coamings are extended forward for some distance beyond the hatch opening to support the rail on which the hatch cover slides when in the fully extended position. The after end of the hatch cover acts as a stop against the forward coaming when the hatch is slid open, and the forward end against the other side of this coaming has the same effect when the hatch is closed.

The rail is a flat piece of light gauge brass or stainless steel screwed onto the coaming and

113

overlapping it by the width of the timber used for the side of the hatch cover. If the hatch cover was built with inside dimensions the same as the outside dimensions of the coaming, it should flush with the edge of the rail when resting on it. A fitting piece must now be made to the exact length of the hatch cover side which, when secured to it, will lap under the brass rail. This can be made from one piece of timber and rebated, or a piece of plywood with a timber strip attached to its lower edge may be used.

Whatever the system, the covering piece must flush with the side of the hatch cover and also provide the running piece which fits beneath the brass rail. Cutting this covering board from one piece of timber can be tricky, as any upward strain may break off the runner under the brass rail. Metal runners can be obtained from ship's chandlers although these, while being more efficient, do not look as attractive as a timber covering piece.

Finishing the hatch cover is a question of trim, using beading or half round to cover any plywood edges and sandpaper and varnish to finish the job properly. If screws are used to secure the covering piece they should be countersunk and dowelled, and a hasp fitted to the after end of the hatch cover so that the companionway can be locked.

Moulded GRP

Once again, the procedure for making a sliding hatch in moulded GRP is no different to that of making a drop-on hatch cover, as described on page 110. However, the mould will need to be adjusted so that the final moulding can accept the side coamings as the hatch slides backwards and forwards. The method of sliding will probably be different, and one system which seems to work quite successfully with fibreglass sliding hatches is to use jib sheet track and slides.

The track is laid close to the fore and aft coamings and secured through the cabin top. The slides should be bolted to either side of the hatch cover in such a position as to match the track. The best arrangement, obviously, is to bolt the slides to the inside of the hatch cover sides, but this will involve making the mould slightly larger than would be the case with a drop-on hatch cover. While the appearance is much better than having the slide bolted to the outside of the hatch cover, the resulting gap will make the hatch cover less watertight than when the sides fit flush to the coaming. Here, obviously, you will

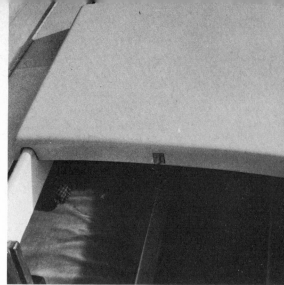

Moulded hatches are usually supplied with the hull and need only to be fitted. Moulding a sliding hatch can be a tricky business; it needs to make a watertight cover over the hatchway as well as fit accurately onto the tracks.

need to make a decision as to whether appearances are more important than practical application or whether, using a little ingenuity, you can adapt your own boat to this system yet make a watertight seal beneath the hatch.

SKYLIGHTS

Like most other boat fittings, skylights can be purchased ready-made, requiring only a few bolts or pop rivets to secure them in place. They are generally constructed of stainless steel with clear perspex protected by some form of grill to allow them to be stood on, and to offer general protection from on-deck activities. These are, of course, very useful and if you have a hole in the deck which needs a skylight it would be false economy not to purchase one. However, they are usually very expensive and where it is not necessary to fit a whole skylight unit or where, say, there is a hatch in place but it is opaque and does not let any light below decks, then the high cost plus the extra work of fitting a complete skylight unit is hardly justified. Particularly is this the case with small boats where a little more light is required in the forward cabin areas but the extra cost of a constructed skylight is not justified.

In this case the translucent properties of fibreglass can be utilised and a skylight, albeit opaque, not clear like perspex or glass, can be easily constructed. This will allow a great deal of light down below with little construction effort

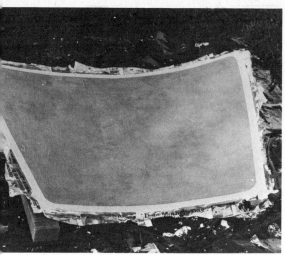

The skylight can be moulded—with clear gel coat—as a separate item and fastened into the deckhead or hatchway rather than bonding it directly.

and with good strength retained in the hatch cover or the deck where the skylight is fitted. Assuming an existing hatch cover is to be adapted as a skylight, then the procedure would be along the following lines.

GRP can be bonded to almost any material, even steel, if the correct procedures are followed and the surface to which the resin is to be applied is dry and clean. So, whatever the hatch cover is made of, it must be thoroughly cleaned of paint, grease, dirt, rust or any other foreign matter which will inhibit the bonding of the synthetic resin. Timber should be cleaned back to its bare surface with particular attention to removing any paint which may have seeped into the grain.

When all is clean, the dimensions of the required skylight are marked on the surface and the aperture cut out. In order to make a good finish to the whole job, particularly in the case of a small hatch, it is as well to clean off the entire inside of the hatch cover and carry the glass right across the top and down the sides. This not only ensures a good bond, but also strengthens the aperture so that it can be walked on without fear of damage.

With the hatch cleaned off and the aperture cut out a sheet of stiff cellophane is taped across the inside, then the first layer of resin applied as described on page 17. The type of glass fibre used is important, for although the woven cloth may give a better appearance, it is generally not as strong as the mat, and strength is quite important if the hatch is to be walked on. The mat is then

laid and thoroughly saturated with the second coat of resin. A second layer of mat is saturated into position and the resin worked firmly to remove all air bubbles. The thickness of the finished job should be not less than 10 mm across the top and even thicker if the aperture is large.

The whole unit is now left to dry and harden. When totally cured it can be given a good finish by sanding, filling if necessary, and rubbing back with wet-and-dry which will bring up a smooth surface free of bumps and irregularities. The skylight area should then be masked off and the remainder of the hatch given a couple of coats of polyurethane paint with non-skid strips secured across the top if necessary.

An alternative method is to mould up a completely new hatch cover using the original as a plug. This necessitates taking a GRP mould from the plug, polishing it up to obtain a smooth surface and then moulding as described on page 21. Before the moulding process begins, however, the skylight area must be taped off on the inside of the mould so that when the coloured gel coat is applied the skylight area is left clear. Once the gel coat has set, the masking tape can be removed and a coat of clear gel coat resin applied over the whole surface.

Now the moulding process is continued as described, with stiffeners laid into the mould if necessary. In the case of a small skylight hatch this may not be necessary, but where the hatch is to be walked on it is as well to run at least two stiffeners transversely across the underside of the hatch cover to prevent it flexing. These can be made up from any of the methods described on page 47.

Moulding the entire hatch cover as a single unit with the skylight, by masking off the pigmented gel coat, provides the most satisfactory result.

WINDOWS

Because boat windows come in many shapes and sizes there are many different ways of fitting them but all of them, no matter what their shape or size, have one common requirement—they must be strong enough and watertight enough to keep out the sea. For this reason, the window material must be strong and unbreakable and the fitting which holds it in place in the cabin or hull must also be strong, to withstand the impact of a wave, and watertight, to prevent leaking. The larger the window the more important the strength of the fitting. I will deal here with what might be termed an average window for the cabin of a medium sized craft.

If the window aperture has already been made during the construction of the hull, then the first step is to match the window frame to the aperture. But fibreglass mouldings often come without window apertures and plywood or steel cabins may well be left blank during construction in which case the window aperture must be cut.

The shape and size of the aperture will usually be determined by consulting the boat plans. If you prefer to cut windows to your own specifications, you should use 'paste-ups' to check the appearance of different sizes and shapes of windows before cutting an aperture. I find black paper best for this job since, viewed from a distance, it makes the 'windows' look quite real and thus makes it easier to assess the appearance of the finished work. The blanks or templates cut from black paper should be stuck in position and carefully aligned before sighting up and marking the outline of the windows.

To ensure the correct shape is cut out, templates should be used for cutting windows. A mock-up with templates pasted in position on the outside of the cabin will indicate the final appearance of the boat before the first cut is made.

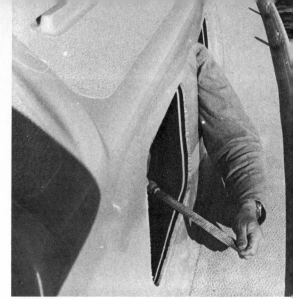

The aperture must be shaped according to the type of window fitting to be used. Careful work at this stage will ensure that the window is a good fit and thus watertight when in position.

Cutting will depend on the type of material involved. For plywood or fibreglass a jig saw or coping saw should do the trick but for steel you will need oxy-cutting gear. When the blanks have been removed the window apertures must be trimmed by filing to ensure that no uneven surfaces or edges remain to make the fitting of frames difficult at a later stage and possibly allow water to seep in.

Although glass is sometimes used for windows, it is a difficult material to work with, particularly on small windows, and there is always the risk of cracking or shattering. Perspex (acrylic sheet) is the best window material for boats and although somewhat difficult to saw, is much easier than glass to work and much safer in the final fitting. A hard cutting disc used on an electric drill will cut straight lines in perspex quite easily and the curved corners can be finished by hand.

The thickness will depend to a great extent on the size of the window and the sort of sea conditions that might be expected. On boats going to sea a thickness of between 6 mm and 10 mm should cope with most conditions although again this depends on size and location. Suffice it to say that this gauge of perspex should suit most windows that are relatively protected and even windows up to 500 mm across in exposed positions, providing they are correctly mounted.

The simplest and currently most popular method of fitting windows is to cut the perspex

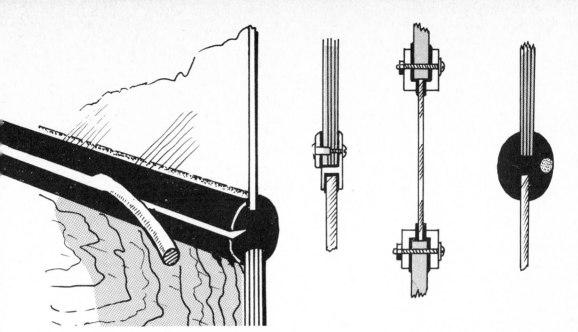

A rubber moulding with a locking strip may be used to secure the windows of small craft, but it will not always withstand the weight of a boarding sea. The bolted metal sections on the right are preferable.

Cross sections of three popular methods of securing windows—left: aluminium or stainless steel strip through bolted; centre: metal and rubber channel, through bolted; and right: patent rubber moulding.

sheet to a slightly larger size than the window aperture and screw or bolt it into place on a foundation of sealing compound. This can be quite satisfactory providing the job is done well, although the final result is not the most attractive and as time goes on there is often a tendency for leaks to appear. Better results will be obtained if you use this method in conjunction with a light frame, but if you are going to go to that much trouble then it is probably better in the long run to have the windows properly constructed in watertight frames.

Plastic framing is virtually useless and should not be used, but rubber mouldings specially made for the job are used quite widely on smaller craft. The moulding is grooved on each side, the inside for the perspex window and the outside to fit onto the cabin skin, and is locked in place by a special device which compresses both grooves onto their respective material. This can be quite a good system and there are a number of proprietary types of moulding available which, when used in conjunction with a good sealant, will provide a reasonably sound, watertight mounting for the windows. However, rubber tends to deteriorate somewhat with weathering and also can leave nasty marks when water washes away some of its deteriorated surface, so

that in the long term this type of mounting tends to create more work than other types of framing.

Without doubt the third method of framing windows is the best. However, it is the most expensive and involves having the windows made up by a firm which specialises in the work. Aluminium or stainless steel frames are used and the perspex is mounted in these together with a light rubber gasket which creates a watertight seal. As a general rule there is nothing more to do once these windows have been made up other than drill the frames and bolt them into position.

Superior in appearance to the other two types of window mounting, they have a longer life providing, of course, that they are correctly fastened and sealed. They also provide good stiffening of the window aperture which, particularly in the case of large windows, is a useful attribute. As with rubber mouldings there are a number of proprietary brands of window frames of this type available and it may well be worth consulting your local dealer on the shape and size of ready-made windows of this type before cutting the window aperture. Using stock sizes will certainly be much cheaper than having windows specially made up to match your particular aperture.

Bolting is undoubtedly the best method of

Sealing the windows must be given close attention, for nothing is worse than a dribble of water constantly running down the bulkhead. A rubber gasket can provide a watertight seal, or the window can be mounted in a bed of mastic compound.

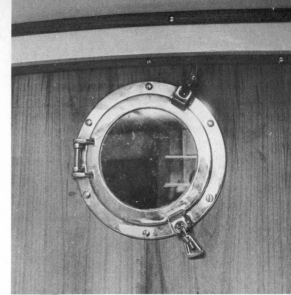

Portholes provide the most secure type of opening window on a boat. They can be obtained in a variety of shapes and sizes.

securing windows in place, although screws (in the case of timber) or tap screws (fibreglass) may also be used if there is not likely to be a great deal of stress on the windows. However, the safest method is to through bolt the frames, countersinking the heads with, if necessary, a covering strip to give a pleasant finish. Castellated or other decorative nuts may be used for an attractive finish. In all cases a heavy coating of sealant must be placed around the fastenings as well as around the window frame to ensure that when tightened up the entire aperture is watertight. Tinted glass is currently in vogue with a lot of boat owners and this can be quite pleasant where boats are to be used in strong sunlight areas.

Skylights may also be constructed in much the same way as windows although they will need to be protected by a metal grille or framework to prevent the perspex being cracked or scratched. A cheaper system for allowing light into the cabin via deck or hatch areas is described on page 115.

PORTHOLES

Since they allow only a limited amount of light into the interior of the boat portholes have gone out of vogue in recent years on both large ships and small craft. However, there is no denying the fact that a good solidly made porthole is a most effective way of keeping the water out of the hull and allowing light in. For this reason portholes—often oval or a similar elongated shape rather than the round portholes of yesteryear—may be found fitted to the hull or cabin sides of ocean craft. Since these units must be purchased as a complete job, fitting them is as described for aluminium or stainless steel window frames—

that is, simply cutting a matching aperture in the hull and bolting the frame firmly into place with generous quantities of sealant.

As a general rule, portholes are more ruggedly constructed with heavier frames and thicker glass or perspex and have heavy turnscrews to hold them in place if they are the opening variety. A rubber seal usually ensures watertightness between the frame and the opening and the screws ensure that a tight seal is made. These units would be preferable to aluminium or stainless steel windows when used in the hull since they are not only more watertight, but more rugged and able to stand up to impact, either from the sea or from coming alongside a wharf a bit too hard. For cabin use, however, they are usually of too heavy construction and too restricting in terms of allowing light into the interior spaces.

VENTILATORS

Ventilators can usually be purchased as a complete unit, making the work of fitting simply a question of cutting a hole in the deck or cabin top and fastening the unit over it. There is a wide variety of ventilators available, some flexible, some rigid, some with water traps and some without. Whatever the case, it needs only for the hole to be matched up to the unit which is then screwed or—preferably—bolted into place. Most modern ventilator units are constructed of

Ventilators are a necessary evil. Every effort should be made to fit a type and size that allows adequate through flow of air, but does not affect the appearance of the boat adversely or create clumsy structures on the deck. The vents on this yacht are barely noticeable.

durable plastic or alloy and therefore suit any type of hull, although where alloy vents are secured to a steel deck an insulating layer must be placed between them to avoid the possibility of electrolytic corrosion.

The choice of ventilator will be a personal one since the two principal aims involved are to allow a good flow of air into the cabin area yet at the same time preserve the pleasant lines of the boat's profile. Nothing is more calculated to make a boat look ugly than unwieldy ventilators stuck all over the deck and cabin. And by the same token, nothing is more unpleasant than trying to live in the stifling interior of a badly ventilated cabin. The choice will also be influenced by the location and intended use of the ventilators since, if they are to be left in position when the boat is at sea, they will need to be of a design which allows air to

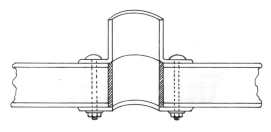

A trunkway may need to be fitted between deck or cabin top and hood liner. It is important that the tightening of the bolts does not compress and distort either upper or lower surface.

flow but keeps water out, whereas the cowl of the standard type ventilator must be removed and the hole plugged if there is a likelihood of water coming aboard.

Fitting the simplest type of cowl ventilator involves merely cutting a matching hole where the unit is to be mounted. With timber and fibreglass boats this may be done with a hole-cutting drill but where this is not practicable—as in the case of ferro-cement—it will probably be necessary to form a hole by making a series of fine drill holes in a circle and punching the unwanted material out. Where the cabin or deck material is fairly thick, in particular with fibreglass sandwich construction, some form of

A modern version of the Dorade box type of ventilator. The drain for the water trap can be clearly seen, allowing the water to run back out on deck.

lining in the hole will be necessary to prevent moisture being absorbed into the sides. It may also be necessary to fit a tubular metal spacer between the top and bottom flanges of the ventilator hole so that when the bolts are drawn up tight, the compression on the top and bottom flanges does not put undue compression stresses on the sandwich construction. A sealant must be used liberally in all areas where water may seep in, including the bolts holding the ventilator in place.

Where the ventilator is to be used at sea a water trap will be necessary to prevent spray being carried down below decks. There are a number of patent methods of doing this, and many proprietary brands of ventilators have some such trap built into their construction. If

119

The vents on this boat are fitted with Dorade-box water traps and need not be removed except for the heaviest sea.

this is not the case, a trap must be constructed when the ventilator is fitted. One of the simplest methods of doing this is to mount the ventilator close to the side of the cabin roof and build the trap into the corner between the deckhead and the cabin side, with a hole at the bottom to drain any water straight back onto the outside deck. A baffle close to the deckhead allows air to circulate into the cabin while water drops to the bottom of the trap and drains out.

If it is not convenient to locate the ventilator in a position to use this system, then a Dorade box can be used which, while efficient, is somewhat bulky and needs to be located in a position where it will not affect the appearance of the boat to get in the way of working gear. The photograph shows the basic design for a Dorade box which can be constructed from plywood or timber, although quite often they can be purchased ready-made in GRP or aluminium alloy. The procedure for mounting this type of ventilator is no different to any other, except for the location of the Dorade box itself over the hole in the cabin roof. This positioning is self-evident from the picture. Water is trapped by the baffle and run off through a hole in the outside of the Dorade box while air is allowed to flow past the baffle and down through the cut hole into the cabin. Fastening these ventilators is simple and similar to most other deck fittings.

EXTRACTOR FANS

Extractor fans fitted inside ventilators are often used in toilets and above galley areas. They are purchased as a complete unit and fitted as described above for ventilators, and will be included in the calculations for electricity consumption.

SELF-DRAINING COCKPIT

The cockpit is the working area of a boat and as such the area which usually gets the most wear and tear. On a sailing yacht it is the area where most on-deck activities take place. The helm is controlled from this point as are the sheets and motor and often halyards as well—plus, of course, any social activities since, unlike on a motor yacht, passengers on a sailboat do not usually spend a great deal of time in the saloon while the boat is under way.

On a motor cruiser it is the area where, if the boat is designed for fishing, the chair is located and all fishing activities are based, while in luxury craft it is the open space used in conjunction with the adjoining saloon area for entertainment. In short, it is the deck space most likely to be used for all but sleeping and eating.

The above factors will illustrate why it is desirable that any cockpit is kept dry, but since in general only the sailing yacht is liable to be taken any distance offshore where she will have to take the weather as it comes, the question of her watertight integrity is normally given greater consideration. A boarding sea must be prevented from getting below; her upperworks must be strong enough to withstand the weight of it; and they and the cockpit must drain freely overboard.

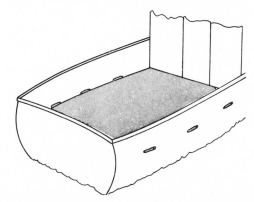

The simplest method of forming a self-draining cockpit is to raise the deck level well above the waterline and allow the water that comes aboard to run freely back over the side.

In this equation the cockpit well presents the greatest danger, and filled with water weighing 64 lbs/cu. ft. it may over-burden her buoyancy. The cockpit will also be adjacent to the companionway leading below, and so there must also be some positive means of preventing water ingress. In a timber boat there is often a full-width beam at this point, which with the main bulkhead forms a strong bridge the depth of the cockpit well. It is therefore known as the bridge deck, and positively separates cockpit from accommodation. The structural details of boats in other materials differ somewhat from timber, but they should have similar arrangements, for strength and to keep water out.

Having contained any weight of water in the cockpit, it must be quickly got rid of, and here the major design requirement is that the cockpit sole is at, or above, the waterline when the boat is under way at her normal angle of heel.

The simplest method of draining off the cockpit is to have drains or freeing ports which allow the water to run straight back into the sea. Pumps are not practical for this work and a bucket brigade is too laborious, apart from being somewhat undignified. However, in order for the water to drain off, it is necessary for the level of the deck to be well above the waterline of the boat. The emphasis is on the term 'well above', for if the draining holes are only slightly above the water level there is every chance that they will drain *into* the cockpit in any sort of a seaway or when the boat is loaded down.

For this reason self-draining cockpits are virtually impossible in small craft. Their relatively low topsides do not permit the cockpit floor to be sufficiently above the outside sea level. The only way to obtain self-draining in these cases is to use the deck itself as the cockpit, closing it in completely and building surrounding coamings or safety rails above it. This, of course, is not practical for anything other than fairly large hulls and most small boats must resort to pumping or bailing if water comes aboard.

Boats of any size, however, can fit self-draining cockpits with relative ease providing the cockpit floor can be kept at a comfortable level well above the waterline. Large craft, particularly motor yachts, can get away with a very simple form of self-draining by sealing off the deck space and placing a bulwark around it. Freeing ports in this bulwark enable the water to drain off without any need for piercing the deck or fitting drains, while the bulwark itself provides the surrounds necessary for keeping water out as much as possible and protecting the occupants.

Recessing the cockpit into the deck, as is common with sailing yachts, is somewhat more involved since it necessitates cutting the deck beams and thus creating a weakness in the tube structure of the hull. This again is no great problem, particularly if the cockpit is installed during the fitting of the deck itself, as compensating members can be fitted in much the same way as for reinforcing the deck area cut away when fitting a cabin or hatchway.

The extent to which the deck beams must be cut away will depend largely on the size of the yacht and subsequently the size of the cockpit. In small yachts it may be possible merely to recess the cockpit floor sufficiently to give leg room, in which case a relatively small opening will be required and the deck on either side of the recess or well will form the cockpit seats.

Where the deck beams are cut a carline is fitted on either side, running from the deck beam at the cabin doorway to whatever beam is selected to form the after end of the cockpit. In small boats this latter may be the transom beam. The cut ends of the deck beams are jointed into this carline and glued and screwed to form a solid unit. At this point the well structure of the cockpit should be measured to ensure that when it is in place it will be well above the waterline at its lowest point.

In measuring, check that the floor of the cockpit has a slight slope either forward or aft (the latter is usually preferable if depth of the cockpit will allow) to ensure that water runs off in the direction of the self-draining holes. An average depth for the well is about 45 cm for

A basic cockpit is merely a recessed area of the deck. If the cockpit sole is above the waterline it can be made to self drain. Failing that a pump will be necessary. Note the low coaming which prevents water getting from the deck into the cabin.

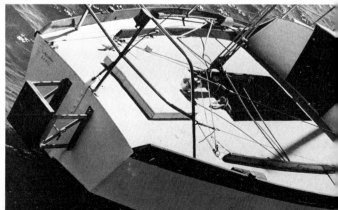

a: *Self draining tubes must pierce the hull skin below the waterline and thus must have a skin fitting when cut off flush with the hull.* b: *The cockpit end of the tube can be bonded with GRP or attached to a skin fitting.*

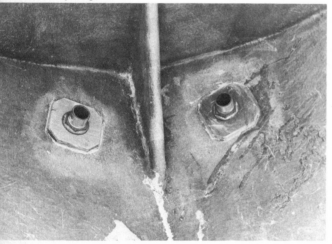

A neatly-fitting built cockpit is attractive and practical. The coaming has been run well out to the sides of the boat for maximum space and the slat seats prevent water gathering.

reasonable leg room and the width will depend on the dimensions of the boat at this point. Allow a minimum width of seat in the vicinity of 30 cm.

The structure of the well is best built ashore and fitted into place by jointing the uprights into the carline already fitted. Some boat owners prefer to build the floor of the cockpit directly into the boat and land it on stringers or landings attached to the sides of the hull, then build the framework up between these beams and the carline. Without doubt this is the stronger of the two methods, albeit involving a bit more work. But if the 'hanging' type of box structure described above is used then some support will be required beneath the floor of the cockpit to take the weight of crew when the boat is being sailed. In choosing which of these systems to use the structure of the hull will have considerable bearing.

With the structure in place the self-draining holes must be cut in the hull and this will involve slipping the boat if she is not already out of the water. Two draining holes are standard and to permit easy flow of water they should be something in the vicinity of 50 mm diameter. Obviously, the larger the hole the faster the water runs out. Skin fittings should be attached to the hull with stop cocks and reinforced plastic hoses run between these and the skin fittings attached to the cockpit draining holes. This, of course, is done before the floor is secured in place.

Now the cockpit can be panelled all round. Ply is suitable, of a gauge somewhere in the vicinity of 15 mm. If there are fittings such as motor controls and gear levers sticking up through the floor, apertures will need to be cut to accommodate them. Obviously, these apertures must be sealed (usually with a flexible rubber covering) to prevent water leaking into the hull when the cockpit is awash. A better system is to transfer the fittings, if possible, to the sides of the cockpit fairly high up as they are less liable to be submerged than those on the floor.

The seats can be secured in a number of ways, the most popular of which is with knees secured through the panelling to the uprights of the well. Some boat owners like full-length seats, others prefer a little space to work and keep the seats to a shorter length, but this is a matter for personal taste. Since water on the seats cannot be drained out through holes in the coaming (the seats are usually below deck level), small holes in the seats themselves will permit the water to run down to the floor of the cockpit unless the seats are made up of a series of timber slats—a popular choice with ocean-going craft as they never retain water, even when the boat is heeled.

Moulding a complete cockpit in GRP is uncommon and difficult. Most fibreglass boats come with the cockpit as an integral part of the deck and cabin mould and this is the only satisfactory way with this material as it makes for easy joining to the hull. When a moulded hull is supplied with no deck or cabin, then a timber or ply cockpit is probably the easiest and best to fit, together with a deck of the same materials. Where the deck is to be moulded and fitted to the open hull the cockpit should be moulded as an integral part of the deck.

However, some moulded hulls come complete with the cockpit shell to be finished by the boat owner. In this case making the cockpit self-draining is simple providing it meets with the specifications mentioned earlier for all cock-pits—i.e. it is well above water level.

The holes for the drains need to be drilled in the cockpit floor and the hull, and skin fittings fastened through them to ensure a watertight fit and a base on which to mount the drainage pipes. This is described in detail on page 97 for other skin fittings and there should be little difference in fitting them to the cockpit. Remember, though, that the drains should be at the lower end of the cockpit in order to drain successfully when the boat is stationary.

Plastic hoses can be used and these should be well secured with stainless steel rings or hose clips. Stop cocks are often recommended, but should not be necessary if you do a good job of fastening the hose, since I have yet to meet a boat owner who turned off the stop cocks on the self-

Plastic tubing totally encased in GRP makes excellent cockpit drains. If the fibreglass casing is well bonded to the hull skin, seacocks are sometimes omitted, but it is safer to use them.

drainers each time he left the boat. They are often in a very awkward corner and if they are not turned off at all times when you are not aboard they might as well not be fitted!

It is quite a good practice to cross the drainage hoses over one another beneath the cockpit. This ensures that water drains out even though the boat may be heeled. There is nothing worse than having a few millimetres of water sloshing around in the cockpit when you are enjoying a pleasant social sail.

SELF-DRAINING ANCHOR LOCKER

An anchor should be stowed where it is readily accessible in an emergency, and while this will often be in chocks on the foredeck, with a light lashing, it may be preferable for the design of the foredeck to incorporate a locker. In the bow overhang it is usually possible to arrange this well above the waterline, and so the locker can also be given a small skin fitting which will allow it to be self-draining. It should be noted, however, that this admirably neat arrangement is in general only suitable for craft with relatively light ground tackle (boats of less than 30 ft over-all), and where a full length of chain cable is carried, weighing several hundredweight, it should be stowed in a chain locker well down in the hull, and also back within the waterline. Such tackle will require a winch, set back from the bow where it may be conveniently worked, and thus also within the waterline; the fall from the winch may therefore be taken straight through the deck to a chain locker below.

Smaller craft without this requirement may also dispense with the full length of chain, and instead use a couple of fathoms shackled to a nylon warp. For the great proportion of inshore cruising in predictably settled weather, this is perfectly satisfactory; the tackle required is far lighter in weight, and the boat will ride more easily to a nylon warp. And at the same time, because of its light weight, it can all be most conveniently stowed in a self-draining locker in the bow, if not on deck. However, such stowage arrangements can limit the size or type of anchor carried, and cannot accommodate a second anchor or extra warp and chain.

The actual shape and dimensions of the anchor locker hatchway will depend on the size and type of boat involved. However, one of the simplest and most practical methods of creating an anchor locker is simply to seal off the eye of the bow from the rest of the forward section of the boat. A waterproof bulkhead only a matter of a metre or less from the stem will create sufficient locker space for most anchors and warps and its depth can be made to suit the individual gear, bearing in mind, of course, that too deep an anchor locker will require a long arm for cleaning or other access purposes.

A triangular opening hatchway in the deck is better than a square one, much depending on the shape of the bow and the size and shape of the anchor. A matching hatch cover must be made to fit snugly onto this hatch and bolt securely into place, for although the finished job will be waterproof and self-draining, it is always best to guard against the loss of a hatch cover if possible. Small bolts or some similar securing device can be used for this purpose.

The locker may be relatively shallow, depending on the amount of warp and chain to be stowed. This is a moulded GRP locker well bonded in place and well secured from beneath. It could alternatively be built in place using a timber framework fastened to the deck and hull.

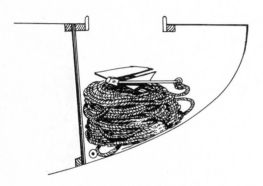

Basic layout of a self-draining anchor locker. Any water taken aboard with the anchor and warp drains off through the skin fitting at the foot of the bulkhead.

The bulkhead will need to be shaped from a template which in turn will need to be made from fairly stiff cardboard to ensure a close fit. The bulkhead can be cut from 15 mm plywood for most medium sized craft but increased in thickness if you feel the job justifies it. It must be angled so that the lower end is forward of the upper or deckhead end and the exact fitting and placement will depend on allowing room for comfortable stowage of anchor and warp. Do not allow too much room or the anchor will charge around when the boat is in a seaway; on the other hand make sure there is room for additional warp if so required. The bulkhead, when cut from the template, should be glassed firmly into position or secured to structural members or landings in the case of timber, metal or concrete boats. Whatever the fastening used,

it is important to obtain a watertight join between bulkhead, hull sides and deckhead.

Welding is obviously the answer with metal boats, and with timber probably GRP tape secured around the edges will assist the glues in making a join watertight. With ferro-cement, a plaster bulkhead will probably suit best.

With the bulkhead in place, rather like the collision bulkhead of a normal commercial freighter, no water can enter the cabin area even if the forward section is flooded. However, to make the anchor locker self-draining, a small hole (about 15 mm diameter) is drilled through the side of the hull at the lowest point of the compartment and a simple pipe skin fitting secured through it. This will ensure that any water that gets into the compartment either directly or drained off the anchor or warp will run immediately back out over the side of the boat again.

COCKPIT GRATING

Nothing adds more to the finish of a boat than timber trim. Particularly is this the case if the boat is built of GRP, metal or ferro-cement. And no timber gives a nicer finish than teak or a similar even-grained hardwood. Teak needs little in the way of maintenance whether it is varnished or not and always rubs up to a beautiful appearance no matter how much it has been weathered.

Small wonder, then, that despite the risk of adding to maintenance problems, most boat owners like a little teak trim here and there to break up the clinical appearance of GRP or similar material. Hand rails, companionway doors and toe rails or rubbing strakes are some of the more common ways of enhancing the boat's appearance by using teak trim, but undoubtedly one of the most attractive as well as most practical is a well-made cockpit grating.

There are a number of timbers that can be used for making gratings but teak, if it is available, is without doubt the best. The description here is for a simple rectangular cockpit coaming, but adaptation of shape and dimensions will provide a grating for any required purpose.

The grating should fit fairly snugly into the cockpit, and unless the measuring is fairly straightforward it may be necessary to make a cardboard template. Particularly is this the case if the final shape of the grating has awkward angles or has to be fitted round some protrusion such as a binnacle. The template should be an exact fit or slightly on the over-large size because the finished grating can be planed down a little if necessary while it cannot be built up if you under-estimate the size. Nothing is worse than a grating that is too small and slithers around the cockpit when in use. The thickness of timber is uniform through the frame and grating, and 25 mm teak will probably suit most craft. The frame should be about 52 mm wide and the grating planks 25 mm wide. These dimensions make joinery fairly easy since teak can be grooved with a 25 mm chisel quite simply.

The best way to purchase the teak for the grating battens is in planks of 26 mm thickness and as wide as possible, and 52 mm shorter than the overall length of the grating. This allows for a 26 mm half-lap jointing at each end. The plank must now be grooved with 26 mm grooves 13 mm deep and spaced 26 mm apart for its whole length. The way to do this is to scribe a line 13 mm deep down each edge of the plank and then mark out lines across the plank at 26 mm intervals throughout its entire length.

Cut across each of these lines with a tenon saw to the depth of the 13 mm scribe line and chisel out alternate grooves with a 26 mm chisel. When

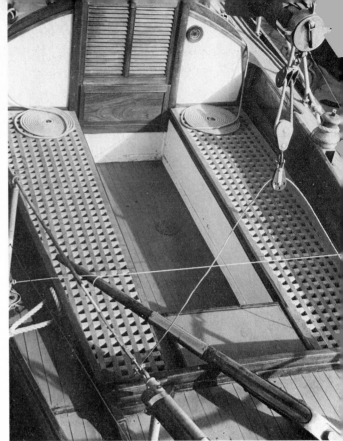

Cockpit gratings need not necessarily be fitted to the sole. They make practical seats which drain off water and at the same time greatly enhance the appearance of the cockpit. Templates will be necessary to ensure a good fit.

this has been neatly completed the plank is then cut lengthways into 26 mm battens with a hand or power saw. If the job has been well done the resulting battens when alternately turned over and placed one on top of the other will match neatly into a basic grating arrangement. Many timber merchants can mill the slots for the battens and at the same time cut them.

Now the frame of the grating is made up, using 26 mm x 13 mm teak planks jointed at the corners. Using a sharp 26 mm chisel and carefully measuring the spacing of the fore and aft battens, rebate the top and bottom inside edges of the frame to a depth of 13 mm to accommodate the half lap joint at the end of the batten. With resin glue and the necessary solvent preparation these battens can now be secured in the frame. When the glue is dry the remaining battens can be cut to fit across with a half-lap joint rebated into the sides of the frame. Some adjustment may be necessary according to the width of the frame but at this stage simple trial and error will take care of such a problem. When all the cross battens are ready and the rebates chiselled out and fitted, the entire grating can be glued up and secured into position. If the jointing has been properly done gluing will be the only fastening required and the whole unit will lock together firmly without any movement whatsoever. The grating should not be varnished as this tends to become very slippery when wet. Teak will weather quite happily without paint or varnish and offer a good non-skid finish.

CAPPING

Generally speaking, capping means covering any exposed area which would otherwise be unattractive or liable to damage. A typical example is the exposed ends of plywood which will readily weather or damage if not covered. With GRP, the edges of a bond such as that between deck and hull are liable to leak or sustain physical damage unless well covered. The uncovered edge of a steel plate may cause injury to crew and must be capped. In effect, any edge or join which cannot be successfully finished and protected will need capping. In addition, capping can be used for decorative purposes such as adding a neat, trim finish to cockpit coamings.

Such a wide variety of uses suggests that there is a wide variety of techniques for capping, depending mainly on the material to be capped. The method used for capping exposed areas of timber is dealt with here. Adaptations for other materials will be relatively simple. Similarly the cross section of a cockpit coaming is used as an illustration but the method used needs only minor adaptation to apply to any other material.

Quite often the thickness of the timber to be capped will allow only a relatively light gauge of capping to be used and this in turn is often not sufficiently strong to serve the purpose of protecting the fitting to which it is attached. Take, for example, the cockpit coaming. The thickness of the timber in the coaming may be only 25-30 mm on an average boat. Capping it with timber of similar width would not be adequate. Firstly, it would offer a very narrow and painful surface on which to sit and, secondly, the light gauge timber used would soon be damaged by sheets chafing it or blocks knocking against it when the boat is working. A capping of less than about 50 mm width is rarely adequate to

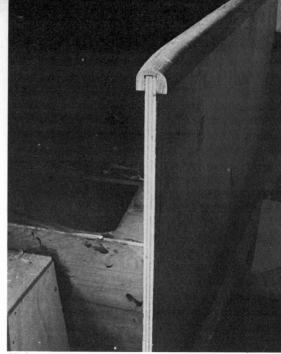

If the capping can be rebated to fit over the ply it provides an excellent finish. Failing this the capping must be built up around the edge of the ply by using battens with capping across the top.

provide sufficient protection, and therefore a coaming must be built up to accept the wider capping.

This is best done by securing a softwood batten around the outside top edge of the coaming. The width of this batten will depend on the width of the coaming and capping to follow. For example, if the coaming is 26 mm ply and the capping 50 mm wide, then the batten will need to be 24 mm wide. Its depth is not over important, although it should be never less than its width. Much will depend on the individual requirements of the boat, particularly the height of the cockpit coaming, as to how solid the capping needs to be. Providing the batten can be smoothed or shaped to a nice finish and be well secured to the coaming to provide a base for the capping, its depth is relatively unimportant.

This batten should be shaped as required on the outside and glued and screwed securely to the top outside edge of the coaming. Because of the curve involved with some coamings it may be necessary to flush off the top surfaces where some twisting occurs in bending the timber. If the coaming is of narrow gauge the screwing will need to be done on the inside of the cockpit and the screws countersunk. However, it is preferable, if the coaming is of sufficient width, to

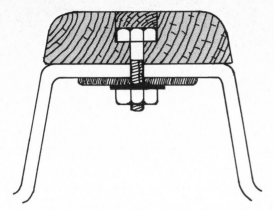

Capping GRP coamings will necessitate the use of a pad underneath. Bolting is better than screwing even though the capping may not come in for over-much stress.

screw from the outside through the batten. All screws must be countersunk and finished either with filler or dowelling.

The capping can be of any timber, but teak is preferable if it is not to be painted. A capping of about 60 mm x 30 mm is a good size for medium class craft, and larger dimensions should be in roughly the same proportion for larger coamings on larger craft. Apart from its weathering qualities, teak tends to be hard wearing. The capping can still suffer considerable chafe from chain or mooring ropes unless protected by fairleads and metal coverings. As in so many cases when fitting out, this is a question as much of personal taste as of practical application.

The top of the capping must be rounded off and sanded down to a good finish. Since it may not be possible to apply the full length of capping at once it may have to be fitted in sections. If this is the case the joins should be placed strategically so that they do not spoil the aesthetic appearance of the job. Where the capping runs the length of the coaming, butt ends will need to be carefully matched so that they fit snugly, particularly if there is a slight curve in the coaming.

When the fitting has been completed the capping is glued and screwed in place. The best procedure is to alternate the screws through the capping into the coaming and then the batten. This distributes the stresses evenly along the whole fitting and ensures that the capping sits down snugly along its full length. Screw heads must be countersunk and finished either with filler (if the capping is to be painted) or

preferably dowels if the capping is to be varnished or left natural. A little planing or sanding will be necessary to flush off the outside or inside edges of the capping and then the required finish applied.

MAST STEP ON DECK

The heel of a mast stepped on deck may be in a socket, channel or shoe, on a flange or in a prvoted tabernacle, depending on the mast design and the use the boat is likely to have. All serve the function of securing the foot of the mast and transmitting the compression loads generated by the rig into the structure of the hull. The step has its opposite number in the chainplates, and together they transmit the drive from the sails to the hull.

The tabernacle was originally designed for the timber masts on craft that might be used inland, where it may be necessary to quickly lower and raise a mast to pass a bridge. As such, it had to be a fairly substantial fitting to withstand the shear loads imposed at the deck, and indeed refined examples of such craft such as the traditional Broads sailing cruiser employ a counterbalanced mast to minimise this stress and facilitate lowering.

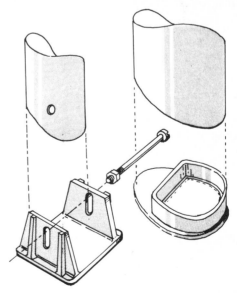

Two typical steps for small yachts.

127

Today's aluminium mast goes some way to easing this problem with its considerably lighter weight, which coupled with strong duralumin castings at the foot has enabled the whole mechanism to be tidied up. With a simple hinge at the foot pivoting on a high-tensile steel bolt, and employing the boom as a sheerlegs, masts of 30 ft can be raised easily. Where this is likely to be frequent, the tabernacle may still be used, but the majority of sailing craft have a fixed or hinged socket, or an adjustable shoe.

The socket is the usual choice for cruising boats where beyond small adjustments to the mast rake, tuning should not involve shifting the foot of the mast. It is used for the great majority of deck-stepped masts on craft over 25 ft. Below this figure, the weight aloft permits the option of a hinge, and with it the ability for the owner to raise or lower his own mast without too much difficulty.

Tuning for the best sail balance and performance may involve a certain amount of experiment with the mast position, and a shoe or flange step allows the foot of the mast to be moved fore and aft anything up to a couple of feet. With this design of step a securing bolt may pass through the foot of the mast, enabling it to be pivoted, or alternatively the weight of the mast is taken directly on the shoe with locating bolts across its fore and aft faces.

In fitting any type of step or tabernacle, first ensure that it is directly located over the support beneath the deck. This is usually in the form of a pillar support or deck girders running across the beam of the boat. Bulkheads are also used in a similar manner to the beam supports. The tabernacle must be so placed that it runs right across the support with its centre over the centre of the support structure. With a bulkhead or beams this means that the tabernacle is mounted on the centreline of the boat so that it is supported evenly by two beams or so that it lies directly over the bulkhead. With a pillar support, of course, the centre of the tabernacle must align exactly with the pillar. Usually a plate base is welded to the top of the pillar to offer a wide support to the tabernacle above.

With the tabernacle in position the whole unit must be fastened together with through bolts in the manner described on page 99 for stress fittings. The bolts must be of heavy duty stainless steel and be drilled through the beams or plate of the pillar. If this is not possible a heavy plate must be placed in such a position beneath the deck that when the tabernacle is bolted through it the stresses will be transmitted to the supporting structure. All bolts must be heavily coated with sealant to make the fitting watertight and where plates are involved, these too must be well bedded in a sealant. Nothing is worse than a constant dribble of water leaking down the mast support and nothing more difficult to cure after the tabernacle is in place.

It follows, as with all fittings, that much will depend on the individual boat as to where and in what manner the tabernacle should be fitted. But bearing in mind the salient points above, it should not be difficult to adopt the method described here to suit any type of hull and deck construction.

COMPANIONWAY DOORS

Both hinged doors similar to those in domestic use, and the washboard type where a number of short sturdy panels slot into reinforced guides on each side of the opening, are used. The type of sailing intended for the boat, the space available for hinged doors to swing and to rest when open, the means for keeping water on deck from getting into the accommodation, the stowage for washboards, and problems of security against break-in and against the doors or boards coming loose and being lost overboard in extreme conditions or a knockdown must all be considered at the planning stage.

Small boats usually adopt the board type of door since the companionway is relatively small and does not lend itself to hanging hinged doors. By contrast, big power cruisers and many big sailing yachts have doorways which are virtually

Step fittings must be solidly constructed and securely bolted through to the mast support. Hinged tabernacles make for easy lowering of the mast.

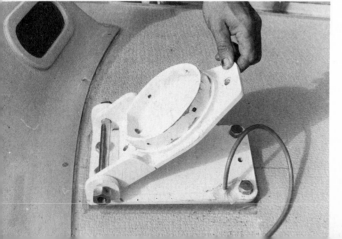

Large motor yachts often fit sliding doors similar to those used in a house.

Louvred doors are not only attractive in appearance but very practical in that they allow a free flow of air into the cabin area.

the same size as those in a house, and closing them off with boards would be impractical as well as unsightly. Hinged doors are used in these cases and, like doors in a home, they may be in one of many shapes or forms, ranging from louvred to glass panelled doors.

Making a hung door is no easy task, particularly if you aim at more sophisticated doors such as a louvred or panelled door. Since these can be purchased ready-made at relatively low cost there would seem little in favour of taking the effort and time involved to make one. For this reason, this type of door will not be dealt with in detail here and I will concentrate on the more common board door. Suffice it to say at this point that a well made and attractively decorated hinged door can be a tremendous asset

to a boat and should be employed if at all possible. In terms of appearance even the smallest companionway looks nice with a trim louvred door and it aids good ventilation as well. But it is cheaper and more practical to purchase the door than to attempt to make it unless you are a shipwright or cabinet maker by profession.

The simple board door, however, is a different matter altogether. In the first place, it is unlikely you would be able to buy one ready-made and, if you could, the chances are that it would not fit your boat since each companionway is different except, as mentioned, in stock boats. Since it comprises only two or more pieces of timber—often ply—it is best to make your own door to obtain the best fit and the result you require. Teak gives an excellent finish to this type of door, so a teak plank or teak veneered ply should be used.

The doorway may already be fitted with guides or runners to accommodate the door boards. If not, they must be fitted to the upright on either side of the door opening. A good system is to rebate the door posts when fitting them. Another is to build a 'channel' to accommodate the boards by bolting two strips of timber to the inside of each door post, with a space between them the width of the boards. Yet another method is to screw onto the door posts two strong metal channel sections which will receive the sides of the boards. There are many other systems to do the job and providing they offer good firm support to the door boards they are acceptable.

The door boards must be cut carefully to plan so that they fit the doorway exactly, allowing only a small clearance on either side to prevent

The simplest form of board door can look attractive with a little trim and finish. The slide channels on this door are adapted from sheeting tracks.

sticking when the wood is wet. Templates will probably have to be cut to avoid wasting the timber of the door panels, since many companionway entrances, particularly on small yachts, are of an irregular shape. Two boards may be enough, but if the opening is large then three may be necessary. Their joining edges should flush exactly and the lower edge be sloped outwards so that rain running down the door does not trickle into the cabin. The top edges should be shaped to fit beneath the sliding hatch of the companionway cover and a hasp attached to allow the door to be padlocked.

So simple is this arrangement and yet so effective that most small boat owners prefer it to hanging doors. From an appearance point of view the boards can be enhanced by decorative trim or by incorporating louvres or some similar design in the panels. Since every door should have some form of ventilator, a little imagination can be used to cut openings which are not only practical as ventilators but also attractive as decoration. Paint and/or varnish can then be used to finish the doors and add even more to their appearance.

The shape of the tiller is less important than its strength, although it can add considerably to the appearance of the boat. An extension or hiking stick is useful on small craft.

TILLER

Providing it is strong enough a tiller can be made from any material, but traditionally timber is favoured because it is warm to the touch, pleasant to handle, and has a degree of elasticity and resilience not found with metal tubing, which is sometimes used. However, tillers have been known to break in heavy weather, sometimes where they join the fitting on the rudder stock, so strength must be considered. The end may be reduced in diameter to fit the grip, as holding an over-large tiller is tiring.

Teak is frequently used but, like other hardwoods, makes heavy going of any ornate trimming or shaping. Ash is as good a material as any since it is an attractive blond wood and relatively easy to work. However, because of the complex curves that may be involved in the tiller,

laminating from several pieces is often done; mahogany and ash, mahogany and oak, or straight oak. The result is an attractive appearance, high strength, and the necessary curvature, which may be considerable. Methods used for laminating are described on page 36. Shaping in a lathe or handcarving the tiller is a specialised job and requires considerable skill.

The basic requirements for a tiller are good strength and attractive appearance plus, of course, secure attachment to the rudder stock. Laminating achieves all these with the least effort since a mould is easily constructed to shape the tiller to the required curve and the actual laminating process is quite simple if it is done correctly. Final shaping and finishing can be done with a plane and sander and the rudder-head fitting bolted securely to the end. The whole job, when finished with clear varnish, is as attractive a unit as will be achieved by any other method of construction and will also be extremely strong.

CHAPTER 6

Interior Fittings

FURNITURE

IN SOME FORMS of hull construction, notably moulded fibreglass, the basic furniture is often built into, and forms an integral part of, the hull structure. Berths, for example, though they may only be in a basic box form and will need to be finished, may be an important part of the longitudinal structure of the boat, so that while they can be prettied up and finished off they must not be removed or severely weakened by cutting. In cases such as this much of the fitting-out work has already been done and all that remains is to finish off with trim—bunk boards, shelves, headboards, etc.

This is not usually the case with a timber hull, rarely with metal or concrete hulls and not even always with fibreglass hulls. So we will not neglect the more involved job of fitting furniture into a completely bare hull.

Moulded furniture

The extent to which the moulded furniture is already fitted will vary from boat to boat. In some cases it will be a basic box structure and nothing more. On the other hand, the use of fibreglass is becoming very sophisticated and since its surface is easy to clean, and the use of different gel coats can create a colour scheme, it makes a great utility finish in a boat. Without timber and fabric trim it is not exactly in the luxury class, but is very practical in terms of keeping clean and some boat owners—particularly those with young families—like it that way.

Thus it is becoming quite common to see interior moulded furniture not only fitted but moulded to a complete finish with recessed sinks, raised moulded fiddleys at the edges, ribbed drainage boards and so on. Since the galley area is not unlike the kitchen of a house it lends itself to this sort of finish and since the moulding process is relatively easy, there is no good reason why the galley furniture should not be completed as far as possible during moulding. In this case there is little to do but add any decorative or finishing touches you may require. Timber trim

always looks superb against the clinical surface of fibreglass, as do stainless steel taps, teak plate racks, etc.

Of first importance when adding trim or fittings to moulded furniture is means of access. More often than not the moulded sections will be in one piece and the inside almost inaccessible, making fastening somewhat difficult. However, lockers under berths are traditionally stowage areas and access is necessary so hatches or openings must be cut. It is always important that the boat's hull skin is accessible since, in an emergency, being able to reach a damaged part of the hull may mean the difference between foundering and keeping the boat afloat. Here again is the need for access through the moulded furniture.

Cutting access holes in the tops or sides of the moulded sections will not weaken them over much providing the holes are not too large and are reasonably spaced. An opening of, say, 25-30 cm length by 12-15 cm height is big enough to offer good access for virtually any purpose, and staggering these holes at about 1 metre centres

Moulded hulls come with varying amounts of moulded-in furniture. Fitting out often means little more than adding trim, fittings and upholstery.

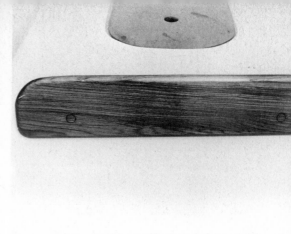

Holes cut in moulded furniture can serve as access to the inside for fitting out and double as locker openings for storage. Neat doors can cover the aperture and give an attractive finish.

Teak trim pieces screwed or bolted through the GRP and finished with dowels add attractive touches to moulded furniture.

will not affect the strength of the section sufficiently to cause problems. The openings may be square or oval and can be finished with hatch covers or cupboard doors, which help compensate for any weakness sustained in cutting the openings.

Pre-built doors or hatch covers can be purchased, in which case fitting them is simple. However, they are not so very difficult to make up from teak finished ply and in this case can be designed to match any other cupboards or drawers. As a general rule, vertical openings are fitted with doors, which may either hinge sideways or downwards, while horizontal surfaces such as those beneath bunk cushions are usually fitted with hatch covers. In this latter case, the hatch covers will need to be recessed or made of very thin ply in order to avoid making a hump beneath berth cushions.

Fitting a ready-made door or hatch requires only careful measurement of the cut hole to ensure that it matches the fitting, and then glueing and screwing the teak surrounds through the fibreglass to a suitable fastening on the inside. The simplest form of backing is a light piece of timber cut to match the hatch surrounds and placed exactly beneath them. Either screws or bolts can then be used to secure the fitting through the fibreglass and the timber backing. An alternative is to use metal pads or washers, and bolt the hatch surrounds through the glass fibre. A good glue will help to make the fastening strong and also fill any gaps between the ready-made fitting and the fibreglass through which it is secured.

Much the same procedure is used for through fastening any trim pieces such as fiddleys, edge trim and headboards. Care must be taken in fastening any heavy trim such as bunkboards as the section of the fibreglass tends to be much thinner here than in areas such as the hull or bulkheads. Where the section is too thin to support the fitting, or where it is flexible, a heavy backing piece should be applied through which the fittings can be fastened. This has the double purpose of providing a backing onto which the fitting is secured and of spreading the load across a larger area of the fibreglass. If the fittings are likely to come under stress then a suitably large backing piece must be used, and this may even need to be of stainless steel. Alternatively the GRP may need to be stiffened by moulded sections such as described on page 47. However, such reinforcement is not often necessary with interior furnishings, being confined mostly to deck equipment.

Where there will be little or no stress on the fitting a good system is to screw through from the inside of the fibreglass using a large washer under the screw head. This enables the fastening to be completely concealed, and although not a very strong method of fastening, can be reinforced by a suitable glue. Light trim pieces such as fiddleys, cupboard doors and glass holders can be secured in this way, but shelves, plate racks and similar fittings which may have to support some weight should be bolted through to a ply pad on the inside of the fibreglass.

Opening a hole in the fibreglass for such fittings as sinks or lockers, if not already done, can be done quite simply with a coping saw. Use a drill to make a series of holes which can be broken together to allow access for the blade of the saw. This should be done in the centre of the

Timber trim, some touches of fabric and a little imagination are all that is required to convert a bare, moulded interior to a warm, livable cabin.

area to be removed and at such an angle that the saw can be run easily into the drawn outline of the opening. This way a neat cut which can easily be matched to a timber trim surround is made.

Sinks can be purchased to size and fitted into the pre-cut hole in the fibreglass of the galley top. A rubber strip about 2-5 mm is fitted beneath the edge of the stainless steel sink before fastening to ensure that water spilled over the edge of the sink does not make its way down into cupboards below. Timber surrounds for sinks are not a good idea as they tend to stain.

Built furniture

When there is no moulded furniture the job of fitting out the accommodation area of the boat must begin from scratch. And scratch, in this case, is the bare structure of the hull. In the case of fibreglass, metal or concrete hulls there will be few structural members onto which the framework of the furniture can be secured and since, with few exceptions, such framework cannot be attached directly to the hull skin, landings must be secured before fitting out is begun. Timber boats have a greater number of structural members and these can be used as landings in many cases.

Since every hull has its own characteristics and since every boat will be fitted out differently, a certain amount of ingenuity will be required in planning where structural members can be utilised as landings or what type of landings should be fitted and where. A book of this type can only deal with an average approach to the

The main structural members of the hull should be used to secure furniture, but if this is not possible landings must be secured to the hull. Here the outline of a set of drawers has been located on a half bulkhead. The stringers and chine will provide many fastening points.

task and individual problems must be solved as they are encountered. Basically, however, landings will be required for all furniture where structural members of the hull cannot be used to secure furniture framework. The more complex structure of a timber boat will, for the most part, provide adequate landings in the form of frames, stringers and so on, but in boats of other material landings such as welded brackets (in steel, aluminium and concrete hulls) and bonded timber or fibreglass brackets (GRP hulls) will be necessary. Such landings must be fitted according to the requirements of the interior furniture and are therefore the first step in the fitting-out procedure.

Materials

The framework for interior furniture can be fairly standard for almost any size of boat. Since little will be involved in structural strength, the only specifications will be for solid construction able to take the use it is intended for. Galley and cupboard framework, for example, can be satisfactorily constructed from softwood (pine) with dimensions around 500 x 300 mm. The main bearers of bunks and doorways should be of heavier dimension, say 800 x 400 mm. Plywood used for panelling should be not less than 100 mm thickness and for large or structural areas such as bulkheads not less than 150 mm although in this latter case the thickness will vary with the size of the boat.

Although some owners do not like using plywood for interior work there is no denying its suitability and ease of use. To begin with, it can be purchased in large sheets, most of which will take care of any single panel of interior furniture. This eliminates problems associated with joining panel sections. It is comparatively stronger than timber of the same thickness which means that lighter gauge facings can be used, and weight in a boat is an important consideration. It can be purchased in different surfaces so that teak, mahogany or blondwood finishes can be used to add to the decor without greatly adding to the price. And if the laminated end is visible and is considered unsightly then it can easily be covered with a beading strip or some similar trim. It must, of course, be good grade marine plywood which has been impregnated against rot. The use of inferior grades will lead to warping or delamination at some later stage.

Softwood is the best timber for constructing the framework of interior furniture since it is easy to joint and fasten. A covering of plywood panels neatly closes in the job.

Treatment

Before any piece of timber is covered or made relatively inaccessible it must be treated against rot. Ply and most timbers except teak are very vulnerable and this insidious pest, once started, will run through the timber work of a boat like a dose of salts. It is a fungus which attacks the fibres of the timber and its spores float freely around inside the hull of a boat, settling on any piece of timber which will give it a chance to germinate. Prevention is the best answer with dry rot for the cure is always severe surgery and in many cases it cannot be satisfactorily cured at all.

Timbers most vulnerable to dry rot are the softwoods used for interior furniture framework and the condition most ideal for the rot to get a hold is the humid atmosphere that pervades the closed up interior of a hull. Prevention begins during the fitting out process with every piece of timber used in the furniture framework being treated before the facing pieces are screwed into place, but after gluing is finished and cured. Cuprinol compounds are widely used; various types are available. Plywood end-grain is invariably a source of trouble and should be thoroughly impregnated, then dried, and finally sealed against moisture penetration.

Good grade marine plywood is often impregnated before it is sold but check on this when purchasing as this is not a universal practice, particularly with cheaper grades. Unfortunately some treatments leave unpleasant stains on the surface of the timber which show up through clear varnish or polish. It is as well to check with your timber dealer when purchasing timber or plywood which will be ultimately varnished to ensure that it is suited to this type of finish.

Joinery

Since the framework of the furniture must be solidly constructed to prevent movement when the hull is working, good joinery is essential. While the plywood panelling will help hold the unit together, the violent motion of a boat in a seaway can put a lot of strain on the framework and loosen fastenings. Good joinery prevents joints working since the stresses are spread through the timber rather than solely on the fastening. The strength lies in the joints, so use of dovetail and lap joints even for the simplest structure will pay dividends later. A complete section on the main joinery work used in fitting out is included on pages 37 and 38.

The easiest method of building furniture involves the use of plywood panels bonded directly to the hull and each other with GRP. Framework can be added where extra strength is required.

Plywood furniture

As mentioned in the last paragraph, it is important that the framing for any furniture is solidly constructed so that there is no chance of any movement when the ship is under way. And as already described, this is achieved by building up adequate framing fastened to the bulkheads, and where necessary to landings and sole bearers bonded to the skin of the hull. The skill with which this is done, and the quality of finish achieved on the furniture thus fitted, is something one will live with from day to day, and so it's worth making a good job. And it might be said that this will also be reflected in the value of the boat, should you ever wish to sell her.

Today, the main material for this work is invariably plywood, and it is available with a number of attractive veneered finishes, in particular teak and mahogany. When considering plywood for boats, there is usually the corollary that it must be marine ply, though it is less frequently mentioned that the word 'marine' may itself include a number of different types of wood. For the skinning of hulls, Brynzeel is one of the best, while in Britain that application is covered by BS 1088 WPBP, each sheet being stamped with the British Standard kitemark. Such ply is expensive, however, and where the wood is not liable to constant immersion in water the normal 'exterior grades' are quite satisfactory.

In building the furniture, small lockers and similar units under no great stress may be built by directly bonding ply panels together with glassfibre tape and resin. But it should be stressed that when doing so, additional strengthening members may be necessary.

Strengthening members may be just fore and aft or cross pieces cut from a reasonably solid timber section or may be shaped plywood inserts, along the lines of miniature bulkheads, which divide the area up into compartments. This latter is an excellent way of creating strength as well as compartments since, like bulkheads, it creates the strongest type of reinforcing that can be fitted to a boat's hull. The method can be used with timber boats also, particularly where furniture has to be fitted to areas lacking in suitable structural members. This is often the case with plywood boats where structural members are widely spaced in comparison to planked hulls and it is also the case with motor yachts which tend to have fewer structural members, particularly in the cabin area, than yachts.

It is important, when using fibreglass bonding to join two pieces of timber, that the plywood is extremely clean and free from any surface grime or grease. While fibreglass makes an excellent bond to timber, the smallest amount of foreign matter will spoil the bond and cause the glass to break away at some later date. For this reason, most interior timber to be bonded with GRP should be new, virgin and unmarked by any foreign matter.

The best procedure with this method is to first cut templates (cardboard or scrap ply) of the ends and front panels. When the panels have been shaped and placed in position they are heavily glassed along all join edges. A particularly strong structural bond is made by jointing the corners, but if this is not practicable, a piece of timber of dimensions somewhere around 5 x 5 mm will provide good corner reinforcement. This work must, of course, be done before glassing.

When glassing the edges use fibreglass tape, mat or cloth and taper the thickness of the bond outward from the join, as described for bulkheads on page 57. This is particularly important with hull bonds as it prevents hot spots in the glass skin.

With the basic box glassed into place, any further reinforcement or compartments can be

Reinforcing by light battens can provide added strength and also landings onto which framework for drawers and shelves can be secured.

Comfortable sitting room is essential with saloon berths, particularly in relation to headroom. Careful measurement will ensure that the occupants are not stooped over when sitting.

fitted prior to screwing the top into place and completing the job. It is not wise to glass the top to the main structure as this will prevent access to the hull other than via cut doors or hatchways and, as mentioned earlier, it is an important safety factor to have all parts of the hull easily accessible.

SALOON BERTHS

Generally speaking, the forward area of a boat is used for sleeping or storage, or sometimes toilet and bathroom, while the saloon is the main living area. For this reason, berths in both areas vary. If fitted, berths in the forward cabin are constructed solely for sleeping and are designed for this purpose, whereas saloon berths double as settees to provide seating accommodation, and are therefore something of a compromise.

Two important factors must be borne in mind when planning to fit settee berths, the first being obviously to utilise the interior space of the hull to the maximum, thus keeping the berths to the smallest dimensions feasible. The second is to ensure that anyone sitting on the berth has room to sit comfortably and is not bent double because of a shortage of headroom or the protrusion of the deck or some similar structural piece. An average of one metre between the top of the berth

cushions and any such protrusion should provide sufficient sitting room for all but the tallest person.

Initially, then, in measuring up for the fitting of the berth a one metre space for headroom should be measured down from the deckhead. This is the highest point at which the berth may be located and therefore all other dimensions must fit with it. It is no good constructing a berth which is comfortable but cannot be sat on, any more than it is to ensure that there is good sitting headroom while the berth is almost on the cabin sole and your knees up round your ears!

Sitting headroom and full-length sleeping room are the two essentials of a settee berth (right).

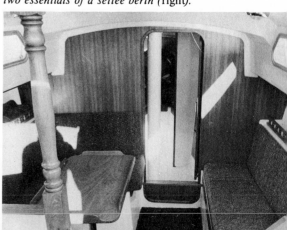

From this it can be seen that a combination of two factors is used when planning to fit a settee berth. Allowance for head room above the bunk and an allowance for comfortable leg room—a minimum of around 35 cm—above the cabin sole. Most boats should have sufficient room to fit these berths, or they are not really suitable for full living accommodation.

Of course, if it is possible to lower the top of the berth farther than the one metre mentioned without upsetting the leg room, so much the better. To utilise the space inside the hull to a maximum the berth should be kept as low as possible without affecting the leg room when sitting. However, some people prefer higher berths for more comfortable sitting and when this is possible it certainly should be done. The measurements given here are the minimum for comfort and anything outside of these will naturally increase the comfort of the seating.

The actual design and location of the settee berth will be individual according to the size and shape of the saloon and your own plans for the accommodation area. If the boat is fairly small then one end of the settee berth will almost certainly be attached to a bulkhead. Allowing for an average of just under two metres as the length of the berth, it should be fitted where it is convenient for use and also takes up the minimum amount of room.

More often than not it will be sandwiched between other fittings such as a bulkhead and the galley, in which case it becomes an integral part of the framework in the saloon furniture. If it is to stand on its own, then it will need to be closed in at each end both from a structural point of view and also to make it look neat. This situation is pretty rare in anything but the largest craft, since space is always at a premium in small boats and butting the berth up against another item of furniture or a bulkhead is a good way to conserve space. It follows that boats of different construction will require a slightly different approach to fitting of settee berths, but the guidelines laid down here, with a certain amount of adjustment to fit individual needs, provide the basis on which comfortable and strong settee berths can be constructed for almost any craft.

It is always better, if at all possible, to construct at least the framework of interior furniture outside the boat in a workshop. This makes for easier and more comfortable working, and usually better tools can be applied to the job than in the close confines of a boat's hull.

If there is no convenient bulkhead the berth may butt up against other furniture or may be free standing with its own headboard.

However, if the deck is in place, and the doors or hatches are not big enough, then the furniture will need to be constructed *in situ*. While this may be a more difficult way of doing things at least it is easier to check that measurements and fittings are correct as the framework is built up. If you build the framework outside the boat be sure that measurements are absolutely exact or the unit will not fit when placed in position in the hull.

While the actual framework of each berth will depend to a great extent on the construction of the hull in the area where it is to be fitted, the basic arrangement should comprise two longitudinal members running the full length of the front of the bunk and supported at intervals by uprights. This framework is then secured to the cabin sole by screws. Transverse members secure this framework to the side of the hull. These should be fairly closely spaced and well jointed both to the inboard framework and to landings on the hull since they not only hold the entire

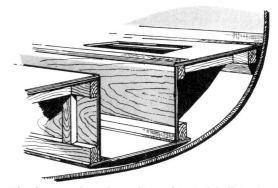

The framework and panelling of typical hull berths, supported on a landing fillet and a fixed sole, both bonded to the skin of the hull. Bonded-in sole bearers may also be used where the sole is removable.

settee berth framework in place, but also support the weight of people sitting on it.

If the ends of the framework are open they will need to be panelled, but if they butt up against a bulkhead or other furniture an outline framework of the berth can be secured to the bulkhead, and used as a landing for the fore and aft framework. It is sometimes useful to divide the underneath of the settee berth into sections for storage, in which case ply panels attached to the horizontal supports and to landings on the side of the hull will do the job. These miniature bulkheads, as it were, also add a great deal of strength to the berth and are often fitted purely as a structural asset.

The front panelling and finish of the settee berth is a personal job and will depend on what sort of finish you require to match the rest of the interior furniture. The ply used for the facing panel is shaped to suit the framework and can be fitted with access doors for under-berth storage if required. The framework is closed in with a panel on the top of the berth. This need only be relatively light gauge ply glued and screwed into position with access holes cut if required and covered with small plywood hatchcovers. Timber or metal trim may be used to cover the ends of the plywood to give an attractive finish.

Berth cushions

When the berth has been secured in position the cushions can be shaped from rubber or plastic foam. The most suitable—and the cheapest—is high-density plastic foam of not less than 100 mm thickness which must be carefully shaped not only to fit the berth, but overlap it by about 10 mm all round. This is to allow for the compression which will take place when the covers are fitted, and ensure that the cushions fit

Cushions can be secured to prevent them falling about when the boat moves by means of Velcro attached to the back. They can simply be pulled off the backrest when required for cleaning.

snugly onto the berth and do not leave a gap all the way round. Unless you are an experienced upholsterer, the covering of the cushions should be left to a professional, since nothing looks worse than an ill-fitting berth cushion cover. Good quality material is essential as well as professional workmanship, for what may appear initially to be a neat, tidy job may stretch and get out of shape after a period of use if the material or workmanship is not first class.

It is a good idea to fit the berth cushions with a plastic zipper running the full length of the back so that in the event of the cushions getting wet—and this is always a possibility—they can be easily dried out. Also, the covers can easily be changed or taken off for washing if they are marked or become worn. Fabric-backed vinyl is often used, and there are rot-proof water resistant weaves for a different texture. Any covers need to be strong so they do not stretch out of shape or break their seams.

GALLEYS

The variations in galley arrangements are so numerous and depend so much on the individual boat that it would take a full book to cover them all. However, as with all interior furniture, most systems evolve from a basic design and we will discuss here the simplest, most basic form of galley. Adaptations or modifications can be made to suit any craft.

Careful measuring and cutting are essential if the foam cushions are to fit exactly, particularly against the curve of the hull. A template is necessary in the first instance.

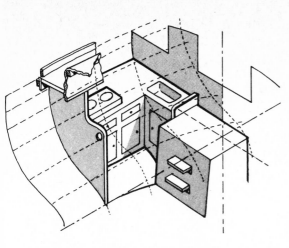

A carefully drawn plan of the galley area will ensure that everything fits correctly and utilises the space available to the best advantage.

The framework of a built galley unit is much like that of any interior furniture, particularly a berth. The main difference lies in the fittings to be attached to the finished unit—stove, sink and so on. Because these are purchased separately the galley structure must be built to measurements which will accommodate them—not, as is the case with a berth, the furniture built first and the cushions cut to match later.

So the measurements for the stove and sink must be known and allowed for in the design. A basic plan for a typical galley, which can be adapted to fit a number of different types of craft, is illustrated. It is a good idea to draw a plan of your own galley to scale before starting work. The use of cardboard templates will ensure that everything fits correctly into place. The most popular position for a galley is at one side of the main saloon, although in smaller craft where space is at a premium a good spot is across the after end of the saloon in way of the main companionway. Again, all a matter of personal taste and what suits the individual boat best.

A neatly laid-out and constructed galley will be a joy forever to the skipper's wife.

The galley furniture may be constructed by any one of the three systems described at the beginning of this chapter—moulded GRP, built timber or box ply. The former will already be constructed and need only finishing, and box ply structures are easily fabricated. A built galley, however, may be a fairly complex structure, depending on its location and shape and the openings required.

The framework of the galley can be constructed entirely of softwood somewhere in the region of 60 mm x 30 mm as it is unlikely to bear any heavy loads. A lap jointed or dovetailed box framework base is screwed (not glued) to the cabin sole. Next step is the landing on the side of the hull for the top framework. This can be timber of about the same measurement bonded with glass fibre to the skin at exactly the right height or screwed to structural members if they are conveniently located. Watch your levels here, working carefully from the waterline level as described on page 49.

Now the plan of the galley should be studied to determine where the drawers, shelves and recesses for stove and sink are to be located. Every opening will require a framework around it if you are panelling with ply of less than 10 mm thickness—it is a good idea to draw a framework plan of the front of the galley and build it separately, fitting it to the main framework when both are completed.

Planning is important in this method to ensure that all work connected with the front of the

Building up the galley on a framework requires careful measurement and strict adherence to the plans, otherwise the stove, sink and other items will not fit correctly.

galley—stove recesses, drawer slides, sink recess, cupboard shelves, etc.—is in the correct position before the front panel is fitted into place. These pieces are small and therefore much of the work can be done in a workshop where conditions are easier and better tools available. However, it does require a little thought in planning to ensure that it all comes together correctly in the final fitting.

It is essential to fit all plumbing and any electrical wiring before panelling in the framework. Particularly is this the case with the skin fitting for the sink outlet. Details of skin fittings are given on page 97. All other adjustments should be made at this time since making adjustments with the panelling in place is difficult (to say the least!). The sink hose should be connected to the stop cock and secured with a ring grip, then led up through the sink recess ready for fitting to the sink itself. If a gas stove is to be fitted a similar arrangement will be necessary for the gas pipes.

The only satisfactory way to fit panelling is to make templates. This will apply to the sides of

Plumbing and wiring must be concealed and must be led through the interior of the galley structure before it is closed off.

the galley unit because of the curve in the hull, particularly to the top, where apertures must be made for the sink, stove, taps and other fittings. Some shipwrights like to secure a landing to the side of the hull to secure the back edge of the panelling, others do not. Much depends on the location of frames and similar structural members and also the span of the panel. The rigidity of the plywood would eliminate the need for support along a short edge. In cutting the top template remember to mark holes for the tap or taps supplying the sink and any other fittings which may be required. This template will be needed later to cut the laminex or formica top, so accuracy is the keynote for a good finish to be achieved.

If the panels are cut from plywood of 15 mm thickness or more, some of the framework described earlier can be eliminated. Each opening is made with a jig saw or coping saw. Since the cut-out pieces for cupboard and drawer openings can be used later for doors these should be cut carefully by drilling 'starter' holes just inside the template line and fitting the saw blade through. The millimetre or so lost in drilling is of no consequence since the doors will be slightly smaller than the opening anyway.

With the quality and bonding power of modern glues only a little screwing will be required to hold the panels in place. This can be done either from the inside (if possible) to conceal the screw heads or from the outside with the countersunk screws plugged with dowels. Some shipwrights like to use beading or some form of capping as ornamental trim all round the edges of the galley. This not only enhances the appearance of the unit but also covers the sawn ends of the panels.

The laminex top is now cut using the original top template after checking to ensure that the fit is still good. As with the timber panels, openings can be cut with a jig saw or fretsaw, again cutting inside the line to allow for any errors and for clean flushing off when fitted. When the laminex is cut it should be given a dry run, placed into position to check all measurements, since once the contact cement has been spread it is very difficult to remove and re-fit it. Ensure that tap holes and other apertures are correctly lined up, and the synthetic surface fits flush to the edges all round the top.

There are many types of glue for this work, the best undoubtedly being the pressure sensitive 'contact' type. With this type of glue both surfaces are covered with a thin, even layer and allowed to touch dry before pressing the laminex down into position. As mentioned, it is very difficult to make adjustments after contact has been made, so make absolutely sure of the fit before applying pressure.

Now the trim pieces are applied. The fiddley is simply a piece of hardwood about 60 mm x 10 mm shaped and finished then glued and screwed along the top of the front panel and protruding about 20-40 mm above it. This retains pots, pans and other galley equipment when the boat is moving in a seaway. The corners can be cut away a little to allow ease of cleaning but all these finer points are a matter of individual taste and can be left to your own ingenuity and taste. Likewise the cupboard and drawer knobs, which may be of standard protruding design or recessed with catches inside, leaving the outside flush and finger holes to operate them.

From this point on the finishing work will vary according to the fittings to be secured. Taps, sink and stove can be placed in their respective apertures and hooked up to their water or fuel systems. Painting or varnishing the exterior panels is described on page 215, and the fitting of extra items of a personal nature will add the finishing touches that can make a well-built galley a showpiece of the boat.

Galley stove

We have already discussed the recess for the stove fitted into the basic galley unit. If the stove is gas-fired a flexible pipe will be run through the panelling of this recessed area to connect up with the stove when in position. The size of the stove has been predetermined and, if it is to be gimballed, space allowed for the gimbals and for the stove to swing freely without being restricted by the back panel other than at excessive angles of heel. The fitting of gimbals is described on page 142.

Some owners are nervous of gas stoves in a boat and rightly so. Apart from the obvious dangers of a naked flame in the highly inflammable interior of the boat there is the possibility of a gas leak creating risk of explosion. Thus great care is necessary in fitting the connecting hoses as well as in locating the gas bottle so that any leakage of gas will be minimal as well as being easily vented away. As with the dangers of fuel leaks in a motor, careful fitting and good ventilation go a long way towards making a gas installation safe.

Stoves come in all shapes and sizes. Fitting large stoves can create problems in small craft, but careful planning will create a suitable arrangement.

In small craft it may be essential to fit a stainless steel or aluminium plate around the galley recess to catch spattered fat and prevent nearby fittings or the hull structure from being scorched. Rather like the drip tray beneath the motor, this metal sheet should be so fitted that spattered fat or oil is run down to a metal tray at the bottom of the recess where it can be removed and cleaned after cooking. Apart from the dangers of spattered fat catching fire, it makes dirty and unsightly marks on nearby bulkheads and fittings. Particularly is this so with the back of the galley area which will probably be fitted with plate or saucepan racks or some other receptacle for utensils. A good plan is to make the removable top of the stove recess into a hinged lid. When the stove is in use the lid is lifted up and thus protects the back of the galley from the spattering fat. If it is too large it can be hinged in the middle to fold into two sections. When the stove is not in use it fastens down to cover the stove and, covered with matching laminex, makes extra bench space for other galley activities.

The question of additional bench space can be important in a small boat and another idea on the same theme, providing the splattering problem is not evident, is to fit the top of the stove recess on stainless steel slides, one of which continues beyond the galley top along the side of the boat. The top when in position conceals the stove and provides extra bench space but when slid to one side allows the stove to be used

141

This sort of innovation can utilise valuable space twice over. When the stove is not in use a cover slides out over it to provide extra bench area.

without loss of working room. The only requirement, of course, is that adjoining furniture permits the top to slide away to the side of the galley unit. As so frequently mentioned before, ingenuity is the key to fitting interior furniture to utilise the space in your boat to its maximum advantage. And nowhere is this more so than in the galley area.

Stove gimbals

The size and shape of stove gimbals vary a great deal according to the size and shape of the stove and its location. Some craft have huge cooking stoves incorporating ovens and rotisseries which obviously need vastly different gimballing from a small two-burner stove used for brewing up the odd pot of char or soup on small family sailing or fishing boats. The former are far too intricate to describe in a book such as this, but are nevertheless only a sophisticated development of the basic gimbals which support any stove in such a way that it can swing freely athwartships as the boat heels or rolls.

One of the simplest forms of gimbal can be easily made from a couple of pieces of light angle stainless steel (for preference) or rod and will meet the needs of most craft whose cooking arrangements consist of the simple two-burner stove. The rod or angle should be bent as illustrated, two matching pieces being constructed to fit one on each side of the stove. The

stove recess must, of course, have sufficient space to allow it to swing in the gimbals or the whole exercise is pointless.

By securing one of the fabricated brackets on either side of the recess, a stand is made on which the stove can be hung. Sockets to take the bolts on which the stove will swing must be welded or in some other way attached to the top of the brackets and similarly these bolts must be secured through the side of the stove in such a way that they allow it to swing horizontally.

To gimbal the stove into position, the bolts are fitted into the sockets and a washer and nut used to lock them in position. The stove is now suspended with room beneath and behind it to allow it to swing as the boat heels. When not required the stove can be easily taken down and stowed by removing the two bolts. An alternative method is to purchase gimballed brackets and bolt them into position so that when the stove is not in use they can be unbolted and the whole unit stowed away.

Some shipwrights prefer the gimballed mountings to be permanently attached to the side of the stove recess and the stove itself permanently hung. However, this takes up a lot of space which is not used other than when the stove is in action. The stove recess, if it is covered, can be utilised as a work bench as described earlier, but usually this can only be done if the gimbals are dismantled. A gimballed stove requires half as much room again as a non-gimballed stove, and since space is always at a premium in the galley, it makes good sense to utilise the extra space gimballing requires, where it is used relatively infrequently.

Careful mounting of the gimbals can conceal them and fit the stove neatly into the general arrangement of the galley. The unit will need to be raised, to have room to swing.

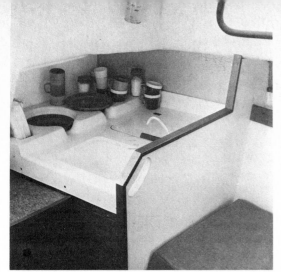

The sink need not necessarily be part of the galley unit. Often it can fill an unused corner to very good effect. On small craft the stove and sink are often mounted on opposite sides of the cabin to balance the interior layout.

Sink

Stainless steel is generally accepted as the best material for sinks, and they may be purchased with or without an integral drainboard. Decide on the type of sink that is required early in the fitting out, and then the galley can be built and the necessary holes cut to suit.

A sink will normally have a water supply and an overside drain, and in a cruising boat it's worth considering a salt water, as well as a fresh water tap. Sea water may be drawn from a separate skin fitting with a pump at the tap, a tee piece may be inserted at the raw water cooling inlet to the engine. The drain pipe should be of a plastic able to withstand boiling water, at least 1 in. inside diameter, and run to a seacock.

Fresh water will normally be drawn from tanks sited low down in the hull, these of GRP, mild steel or a flexible synthetic rubber, with ¾ in. or 1 in. bore reinforced plastic tubing supplying the tap. Small craft taps usually incorporate a small hand lift pump adequate for most needs, and with the advantage of in-built economy. But where a shower is installed or hot water is 'on tap' an electric lift pump is usually fitted, producing sufficient pressure for those services. Such pumps are also fitted with a pressure switch which responds to the opening of a tap, and so given a supply of electricity, their action is automatic.

Given the plumbing, hoseclips and fittings, and assuming that the relevant skin fittings have been installed, any problems in fitting the sink are often those of access. And the drain, by the way, should be above the waterline of the boat when she is heeled. Mounting holes for the taps may be pre-cut in the rim of the sink, or they may be mounted through the adjacent panelling; use large washers under the nuts where this is ply. Have more than adequate pipe runs so that joints can be re-made if necessary, and so that there's room to manoeuvre the pipes in the confined space under the sink. Taps should be bedded on rubber washers or sealing compound, and the same of course for the flange round the sink.

Combined stove/sink

As mentioned before, the fitting of space and labour-saving ideas into a boat's galley is limited only by your own ingenuity. Since space is always at a premium, but particularly in small craft, it is well worth while taking time out to sit down and scratch your head to come up with some idea which may save space in return for relatively little effort. There are unlimited numbers of ideas and adaptations to the basic galley unit described in this book, and it would need another book simply to describe them all. However, typical of the sort of ingenious idea which can save space in a small craft is a combined stove/sink unit which is described here with the intention of triggering off similar ideas for your own boat.

The sink may be of standard design, even perhaps already moulded into the boat if she is of fibreglass construction. The stove needs only to be matched so that it is a few centimetres larger all round and mounted on a board with rubber feet which fits well over the sink aperture. By hinging one end of this stove base so that when lowered it sits squarely across the sink you have literally halved the space required for both units to be installed in the galley.

When the sink is required, the stove can be

Where a sink is required to fit a specific measurement it can be moulded from GRP by making up a simple male mould such as this.

hinged upwards and secured by some form of catch on the bulkhead or side of the cabin and when required for cooking can be lowered into position over the sink. The only problem in fitting will arise with the location of taps and a suitable bulkhead or upright onto which to secure the raised stove. But allowing for these problems should not tax anyone's resourcefulness too severely!

Take care that when the stove is alight the flame or spattering fat do not damage any nearby material, and ensure that when the stove is clipped up it is held securely against the motion of the boat.

Plate and cup racks

The ideal plate rack is one which accommodates the largest number of plates in the smallest space. There are many fancy designs for cup and plate racks and without doubt some of them are most attractive and useful. Boatbuilding books are full of such designs but we will content ourselves here with, as usual, the basic format and leave any further development to your own inventiveness.

Plate racks are simply box structures made to take plates of different sizes and permit them to be lifted easily in and out. They can be made out of almost any spare plywood and, like a number of small interior fittings, are an ideal way to use up ply offcuts. As a rule the rack is made separately and screwed into place so that it can be easily removed. The base should be of fairly firm ply, say about 10 mm thickness, and cut to the shape and size of the space it is to fill. Then each of the sizes of plates (and cups) to be accommodated is marked on this base board and

The size and capacity of plate and cup racks will vary from boat to boat, but the basic design remains the same. This is the simplest form of rack for bulkhead mounting.

the partitions located to allow about 5 mm clearance on each side of the plate.

This will permit easy movement of the plates in and out of the racks yet prevent any movement in a seaway. Similarly, the openings in the front panel should be sufficient to allow a hand to take a firm grip on each plate yet not big enough to allow the plates to slide out of the rack when the boat is moving around. In the case of the cup rack the opening at the front can be quite small as the handles will protrude and the cups can be lifted out without the need to put fingers into the rack. An opening of around 100 mm for plates and 20 mm for cups will be fairly close to the mark.

The height of the racks will depend on personal requirements and the space into which the racks are to fit. If there is unlimited space the controlling factor will obviously be the number of plates to be kept in the rack. The location will also have a bearing on the height since there must be room not only to fit the rack but also a few centimetres of space above it to allow lifting in and out. Cups take up the most space so perhaps the cup rack will be the controlling factor as far as height is concerned.

Templates cut from cardboard will avoid any wastage and make the actual cutting process easier. The top corners of the spaces in the front panel can be rounded out to make for easier lifting of the utensils. Quite a good idea is to glue or staple the templates together then fit the whole unit into place to ensure that no adjustments will be needed after the ply has been cut.

With all sides and partitions cut the base is made up by gluing and screwing a light framework (say 20 mm x 20 mm softwood) to the base panel in way of the sides and partitions. Similar pieces can be cut to make the uprights for the corners and landings for the partitions. Then it becomes merely a case of glueing and screwing the unit together.

Cutting board

Since space is at such a premium in a small boat, refinements such as cutting boards must be portable and not take up too much space. One idea is to fit the cutting board in the space taken up by the sink. In this way the whole of the galley bench still remains available for whatever culinary activities are in progress, while cutting can be done without interrupting these activities or having to clear a space.

Another innovation which saves space—a cutting board which slides beneath the galley bench.

The base of the cutting board is shaped from timber or ply around 15 mm thick to fit exactly into the top of the sink. The cutting board itself is made from about 30 mm thickness timber to whatever size is required, as long as it is larger than the base piece. Both pieces are then glued and screwed together so that the base fits into the sink while the cutting board overlaps all round.

A good tight fit between the base and the sink will ensure that the board does not move when in use, and to achieve this tight fit you may need to round off the corners to match the shape of the sink. Timber should be used for the cutting block as opposed to plywood, as the top veneers of the ply tend to get damaged by knife cuts and disintegrate, spoiling the surface and the appearance of the board.

Screws should be inserted through the bottom piece of timber so that the cutting area is left unmarked. Teak is probably as good a timber as any since it does not require varnishing, but most timbers are suitable for this job.

CUPBOARDS AND LOCKERS

On board a boat, cupboards and lockers are virtually one and the same thing. If there is a difference, perhaps it is that cupboards are generally built into the boat as a complete structure, whereas lockers tend to utilise spaces already formed—beneath bunks and where awkward corners of the hull have been closed off. And then again, cupboards are invariably closed by means of a door while lockers may be open.

Either way, both cupboards and lockers are a most important part of the interior fittings because they provide the all-important storage space which is always at a premium, no matter how big the boat and how spacious the interior. Unlike a house, where much of the storage can be done on shelves or on top of the cupboards, a boat must have enclosed storage space or everything will be all over the cabin the minute she heels or rolls in a seaway. A certain amount of shelf space can be utilised for small items providing there is a fiddley around the edge of the shelf, but most items of equipment as well as utensils and food must be stored in closed compartments and this means either a cupboard or a locker.

Lockers

The easiest way to create a storage space is to form a locker which usually involves closing off a section of the hull. There are many awkward corners in a boat hull—particularly a sailing boat—and while it may be too difficult to fit useful furniture into such a space, it is simple enough to close it off and create storage room.

The classic example of this is beneath settee berths where the curve of the hull creates an awkward shape for anything but storage: likewise in the eyes of the bow where the awkward triangular area is utilised for stowage of anchor and warp. Nooks and crannies beneath the deckhead are often closed off to form lockers and any seating or other fitting which leaves space beneath can be turned into a locker compartment.

Thus fitting a locker simply means closing in the area to be used, leaving either an open

Almost any corner can be utilised as a locker providing it has an opening for access. With storage space always at a premium on a boat, no area can be wasted.

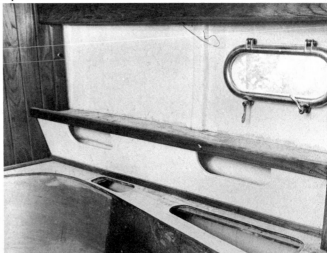

hatchway or a door for access. With timber hulls there may be sufficient structural members adjacent to the area to enable a simple panel to be fastened in place. With most other types of craft a landing will probably be necessary to take the panelling. As a general rule a light timber landing around 25-35 mm square is all that is required unless a large area is being closed in, when heavier gauge landings may be required. The landing can be glassed or bolted into position and the panelling screwed to it. The hull forms the remaining sides and top and bottom of the locker unless the shape requires one or more of these to be panelled in. In this case the landing will be more of a framework construction.

Cupboards can be fitted in many parts of the hull, depending on how high they are to be. A full-length hanging cupboard requires a lot of space whereas a medium-sized cupboard fits more easily into the hull and can still hang most clothes and wet weather gear.

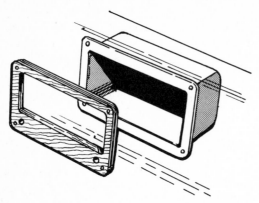

A locker can be built or moulded to a particular size and shape and covered with a facing panel to prevent the contents pitching out. This is often done where the area is such that an unlimited locker would be too large or too deep for practical use.

Many lockers have only an access hatch (around 20 cm x 10 cm is a good size for small lockers) of an oval or rounded rectangular shape left open for easy use. Others are square or rectangular and have a fitted door or hatch to close off the locker area. These doors may be hinged or simply slotted into position as described on page 128.

Cupboards

Cupboards range in size from small compartments much like lockers to large, even full-height units for hanging clothes. In all cases they are built up on a jointed framework and may be totally capsuled or built against the side of the hull and the cabin sole. Obviously it is easiest to utilise parts of the hull in constructing the cupboard as it reduces the workload and the cost. But some boat owners prefer to line the

back and bottom of the unit, or build it as a separate and complete unit so that anything stored is not in contact with any part of the hull. This is important if bilge water is inclined to run up the side of the boat when she is heeled or rolling, or if you have a leaking gunwale or deckhead.

The construction of the unit will again depend on each individual boat and the area into which the cupboard is to fit. For example, two adjacent bulkheads will provide the sides of a full-sized cupboard with, perhaps, the deckhead and cabin sole providing top and bottom. Then the only work that has to be done is to build the framework of the front of the cupboard and fit it with a door, much the same as a locker. On the other hand, there may be nothing but the hull skin available in which case the entire unit, except for the back, must be constructed and fastened to landings on the hull.

Thus construction of a cupboard unit is much like that of a galley as described on page 138 with, perhaps, the exception of recesses and holes for the various galley fittings. But the basic framework can be built up as described by jointing a timber framework or, in the case of GRP hulls, by glassing timber or plywood panels into place.

Since cupboards usually form part of the built-in furniture of the boat, they can be finished to match the decor. The front panel will probably be of teak veneer or some similar decorative wood, or faced with laminex if the cupboard is part of the bathroom or galley equipment. Doors should also be nicely finished to enhance the appearance and often jalousie or louvre doors are used.

Shelves can be fitted beforehand if the entire cupboard is built as a separate, complete unit and then secured in place. Where the unit is built to the hull, however, it will be necessary in some cases to fit landings and this must be done before the unit is panelled in, or you will be working under great difficulty. Some cupboards will be fitted with low shelves; some, perhaps, with no shelves at all. Since the whole reason for cupboards and lockers is storage of gear out of sight, each unit must be constructed to fit the purpose it is intended for and the gear it is to conceal.

Locker doors

There are a number of ways in which open lockers can be closed off, much depending on the size and shape of the opening and the material from which the surrounding panel is constructed. One of the simplest methods which can be used where the locker is enclosed by panels of GRP or plywood is a simple lift-off door which involves very little work in construction and yet is quite secure and quite decorative when finished, and can also be used with locker openings of different shapes.

The door panel is a piece of timber or plywood of around 15 mm thickness cut to overlap the

A lift-off door panel as described in the text is particularly useful with motors or other compartments where wide access is required. A hinged door (background) does not open as wide in confined spaces.

locker opening by about 20 mm all round. Since this is to be the finished face of the locker door, one side should be prepared for finishing by sanding back, smoothing off the edges and rounding corners. Obviously the best results come from a good quality piece of timber with a nice natural finish, but if needs be a veneer can be glued onto the face side of the door or it can be painted to match the interior decor of the boat. Finishing is described on page 214.

A second sheet of timber—this can just be ply since it will not be seen—must be cut to the shape and size of the door opening. The thickness of this piece of ply should be slightly greater than the thickness of the material from which the locker is made. When glued and screwed to the inside face of the door it should fit snugly into the opening with the face piece overlapping. A couple of small metal plates screwed onto this inner piece of ply at the bottom edge and overlapping slightly so that it fits over the bottom of the locker opening will provide the means of securing into place. At the top a catch of some description can be used to secure the door in place and this can be of any desired type.

Some boat owners do not like protruding knobs and I must say I am one of them. Where knobs are not necessary, and in this case they are not, a hole of about 30 mm diameter bored out of the locker door close to the top edge will allow finger access to operate a catch fitted inside and adjacent to the hole. A hole of this type has the twofold effect of preventing protruding knobs sticking out from the cupboard door and also of allowing good ventilation of the locker. If knobs are preferred they are simply bolted on in the position required. As with so many interior fittings, the final finish of the locker door will depend on the interior decor of the rest of the boat.

Cupboard doors

While the construction of a cupboard door is in principle straightforward carpentry, if it is to be square and true, and remain so in use, good joinery is required and it cannot be effectively glued up without a pair of sash clamps. The corners of the frame should be morticed, or mitred halvings, and a rebate around the inside edge of the frame will enable a panel to be fitted to stiffen the frame and hold its shape. For these reasons a number of timber merchants now offer ready-made doors, or they can be made up to

147

Louvred doors are particularly good for cupboards as they allow for good ventilation and avoid the mustiness that comes with sea air or damp gear.

Side shelves can be closed off with a simple fiddley as the table is.

Side shelves can also be fitted with a facing panel which, in effect, makes them into a nest of lockers.

your own specification, and their machinery enables them to do this with relative economy. An additional advantage here is that a specialist is often able to offer ready-made louvred doors of the type pictured above, and these are to be preferred in the poorly ventilated confines of a boat.

The frame of a ready-made door may be planed to size so that it is a snug fit within its aperture; there should be at least 2mm clearance all round. Thin spacers of this thickness can then be placed under the bottom sill, and the door and its frame marked for the hinges. Butt hinges are best, and each half will require a neatly cut recess in frame and doorpost. Make a trial fitting with a couple of screws, adjust as necessary, and secure the hinges. Lastly, fit the catch.

SIDE SHELVES

Widely used on every type of boat, particularly small craft, shelves are easy to construct and fit. As a general rule they will run fore and aft but that is not always the case. They can be fitted into almost any spare spot and have only one basic difference in construction to the shelves normally fitted in a kitchen—that is the fiddley or rim around the edge which prevents everything from rolling off the shelf.

A landing must be provided for the shelf and in the case of metal or timber boats this may either be fitted to the hull skin, in which case the frames will be rebated into the shelf itself (by no means a bad idea since it helps prevent things sliding around) or to the inside of the frames. With fibreglass hulls a landing must be bonded to the hull skin to take the shelf.

A narrow shelf, for example, intended purely to hold salt and pepper shakers, cigarette packs, magazines and so forth, needs only a landing about 25 mm wide and about 35 mm deep onto which the edge of the shelf can be screwed and glued. Wider shelves and those designed to take heavier items, such as tools, will need a wider landing—say 40 mm wide by 60 mm deep—onto which its inner edge can be screwed and glued. A wise precaution always, where the shelf is wide or may take heavy loads (even someone grabbing at them when the boat moves violently), is to fit two or three brackets on the underside. These can be made simply by shaping a couple of timber or ply knees, screwing and glueing them to the underside of the shelf and fastening them to the side of the hull or a conveniently located frame.

The shelf itself can be of plywood or timber. In the former case, trim will be necessary round the edge to conceal the laminations. Ply 5–7 mm ($\frac{1}{4}$ in.) thick should be sufficient for most purposes and the shelf will need to be shaped to fit the side

of the hull if it runs along a curved surface. In this case the landing may need to be planed flat as the curve induced in it will tend to upset the horizontal of the upper edge and the shelf will be all askew unless the landing is levelled off.

FIDDLEYS

Fiddleys (or fiddles) are the small raised edges on tables, shelves, galleys, and similar surfaces which hold things in place when the boat is moving in a seaway. There are a number of different types of fiddley, ranging from a metal rail arrangement used around stoves to stop saucepans falling off, to large, attractively finished timber fiddleys which are fitted around the edges of berths and settees to hold the cushions firmly in place. It follows, therefore, that the fitting of a fiddley will depend partly on the purpose it is to serve, the object it is to be fitted to and the requirements of each individual boat.

Bunkboards or leeboards may be fitted to seafaring berths to retain not only the bunk cushions but also the occupant. Larger craft, where berths are separate from the settees of saloon accommodation, may use a fiddley only a few centimetres high to hold the cushions in place.

Galley fiddleys are usually part of the construction of the stove but if not can be fitted simply as a surrounding rail of metal about 3-5 cm high. It will obviously need to be welded or bolted into place and must be so shaped that a number of saucepans can be placed on the stove at one time. A fiddley which enables only one saucepan to be used limits the galley activities.

Fiddleys around galley benches, saloon tables and chart tables as well as other flat surfaces where relatively light gear is used can be cut from timber or ply of about 10 mm thickness and of a suitable height, say 30 mm. Fiddleys around tables should not be brought right to the corners forming a complete tray as this makes them very difficult to clean. A small aperture left at each corner will enable crumbs or other items to be easily swept off. Leeboards used to hold bunk cushions in place should be cut from attractive plywood or timber of 15–20 mm thickness. A good height for such boards is around 10 cm, since this enables the cushion to project well above them and avoid a hard edge. Obviously this will depend on the individual thickness of the cushions.

Fiddleys around a table are essential, but must be fitted so that they do not intrude on the appearance or the use of the table. The pinrail (background) acts as a fiddley for the side shelf.

Since a fair amount of strain can come on fiddleys they must be well secured. In the case of tables and galleys they may be screwed into position, but bunk leeboards and similar large section fittings must be through bolted with, in the case of GRP, suitable pads beneath. The fastening procedure can be considered similar to that described for stress fittings on page 99, but since the strains on a fiddley are likely to be only moderate, the dimensions can be reduced. Bolt heads should be countersunk and covered with a dowel as described on page 31 and the whole fiddley finished to whatever degree required. Hand sanding and a number of coats of varnish will undoubtedly give the best finish for interior work.

The fiddley may often be purchased ready-made, in which case it may come in any one of a number of forms. Without doubt the most attractive is the pin rail which is very hard to make and thus should be always purchased ready to fit in place. The best system of fastening this type of fiddley is to screw (and glue if required) into place. With GRP and plywood shelves it may be possible to screw through from the underside of the shelf or table which avoids the need for drilling and dowelling down through the fitting. However, where the screw cannot be fitted from beneath, it will be necessary to drill through from the upper surface, in which case the screw head must be countersunk and dowelled.

Fiddleys such as the pin rail can add a great deal to the appearance of the boat, and careful choice and fitting of such items can be a simple and relatively inexpensive way of serving two purposes—fitting a practical fiddley while at the same time enhancing the appearance of the interior furniture.

SELF-LOCKING DRAWERS

Whether under bunks, wardrobes, galleys or in some other corner of the accommodation, sliding drawers provide much of the readily accessible storage space in the interior areas of a boat's accommodation. These drawers are no different, basically, to the drawers used in normal furniture in the home but the humbug with them, unless they are locked all the time, is that they slide out whenever the boat heels or rolls. A simple device incorporated into the structure of the drawer when building it will prevent this and is fairly universally adopted on craft of all sizes.

The bearers for the drawers are built into the framework of the unit when it is first put together. There are a number of designs, but the simplest is a box shaped structure the size of the drawer opening containing two timber runners at the bottom along which the drawer slides. These runners are rebated to accept the bottom edges of the drawer as illustrated and the whole box structure made to suit the depth of the drawer itself.

The self-locking device employs part of the front structure of the drawer and the lower front

A nest of self-locking drawers with a small cupboard. The rebate beneath the front panel of the drawer locks into a matching batten in the framework when the drawer is closed.

edge of the opening. The whole drawer is built about 15 mm less in height than the opening to allow the drawer front to be lifted when it is pushed in. Behind the front panel the lower edge is rebated about 10 mm to fit over a batten of the same dimensions fitted onto the lower edge of the opening. When the drawer is closed this raised edge fits into the rebated edge of the drawer, thus locking the drawer in the closed position. To open the drawer it must be lifted to clear the raised edge and then pulled outwards like any normal drawer.

The drawer can be made to any dimensions to suit any furniture. The locking device on the front lower edge is the only part that needs to be specially fitted. Drawers already constructed in the normal manner can be easily adapted to the self-locking type.

BACK RESTS

One of the most comfortable additions to interior furniture is a set of back rests to pad the backs of the saloon settee berths. As often as not, these berths have lockers or cupboards behind them which do not make the most comfortable support for the back when sitting upright. Back rests are easily made out of lightweight high-density foam covered by your local upholsterer. A thickness of 50 mm is usually sufficient and the shape can be cut from a template to fit exactly along the back of the berths.

Always use high-density foam as the normal plastic foam in the relatively light thickness will allow knobs and protrusions to be felt through it. The covering can be of any material to suit your own taste, but wool fabric is without doubt one of the most comfortable and most durable.

The biggest problem in fitting back rests is to

One method of securing the back rest cushions in place.

keep them upright. Since they are located almost vertically in the boat's hull it needs only a slight roll to send them flying, and in yachts a sudden heel can have all the back rests in a heap on the lee side within seconds. A simple way of securing them into position is to attach small strips of Velcro to the cushions and the supporting panel behind them. The Velcro can be matched in colour so that it is hardly noticeable and glued onto the back panel with a light contact glue. There will be relatively little strain on the strips and gluing them with a heavy glue may make it difficult to remove later.

The facing half of the Velcro is stitched in a matching position onto the back of the cushions. Once pressed together the Velcro will hold the back rests into position against the heel or roll of the boat and yet if they need to be removed for any reason, a light tug will pull them free.

This system can be used for holding many things against the boat's side or bulkheads, for example, to secure curtains in place, thus avoiding the need for screw fittings. However, remember that Velcro is a light securing medium and heavy objects will not be supported by it against the violent motion of the boat. In terms of furnishings it is ideal, and used in the way described can be easily removed if for any reason you change the interior layout.

FORWARD BERTHS

There are big differences in the construction of berths, mainly as a result of their location in the complex shape of the boat's hull. Main saloon berths are fairly straightforward as they are situated where there is good space and the curves of the hull are not too severe. Quarter berths are often formed as part of the cockpit structure, but forward berths are on their own since, being in the bow section, they are affected by some of the strongest curves in the entire hull.

The standard form of forward berth is two single berths, one on each side of the hull, which meet at the forward end. As such they can be easily converted into a double berth by filling in the triangular area between them at the after end. A popular arrangement with small craft, both power and sail, is to utilise the triangular shape between the berths for some other purpose— often a toilet—which can be covered when not in use by the filler piece, fitted with a matching cushion which then makes a double berth out of the whole forward section.

Basic construction of forward berths.

The construction of the forward berths is fairly straightforward since, because of the narrow confines, the support beams for both berths can be run directly from one side of the hull to the other. This means that the first step is to measure carefully the hull and fit landings (unless there are conveniently located stringers) along the full length of each side, glassed or screwed into position to take the beams. Levels are important here as you won't want your crew or passengers sleeping with their feet high above their heads and the sheer of the boat is fairly marked at this point.

Your starting point can be the bulkhead which separates the forward compartment from the rest of the boat. The height of the berths can be determined and the landings run up each side of the hull from this point. These landings should be of reasonably solid dimensions, say around 40 x 55 mm and laminated to take the hull curves if necessary. The beams can be either screwed and glued on top of them or half-jointed and then glued and screwed.

To make a solid job which will withstand any person's weight, the beams should be cut from about 50 x 70 mm softwood and spaced at about 30 cm centres. Fit them first with a dry run, as exact fitting and levels both ways are important. Once you are certain that everything is lined up and level the beams can be screwed and glued (jointed for preference) to the landings. At this stage all the beams from forward to aft across the width of the hull are fitted. The area between the berths can be cut out later.

Now the fore and aft bearers must be cut. These can be of the same size timber as the beams and will form the inner edge of the berths. They should be laid onto the beams initially and then cut for jointing. This must be done carefully since awkward angles will be involved. The beams can be recessed *in situ* and the bearers again laid across to ensure exact lineup before marking and recessing for the lap joints. Once the cutting and shaping has been completed the bearers are glued and screwed into position.

At this point uprights can be secured to form the triangular area between the berths. The uprights can be of similar dimensions to the beams and bearers. A floor framework may be necessary but can be of lighter timber as it is merely to hold the uprights in position and will carry little load. The entire framework should be jointed into position and glued and screwed to make a solid unit. Now the after beams can be sawn away between the bearers, at which point the framework of the berths is complete.

access opening must be near the skin fittings to allow the seacocks to be operated.

If the berths are to be made into a double berth the side panelling will need to be cut short at the top of the bearers and the latter rebated to take a fitting piece of ply which will fill in the triangular space and can be removed when not in use. A matching cushion can be made to complete the job and convert the twin berths into a double berth.

The area between the forward berths can be utilised for storage or a toilet and closed in by a plywood panel. A fitting cushion transforms the whole unit into a double berth.

Panelling-in may require templates to ensure a good fit for each section. Panels are glued and screwed to the framework.

Panels, usually ply around 15 mm thickness, are fitted to the sides and top. The sides should be brought up some 50-60 mm above the framework and capped to make neat fiddleys which will hold the berth cushions in place. The top panelling is screwed to the framework and if access is required (beneath the forward berths is an ideal storage space for ropes and other gash gear) small hatches are cut in the way described for main saloon berths. If a toilet is to be fitted between the berths it will be necessary to place the skin fittings in position before building the berths, or at the latest before panelling. An

With GRP hulls much of the framework described here can be eliminated by using the method described on page 135 of glassing the ply panels directly to the skin. Providing the ply is of good section (say 20 mm) and is well braced, this method can prove quite efficient.

MOTOR CASING

It would be literally impossible to describe in detail the construction of a motor casing or cover since the type, shape and size vary enormously from boat to boat. A yacht with a small auxiliary, for example, would probably have the engine mounted beneath the cockpit and protruding only slightly into the cabin below the companionway. In this case the casing would in effect merely be a cover and would form part of the main companionway. By contrast, an open fishing boat may have the motor set in the centre of the cockpit well and the whole unit would need to be covered, requiring a fairly large box-type construction.

Easy access to all parts of the motor for repairs and maintenance work is important. The motor casing must be designed so that when lifted off it exposes much of the machinery.

And the other extreme, of course, is the motor yacht of some size which would have its motors enclosed in a separate compartment, in which case it would be necessary to construct bulkheads at each end of the compartment rather than a box enclosing the motor itself. So the casing enclosing the motor is something that is far too individual to detail here, although perhaps it is important to mention a few pertinent facts which will apply equally to any motor box, cover or compartment regardless of size or shape.

The first factor is that the framework must be securely jointed and glued and screwed. Lap joints or even dovetail joints should be used as the vibration from the motor will gradually loosen any but the most secure joints. Secondly, insulation is essential if noise and fumes are not to ruin any boating activities for all on board. And, thirdly, there must be adequate ventilation, for unless the motor can breathe it cannot work efficiently.

Because of the vibration problem the framework should be of heavier gauge timber than for most internal furniture. This has the twofold effect of making a more solid job and also allowing deeper and thus more secure jointing. A large part of the casing must be readily removable to enable good access to the motor for repair and maintenance work, and it is a good idea to have an inspection hatch or some

similar small opening allowing access to such things as dip stick, main switch, batteries and other parts which require routine attention at frequent intervals.

Panelling can be of any material but again it is a good idea to use heavy gauge material since not only does it stand up better to the vibration, but also helps deaden the noise. The framework will help to absorb some of the vibration and the panelling makes a fairly effective silencing medium providing it is well screwed together to totally enclose the motor compartment.

This, of course, creates problems with ventilation for, as mentioned, a motor must have a good supply of air to breathe and function properly. Just how the air flow is arranged will again vary from boat to boat. The simplest system is that used in big motor cruisers where deck or side vents suck air directly into the motor compartment from outside. With small auxiliaries the problem is more difficult since the motor may be low in the hull and fairly well boxed in. A clear space through the bilges can provide the necessary air channel, as long as the bilge is dry and clear, but some form of duct that will permit air flow in all circumstances is required. Ventilation also helps to dissipate engine heat and any fuel vapours, however it tends to reduce sound insulation to some degree.

Nothing is more calculated to ruin a pleasant day on the water than a lot of motor noise, so insulation of the motor compartment is an important factor in its construction. There are many insulation materials, but care must be taken to use those which are not affected by heat. Styrofoam is one of the more popular of the synthetics, although asbestos is probably safer. You should consult your local dealer when planning insulation for the motor compartment since these synthetic materials are being improved all the time and he may have a more suitable one than those that are currently in use.

Access to the motor adds yet another headache to the construction of the motor casing. In the two extreme cases—big cruiser and small fishing boat—there are few problems, since you can usually crawl into the big boat's motor compartment to carry out maintenance work and in the case of the fishing boat you just lift the total box-type casing off and leave the motor exposed. But once again the problem arises with small motors, particularly auxiliaries. Being pushed into difficult corners they are almost impossible to get at other than through the side or front of the motor casing. Since access is very important, particularly in an emergency such as fire, the motor compartment must be readily opened up without having to undo a multitude of screws or bolts.

A popular system is a removable panel behind the companionway step, and/or the entire cockpit sole. The latter access is more frequently found aboard motor cruisers, but on a sailing boat where there may be a self-draining cockpit a lip and seal will be necessary around the hatch opening to keep out water. Thumbscrews or wing nuts may be used to pull the hatch down firmly, and so that these fittings do not intrude the hatch is then usually covered with a teak grating.

CHART TABLE

Almost anything will serve as a chart table. In small yachts it is not uncommon for the dinette table, the galley bench, the engine cover or any other flat surface to be pressed into use as a chart table when space does not allow a permanent area. This seems rather a pity since a chart table is one of the easiest items to install in a boat and it can make the navigator's life so much simpler to have a decent place to work.

Probably the most basic form of table is a flat piece of timber which can fit across the top of a bunk or onto some similar piece of interior furniture. Under difficult or cramped circumstances the ice box or even a settee berth can be used to support the board with a couple of bolts fitted to secure it into position. It can be stowed

The ultimate chart table—full size with navigating instruments clustered around it—is possible only in the largest yacht. Most small boats compromise with the chart table utilised for other purposes.

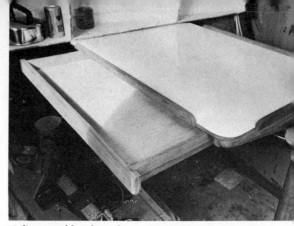

A dinette table adapted as a chart table. The dimensions of the table are half a chart, and a chart drawer is fitted beneath.

away under bunk cushions or in any available space when not in use. Providing it is the right size and conveniently located you need do nothing more than fit it into position when laying off courses or plotting, then stow it away when finished.

The size of the table should be not less than half that of a naval chart. While the sizes of charts do vary, measurements of 60 x 70 cm will cover most normal Mercator charts. Adopting this size means that you need not fold your charts to other than their original folds. This prevents bad creasing which makes the chart difficult to work on, particularly with parallel rules. The table should be covered with a rubber mat to prevent the chart from moving and also provide a soft underlay to absorb the prick of the divider points. A fiddley of light beading round the edge prevents pencils and rubbers from rolling off when the boat is moving in a seaway.

The question of what mountings to put under the table will depend on where it is to be fitted. Naturally if the boat is spacious enough a separate corner with the chart table permanently fixed in position is the ultimate but that is usually only the case in large craft. However, a little ingenuity should quickly provide a spot where brackets can be fitted so that the table top can be neatly dropped into position when required. It should be of a height that makes for comfortable working for the navigator either standing or sitting.

COMPANIONWAY

The companionway provides the main access to the cabin and is usually in the form of steps or a ladder arrangement. Much will depend on the shape of the doorway, the depth of the step down

The companionway will vary in size with the depth of the cabin. In smaller craft one single step is often all that is required.

A typical companionway ladder.

to the cabin sole and whether or not a sliding hatch is fitted.

As a general rule the steps are constructed as a separate unit which can easily be moved to allow access to space beneath and behind it, although some boat owners adapt engine covers and even galley benches as part of the companionway system. For the purpose of this book I will consider the companionway to be a neat timber ladder arrangement which, by adapting the design and dimensions, should fit most craft.

It is obviously important to draw up a design for your companionway to ensure that it fits snugly between the doorway and the cabin sole. The angle at which it rises is not over important, and some companionways are almost vertical. However, more comfortable access, particularly for non-boating guests, is achieved if the angle is moderate. This, again, will depend on what lies beneath and behind the companionway, since it may need to be built around an installation such as a motor casing.

Drawing up a plan of the companionway from a sideways elevation will indicate both the angle and the profile of the step. It is important that the ends of the companionway are comfortably snugged up at the top and bottom so that there is no movement when the weight of a body is placed on the top step. If it is to be removable, as most are, small door bolts are probably the best means of securing the companionway into position and these should be fitted at top and bottom on both sides to secure it firmly.

A good sized timber for companionways is around 22-25 mm in thickness. This can be used both for the sides and the steps, so that in effect the unit can be cut completely from one or two planks. The width of the sides will vary according to individual requirement but about 20 cm is a good size if room permits. A template must be made to ensure a good fit and both sides can be cut from this template. The angle of the steps to the sides must be carefully measured and marked to ensure that they are correctly aligned with the levels of the boat.

The sides should be cut, planed and sanded to the required finish and rebated to take the steps. The joints for the steps may be stub mortise and tenon or dowel joints. I find square dowel joints are easy to fit and make a nice finish but it's a matter of preference. Sufficient to say that the joint must be solid and well fitting, and glued firmly into place so that it will take the weight which will be placed on the step. The steps are glued into one side and then the second side tapped into position, the whole lot being secured with a Spanish windlass to keep it tight until the glue has set. Apart from the bolts mentioned earlier, other fittings will be of a personal nature although often hand grips are useful if the companionway is of any length. These can be cut into the sides between the steps and give an authentic nautical look as well as providing firm hand holes for climbing the companionway when the boat is moving in a seaway.

The finish will need to be matched to the interior decor of the boat, but nothing looks quite as nice as a well varnished companionway of teak or a similar attractive hardwood. To prevent wear or scratching of the steps strips of non-skid material or serrated rubber sheet can be glued on and also prevent any chance of a foot slipping off the step, particularly if the companionway is steep.

ICEBOX

There are two ways of going about fitting an icebox, much depending on its size and location in the boat. It can be built separately in the workshop to virtually any size required or it can be built *in situ* in the hull to fill a spare corner, in which case its size and shape will be governed by the area it is to fill. While obviously a square icebox built in the workshop and fitted in the galley or other suitable spot will be the most convenient and will most resemble the domestic refrigerator, using up spare space in the hull for an icebox is very useful and practical even if the shape and size may not be exactly what you require.

Fitting in situ

Of the two methods, the easiest is the icebox fitted *in situ* since much of the work is already done. The hull forms one side of the box and often a berth or cupboard the other. All that remains, in effect, is to add ends (often only one end) and insulate and line the box. Let's assume that we are fitting an icebox beneath a berth. It should not require any great amount of imagination to adjust the details given here for any similar situation.

The hull skin can be of any material and it should need no lining. In the case of timber hulls the projecting structural timbers may make the insulating work a bit more difficult but patience and a good pot of glue will take care of it. With steel or ferro-cement hulls the choice of glue will also determine the quality of the job—probably a PVA or similar glue will be best. Whatever glue is used, it will be necessary to clean off the hull skin and surrounding woodwork to give the glue a good surface on which to bond.

Before lining with insulating material, drainage must be considered. Some boat owners prefer not to fit a drain to their ice boxes, but simply mop out by hand any accumulated water. Their argument is that ice box water can contain small scraps of food which when drained into the bilge get caught up and deteriorate, making the boat smell. It is a good point for this does, in fact, happen. However, rather than bail out the icebox by hand, which is a messy business, a

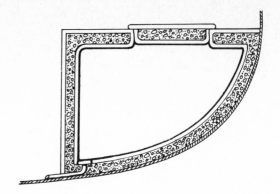

Cross section of an icebox fitted beneath a berth indicating the location of the hatch and the drainage outlet. Racks may be fitted as required.

strainer over the drainage hole, or else draining the water into a separate container rather than the bilge, will resolve the problem.

The insulation for the icebox can be any one of a number of materials, but the cheapest and one of the best is expanded styrene foam (polystyrene). This can be obtained cheaply in sheets, and should be 50 mm or more in thickness. Obviously the thicker the better, but if you use material that is too thick you will wind up with very restricted space inside your icebox. The foam should be laid onto surfaces all round the inside of the icebox and carefully fitted so that the insulation has no breaks. The same procedure is followed with the hatch cover or door of the icebox, making sure that when closed the insulation is fairly tight-fitting. Not completely tight-fitting in this case, as a thin cover of fibreglass still has to be placed over the foam.

Before styrene foam can be glued or glassed into place it must be sealed, as it reacts with the polyester resins normally used in GRP. Fortunately, however, it does not react with the epoxy resins or paints, and one of the proprietary sheathing kits now on the market can be used to give it a hard and serviceable finish. This may in itself be sufficient, but if not a GRP liner can then be laid up inside, and this is best cut from woven glass cloth.

A first coat of resin, mixed as described on page 17 or according to the manufacturer's directions, is then applied to the sealed foam insulation, the glass mat pressed into place and the second coat of resin worked through it. A covering of flowcoat or gelcoat will help seal off the GRP and give a pleasant appearance to the interior of the box. It goes without saying that

A neat icebox made of ply panels glassed to the hull skin. This will double as seating at a dinette table.

fitting the hatch or door of the icebox will need some thought as the work progresses but this should not tax your abilities too far. Trial and error is probably the best way of getting a good fit depending on the particular closing device and the thickness of the insulation.

The drainage hole, of course, must be kept clear during the lining operation and sealed into place with the resin. A simple sink strainer secured to the plastic hose with a jubilee clip serves the purpose, the strainer being glassed in with the final coat of resin. When the GRP has cured and hardened sufficiently, light sanding may be necessary to smooth off any bumps or projections, and a stainless steel or galvanised rack fitted to hold the ice block if such is required.

Separate icebox

An icebox can be made of any material, but the most common are plywood or GRP, sometimes a combination of both. The GRP unit must be moulded and this can be a fairly expensive and time-consuming operation as two moulds will be needed—a male for the inner container, and female for the outer skin. So while fibreglass is without doubt an excellent material, it is also the most costly and time consuming. Plywood on the other hand is cheap and easy to use and can be finished with GRP, either by sheathing completely or using the synthetics to seal corners and line the insulation.

There are many ways of going about building an icebox from either or both of these materials. Two containers are required, one outer and one inner, with not less than 50 mm space between them into which is packed insulation. How you

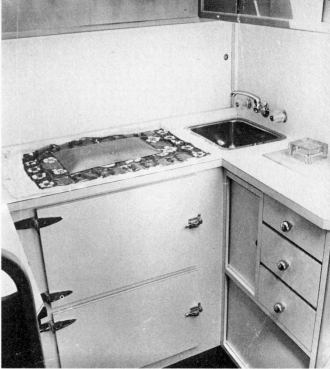

The icebox can be built to match the surrounding galley furniture. Rather than utilising the hull space, this type of icebox is self-contained. Refrigeration capsules can be fitted to convert the icebox into a normal domestic refrigerator.

go about the job will be dependent on your ability, your requirements and the materials you intend to use. If you are a carpenter you will obviously go for plywood, if you fancy yourself at GRP work you will use that material and on the other hand you may opt for a combination of both. This latter is often the best solution in which the outer casing of the icebox is made of plywood just as would any other piece of box furniture. Sealing the corners adds to the strength and prevents water seeping into the ends of the ply and GRP tape is without doubt the best for this.

With the outer casing constructed (it will make life easier if you keep one side off until the lining is finished) the insulation and fibreglass liner are applied as described for fitting the box *in situ*, allowing of course for drainage and the door or hatch cover.

The icebox can be easily converted to a refrigerator by fitting one of the small electric freezer units available on the market. However, check your power supply and particularly battery capacity before installing one of these units, as they can be heavy on power if used consistently.

Overboard discharge toilets are nearing the end of their days. Already they are banned on many waterways and it is only a matter of time before they may be illegal in many inshore waters. Self-contained portable toilets or conventional toilets with holding tanks in the boat will then become the future trend on board small craft. Apart from the pollution aspect, self-contained toilets of either type are a safer proposition for boats since they avoid the need to puncture the hull skin, with the problems that this entails. For these reasons I will deal only briefly with installation of a flushing overboard discharge toilet, but in any case, fitting such a toilet is a simple process as they are usually purchased as a complete unit ready to hook up to intake and discharge skin fittings, described on page 97.

The intake pipe is usually of smaller diameter than the discharge pipe, as the latter needs to be of a gauge that can cope with solid matter. For the same reason, the discharge pipe should lead through the hull in a fairly direct line since bends and turns in the pipe will create areas susceptible to blockage. Nowadays plastic or rubber pipes are used on all toilet fittings, and there is a tendency for this material to kink when turning

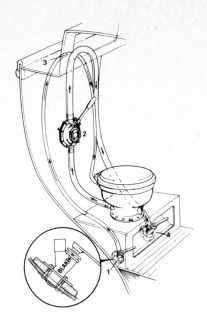

Toilet installation showing swan-neck, inlet (1) and discharge (4) seacocks, pump (2), and air bleed valve (3) to break vacuum after pumping stops. Seacocks must be accessible.

A standard discharge toilet which flushes directly through the hull skin.

too sharp a corner, adding to the possibility of a blockage. The intake pipe need only be of a diameter to allow sufficient flushing water to be drawn in and in any case the size of both these pipes is usually controlled by their connection on the toilet unit.

There is a school of thought which requires both discharge and intake pipes to be brought up the side of the hull well above the waterline to form a gooseneck which will prevent an inflow of water and possible flooding of the boat. While most good quality toilets have an inbuilt valve, such valves are not completely reliable and in any case are not intended to withstand the possible inflow of water from outside the hull. Certainly, this system guarantees that the boat will not be flooded via the toilet system, but unless it is concealed behind some lining, it is a fairly ungainly looking arrangement.

If the toilet can be mounted so that it is above the waterline when the boat is stationary, then the risk of accidental flooding is removed. Discharge and intake pipes can be run directly through the hull via skin fittings below the waterline without any risk. However, as mentioned in the section on skin fittings, a stop cock is essential wherever the hull is pierced and

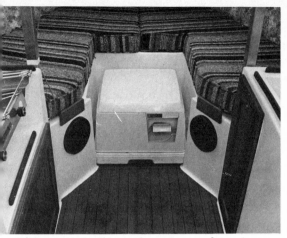

Self-contained toilets are becoming mandatory in many areas. These are much simpler to fit as most are portable and need only to be secured in place while the boat is at sea.

you should always develop a routine whereby stop cocks on toilets are turned off whenever the toilet is not in use. This will eliminate any possibility of leakage or accidental flooding due to failure of part of the plumbing system.

The fitting of the toilet bowl itself usually consists of bolting onto a piece of timber located in the required spot. Toilets take up a lot of room, not so much in themselves as in the fact that they demand a certain amount of room to move as well as privacy, both factors which involve taking up valuable space. Large craft can fit a completely enclosed toilet compartment, in which case the toilet and other bathroom fittings are not unlike those of a bathroom in a house. Small craft, however, often cannot afford the space of a separate compartment and therefore the toilet must be concealed beneath bunks or pushed into a spare corner, such as between the forward berths.

INTERIOR LINING

Some boat owners have no wish to line the interior of the boat, preferring to use the full width of the hull for accommodation. On the other hand, materials such as bare fibreglass, concrete and steel present a fairly unattractive finish and need lining to enhance pleasantly designed and built furniture. Of course lining the hull reduces the interior space somewhat, particularly when frames and stringers must be covered. Assuming a frame to be of 70-100 mm in

depth, lining both sides of the cabin takes away perhaps 200 mm of the width of the boat which is not a good factor from an accommodation point of view.

However, there is no denying the attractiveness of neatly installed lining, so the question is how to reduce as much as possible the loss of interior space. One method is simply to cover the sides of the boat with a form of carpeting or vinyl between the frames. In the case of fibreglass where there are no frames this is often a good solution. In some cases just painting will do the trick. But for most craft a properly fitted liner of plywood or some similar material is necessary to cover up the less attractive parts of the hull construction.

Panelling with light gauge ply makes all the difference to interior appearance. The panelling can be applied before the fitting of interior furniture, in which case the installation is fairly easy as large panels cut from a template of the side of the hull can be fitted without much problem. On the other hand, much of this lining is then wasted as it will be concealed by the furniture and a better method, albeit requiring a little more effort to fit, is to line the areas around the furniture after the boat has been fitted out.

An interior liner gives a clean, finished appearance to the hull and conceals unsightly fittings such as wiring and fastenings.

It is usually best to install all fittings before the lining, since fastenings must be made to landings or structural members and if these are covered by a liner you will have to cut holes through it to secure the fittings. Light fittings may sometimes be secured to the liner, but for the most part cabin furniture must be secured to the hull by way of landings or structural members. Where fabric or vinyl lining is used the problem is not so acute since fittings can be secured through the liner.

If a fabric or vinyl lining is used it is probably best to line the entire cabin area before beginning to fit out, but since this type of lining is usually only suitable for craft which have few protruding structural members, landings will have to be secured to the hull before the lining is put in place.

Another important factor to bear in mind before installing a hood liner to the deckhead of the cabin is to ensure that any deck fittings such as winches or grab rails are in place before the liner is installed since they will almost invariably be secured by through bolts. Much the same applies to electric wiring and other attachments which should be in place before the liner is fitted. The unsightliness of bolts and nuts or electric wiring will otherwise completely nullify the purpose of the lining. Quite apart from the appearance, the liner is never strong enough to withstand the stresses that come onto deck fittings and may well be crushed if the fittings are through bolted onto it.

Fibreglass manufacturers sometimes provide a complete interior lining with the boat. In this case, the only problem will be securing interior fittings through the liner to structural members on the hull behind. Moulded liners such as these make first class interior lining, but are generally beyond the scope of a home fitting-out job, since in order to make such a liner a plug would first need to be made—a long, expensive and wasteful system if only one liner is to be produced.

Fabric liners come in a range of materials, mostly waterproof, and are reasonably successful in providing a neat, attractive finish to the interior of the boat if the structural members are not too much in evidence. Lining a fibreglass hull with fabric is quite simple, entailing only a satisfactory method of glueing the fabric in place. Steel and concrete hulls are similarly suited to this method, although a few stringers may protrude through or beneath the fabric in the case of a steel hull. Vinyl is sometimes used and even quilted material or waterproof carpet has its place according to your taste on interior decoration. For the most part these materials are provided with a waterproof finish and are simply glued into place on the hull side.

Because of the difficult curves and shapes involved in a boat's hull, the best method is to cut templates before attempting to cut the material and thus avoid waste. By strategically cutting the templates, joins can be kept to a minimum and probably concealed. Failing that, they can be covered quite tastefully with light timber strips. Contact glue is probably the best adhesive for this job, but reference to the manufacturer's instructions will resolve any problems that may arise from glueing onto different hull surfaces. Trimming around windows, furniture and doors can be left until the glue is dry and then timber or aluminium strips used to finish the job.

In areas such as bathrooms and around the galley, it may be more practical to use a laminex or vinyl liner. Laminex is cut and glued in exactly the same way as described on page 216, and vinyl can be secured the same way, although it will be necessary in this case to ensure that the surface onto which the vinyl is being laid is well smoothed out as any unevenness will show through the finished job. In larger craft where a more exotic finish is required, tiles may be used and the application is the same as for a similar job in the home. It is not unknown even for some larger craft to have ceramic tiled bathrooms and there is no reason why not if that happens to suit your boat, pocket and taste.

In most cases, however, with small to medium size family boats a plywood lining is the simplest and most effective way of making the interior accommodation areas attractive. The plywood needs only to be light since it will take few stresses, and can come in virtually any finish from an attractive timber veneer through to decorative plywood which can be later painted to any suitable shade. The plywood must be marine grade and preferably impregnated with anti-rot

Timber panelling on the sides and laminex as a head liner make an attractive and clean finish.

chemical. The gauge of the plywood will depend mostly on the area to be covered, since too light a ply covering a large area may buckle slightly as it is fastened.

The ply panels are cut from templates and can be screwed directly to frames or any other structural members on which they land. Where two panels meet a light batten can be glued or screwed into position to cover the join and the use of different coloured timbers at this point can add to the appearance of the panelling. Where the lining meets with shelves or other items of furniture a similar batten or length of quad can be fitted to obtain the same well-finished effect.

If there are no suitable frames or stringers then landings will need to be constructed of light timber (say 30 mm x 15 mm) and secured across the hull sides to take the lining. The screws used to secure the panelling should be countersunk and covered by a trim strip, or else some form of ornamental screw used to add to the appearance of the finished job. The use of different coloured timbers and ornamental screws can do wonders.

The cabin deckhead is often sufficiently attractive without the use of liners. Particularly is this the case with timber boats, where the deckhead beams add a lot of character to the boat and where ornamental knees are often used at the extremities. A popular arrangement, and one which takes a lot of beating from an appearance point of view, is to paint the deckhead panels between the beams white and leave the beams themselves natural timber with a coating of clear varnish. Steel, concrete or moulded GRP deckheads can be smoothed and painted with matt 'speckled' paint as an alternative to lining.

Light fittings, such as racks, may be fastened to liner but most heavy fittings must be through bolted.

DINETTE

One of the currently popular interior arrangements is the dinette. This is a useful piece of interior furniture which has a twofold purpose providing a table and seating for four people during the daytime, and collapsing to form a double berth at night. In very small craft there may not be sufficient beam to form a double berth, so the dinette seats two at a table during the day and forms a single berth at night.

Although there are many different versions of the dinette, the basic principle involved is the construction of two thwartships seats with a space between them. When in use as a table this space provides leg room under the table. When converted to a double berth, the table is lowered to fit across this space and provide the completely flat surface area on which the double berth cushions can be placed.

Obviously, the first measurement is the longitudinal one since the berth must not be less than 2 m in a fore and aft direction or it will not provide full adult sleeping room. If the width of the table is not less than 80 cm—which enables it to carry a chart and thus serve a further purpose as the navigator's table—the seats will then be around 60 cm each in width. Since there is a slight overlap, the dimensions of the seats will actually be a little wider, offering plenty of room for sitting comfortably, as well as room for a back rest cushion.

The length of the table—or width of the berth—will depend on the room available in the cabin area, although a minimum of 120 cm will be necessary if two people are to sleep comfortably on it. Obviously, the wider the berth, the more comfortable the sleeping accommodation. Most dinettes form one side of the saloon area, so in medium and small craft the through-companionway will need to be offset to allow full width to the dinette. Bear in mind, when measuring up for the dinette, that headroom may be limited close to the side of the hull in some craft, where side decking protrudes down into the cabin space. This will not affect the sleeping room, but will intrude on the room around the table if the persons nearest the side of the hull cannot sit upright.

Since the dinette is invariably secured to the side of the hull, and since it is likely to come under some stress, it must be fastened to structural members such as stringers or frames or, if these are not available, then to landings

161

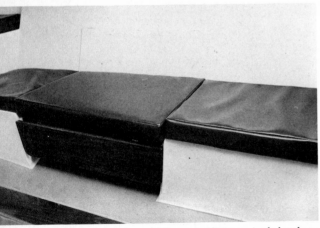

The simplest form of dinette, utilising a single berth: a., the table is supported by collapsible legs and slide bolts at the hull side. Note rebated ends of seats to take table; b., with the table dropped the berth is formed. A hinged section of the table allows a good size area when the table is used, but matches the berth size when dropped; c., a cushion fitted over the table completes the berth. Slide bolts hold the dropped table top firmly in position.

secured to the hull. A framework can then be built to the desired dimensions or the ply panel method of constructing interior furniture (page 135) employed if the hull skin is GRP. Steel and ferro-cement craft will probably need to weld landings or lugs to the hull framework to which timber landings can be bolted.

The design of the dinette is a question of personal taste and the shape of the hull area into which it is to be fitted. If there is sufficient room, the seating can be extended along the side of the boat, joining the two end seats to form a horse-shoe arrangement with the table supported on a pillar in the centre. Small craft, however, will be restricted to the arrangement described earlier of two thwartships seats with the table between, all secured directly to the hull side. The seats can be utilised as storage compartments with access through a hatch in the top and can be permanently fastened. The table, of course, must have a temporary fastening since is must be unhooked and lowered when the unit is converted into a berth. Draw bolts between the underside of the table top and the hull side are a typical example of the simple fitting that can be used here.

When the table is lowered into position on the seats it must be landed firmly into a rebate or onto brackets, as it will be carrying the weight of two bodies. A telescopic pillar is another method of making the table top firm in both the raised and lowered positions. Whatever the fitting, it goes without saying that it must be secure and capable of withstanding the weight which will come onto it both as a table and as a berth. The seats must be rebated sufficiently to allow the table to fit flush or there will be an uneven bump in the bed! Fiddleys fitted to the table will also tend to make an uncomfortable bump, but by carefully cutting the cushions so that the fiddleys fit into the space between them, and using high density foam of good depth, the bump can usually be absorbed in the softness of the cushions.

As mentioned, each individual boat will fit a different type of dinette in order to best utilise the space available for it. But providing the basic points mentioned here are followed, adapting a simple design to almost any hull should not be difficult. Dimensions of timber used should fall into the following categories: framework, softwood around 60 × 30 mm, slightly heavier if it is to cover a long unsupported span. Ply not less than 30 mm thick.

CHAPTER 7

Installing the Motor

INSTALLING A MOTOR is one of the more complex jobs in fitting out a hull, but like most things, if it is tackled one section at a time there should not be too many problems. Up until now we have been discussing most of the other elements and fittings within the boat, but in the majority of craft the engine should be one of the first items to go aboard at a time when the area around it is freely accessible. At that time there will be least difficulty in fitting the bearers, and the lower sections of the hull can be easily reached to align and install the sterngear. And once the motor is in position, everything else can be built up around it.

If the boat is an established design, the type of motor and sterngear will probably be specified on the drawings. This is of particular importance with a powerboat, and if planing performance is the objective a marine engineer or experienced naval architect should be consulted to achieve the right equation between hull form, weight, estimated speed, horsepower, reduction, shafting and propellor.

While these criteria need to be more precisely calculated for higher speeds, they also apply to the slower displacement motor cruiser and the sailing yacht with auxiliary. These two classifications cover the majority of craft afloat, and for the purposes of this discussion we will take 40 ft as a maximum overall length and 10 knots as a maximum speed. That bracket will also restrict our need for horsepower, and a maximum will be well below 100 h.p.

First, then, we must decide on the size and speed of the propeller necessary to drive the hull, a factor governed by the size of the aperture at the transom, or the clearance beneath the hull. From this, and the details of the boat, the propellor manufacturer will be able to quote the power required and also the propellor. He will also quote the propeller r.p.m. which will enable the correct engine/gearbox combination to be selected. Fuel cost has recently increased the popularity of diesels, but the petrol (gasoline) motor remains lighter, quieter, smoother running and cheaper in initial cost: it is well suited to the small powerboat.

Most boats place a premium on space, and so in addition to the conventional shafting systems we shall be discussing here, options include hydraulic drive, V-drive, Z-drive and the various sail or S-drives. A hydraulic drive allows the engine to be sited almost anywhere on the boat and often athwartships by the transom, while the V and Z-drives also place the motor well aft. An S-drive is usually supplied integral with its motor, and can greatly simplify installation. The layout of the boat coupled with the manufacturer's data will indicate whether one of these systems will be suitable, but in terms of cost as well as reasonable simplicity the traditional straight shaft remains a sound choice.

ALIGNMENT

The first decision to be made with normal shaft transmission is that of alignment—the angle of the propshaft in relation to the waterline, and also to the engine. Ideally the two should be the same, so that there is a straight-line coupling to the motor, eliminating the need for a constant velocity joint or a universal coupling. A drop-centre gearbox can on occasions ease this problem. The maximum 'down-angle' aft quoted by most engine manufacturers is 10°.

The job of alignment is eased in hulls with a keel, skeg or deadwood, where the location of the rudder and the shape of the skeg will indicate the position of the propeller, and therefore where the propshaft penetrates the hull. At this point the shaft will be carried in a cutless bearing at the end of the stern tube, and by simple measurement one can locate the bearing and the hole for the shaft.

Spot the centre of the hole and drill a small pilot hole, and then with a tank cutter open out the hole to the clearance diameter of the propshaft, or to the diameter of the register on the forward boss of the bearing. The bearing can now be temporarily screwed to the skeg, with the screws not quite pinched up, and a length of dummy shafting inserted of the same diameter as the shaft and long enough to reach the engine bearers. Arrange a temporary support

A dummy prop shaft is inserted through the angled hole in the after run of a sailing cruiser preparatory to establishing the alignment of the stern gland and shaft bearing with the motor.

for the shaft at the forward end of the engine position, and you now have a datum level for the complete installation. The sterntube will be brought inboard from the threaded boss on the cutless bearing, usually to a small web frame which will also form a mounting for a stern gland and greaser; the tube can be passed over the dummy shaft to establish the size and location of the frame. And the motor template can also be set up on the shaft to determine the size and position of the engine bearers.

Many motor cruisers and numbers of high-performance sailing boats have few underwater appendages on which a propeller and its bearing might be mounted, and to support the end of the shaft a separate external bracket and bearing are required. This is usually a P-bracket, or where the strut has a bipod support it is known as an A-bracket (see photos on page 172). From the illustrations it will be seen that the propeller shaft passes through a gland and shaft log in the underwater run of the hull, and that the positioning of the hole for these components is precisely related to the overall alignment. As we now have no datum on the hull for the shaft, the position of the bracket and the hole cut for the shaft log can only be established from accurate drawings, and if none exist one should be made of this section of the boat. That will present the oppor-

tunity to also include the motor, scaled from the maker's data, and at the same time to predetermine the angle of the shafting.

By measurement from the drawing, holes may now be cut in the run of the hull for the P-bracket and the shaft log—that for the bracket a snug fit around its shank, and that for the shaft extended to an oval shape through which it may run at a shallow angle. Open out the oval hole in the hull so that it will accommodate the angled shaft with about $\frac{3}{4}$ in. clearance all round, and then a dummy shaft can be inserted via the P-bracket and up into the hull, with which you can begin to establish the alignment.

At this stage the P-bracket will be only lightly secured to a small web within the hull, and the shaft log and gland may be slid over the dummy shaft for a trial fitting on the inside skin of the hull. To correctly support the shaft the log will often require a small timber mounting block to carry it clear of the hull, and this should be cut and positioned to bring the shaft central in the hull aperture. By adjustment here and at the bracket the shaft may now be aligned at the correct angle, and the bracket and the log finally fixed.

As before, the motor template can now be offered up to the dummy shaft, and the engine bed dimensions formed to suit.

MOTOR TEMPLATE

Templates are widely used for fitting various parts of a boat's interior equipment—there are templates for bulkheads, templates for galleys and indeed templates for just about every item of interior furniture, yet rarely do you hear of a template for a motor.

Nothing could be more awkwardly shaped and lend itself less to the making of a template than a boat's motor. And yet, because the motor is usually fitted into a tight corner of the hull, particularly in yachts, an accurate template is essential. It will not only be required for the fitting of the motor into the space allowed, but also for the location and height of engine beds and the alignment of shaft and stern tube. In short, unless the boat is already set up for the motor, a template will be invaluable from the first step in this, the most tricky fitting-out operation of all.

Simply transferring measurements from the motor to the hull will often be too difficult as

The template constructed from chip board. Note the location points of the 'feet', drilled out so that the position on the beds can be marked.

motors tend to be of awkward shapes and have a lot of ancillary gear attached which increases their dimensions considerably. While it would be beyond all practical reason to attempt to make a total mock-up of the motor, a template can be fairly simply made which, providing it is done carefully, will indicate the extremities of the motor and gear in all directions and thus serve as well as a mock-up for fitting purposes.

The first essential will be to obtain both a profile and cross-section plan of the motor from the manufacturer. If this is not possible you will need to measure up the motor itself, taking extreme measurements of all dimensions. A couple of sheets of plywood or pineboard are all that is required. The first should be used as the template for the profile of the motor which must be scaled up to full size if taken from the manufacturer's plans. If plans are not available, a rough outline can be taken from the motor itself and an accurate template made by measuring all extremities in terms of height and depth of the motor above and below its centreline.

Ancillary gear which sticks up above or below the profile of the motor must be included even if it does not always take up this position—for example, the decompression levers on the head of a diesel. When the template is made, these should be in the vertical position. If the motor is a tight fit and allowance is not made for them you will find you cannot raise the levers when the motor is to be started as they are too tight under

the deckhead. In short, the dimensions drawn on the template must be for maximum extremities under any condition. The shaft line, which indicates the line of the propeller shaft and thus the installation angle of the motor, is marked on the template so that the motor can be correctly aligned on its beds.

The number of cross-section templates may vary according to the shape of motor and fittings. Probably two will be necessary, one located at each pair of mounting feet so that the motor can be correctly aligned on the beds. It may be necessary to fit a further cross-section template if there are extreme dimensions at other parts of the motor. It follows that making up the template will vary greatly from motor to motor. Compact, box-like motors will easily be covered by the template construction described above. Motors with a great deal more gear on them may need more cross-section templates and this will also depend on how tight is the area into which the motor is to be fitted. If the sides and top of the engine compartment are critically close to the motor—which they should not be since access room will be necessary for repairs and maintenance—then a number of cross-section templates will be needed to ensure that each individual part can fit freely into the space provided.

The template must be set up with each cross-section at right angles to the profile and glued and screwed into place. It is important, obviously, that the cross-section templates are exactly at right angles to the profile or the whole object of the exercise will be lost. It may be worthwhile adding more templates of individual parts, such as the mounting feet, in order to make fitting on the beds easier, but this again will depend on each individual boat and motor.

If the motor beds are in position already, then the template is used simply by placing the locations of the feet on the template against those on the beds. If the template has been accurately made it will indicate clearance all round the motor as well as any misalignment that may have crept in. This is a good time to make adjustments, for moving the template around will be a lot easier than moving the motor, and any alteration to the beds or surrounding areas can be made while the compartment is still empty. The alignment of the motor on the beds can be checked against the marked shaft line on the template. The previously fitted piano wire should match the shaft line exactly. If it does not, then adjustments to the beds can be made with relative ease.

If the motor beds are not in place their location will be indicated by the feet on the template. By matching the shaft line on the template with the piano wire, as described above, the exact position of the motor is indicated, and the beds can be measured accordingly. If you prefer to fit the beds by using measurements from the plans, the template can be used as fitting of the beds progresses to check that they will be in position when completed.

THE BEDS

There are a number of different ways in which motor beds can be mounted in the hull, much depending on the material from which the hull is constructed. In the case of timber hulls, for instance, the engine beds can be fitted over floors already in position to form a firm composite unit with the construction of the hull. Steel hulls will probably have flanges welded to the bottom framework to which timber engine beds can be bolted, while moulded fibreglass hulls often have nothing at all in the way of structural members and the beds are glassed directly to the hull.

Whatever the system, the engine beds are usually of heavy section hardwood and only their shape and location will vary from boat to boat. In the case of timber hulls fitting may involve a fair amount of cutting and jointing to set the beds securely onto the floors. Suffice it to say that in all cases the beds must be firmly secured no matter what method is employed as these are major structural members which transmit the thrust from the motor to the hull of the boat.

Measurements for the beds can be taken from

Motor beds may run fore and aft or athwartships, much depending on the shape of the motor and the area of the hull where it is mounted. Heavy GRP reinforcing spreads the loads from the end of the beds into the hull skin.

the plan or by using a template as described earlier. Since the timber used is of considerable dimensions and usually hardwood, adjustment to the size and shape of the beds will be difficult at a later stage and therefore some time and care must be taken in getting the beds shaped and jointed exactly before they are bolted into position. While minor adjustments to the angle of the motor can be made by using shims, such adjustments are very limited as they can only raise the motor and not lower it.

When the beds have been prepared, try a dry run to ensure that everything is correctly aligned. Secure the beds lightly into position and mount the template of the motor onto them. A complete check on the alignment of the shaft and clearance of any protruding part of the engine equipment can now be made and any necessary adjustments to the beds carried out. This is probably the most important stage in installing the motor, since once the beds have been secured in position adjustments will be very difficult.

Provision must be made for bolting the motor to the beds since no other means of fastening is adequate. The precise location of the engine feet

The beds must be shaped to fit accurately into the hull or hot spots of pressure will be created on the hull skin. If possible, beds should be fitted across floors or bearers.

The engine beds may need slots cut for the mounting bolt nuts before they are fastened in position.

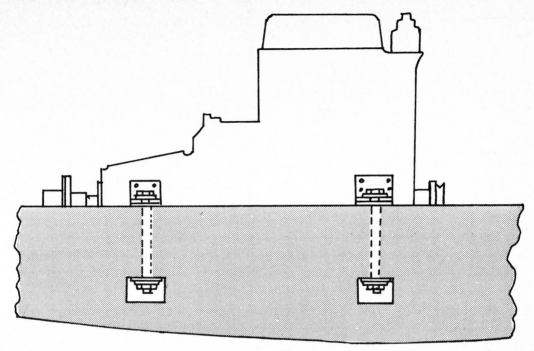

The motor must always be through bolted as vibration will loosen other types of fastenings. Since the beds are of heavy section, slots are cut to accept each nut and its locking plate.

can be marked on the beds during the dry run and the bolts securing the motor in position must be prepared before the beds are fastened to the hull. Since the underside of the beds is rarely accessible, either the bolts must be permanently fixed in their drillings, thread uppermost with a locking head under their heads, or the bearers may be morticed for the nuts, as in the above sketch, and the nuts fitted with locking plates. This method has the advantage of easily removeable bolts, so that if need be they may be renewed, and obviously the threads need to be cut and finished to exactly the right length.

Bolting is also the only safe method of securing the motor beds to the structural work of a timber hull, since vibration can loosen other fastenings. Likewise, through bolting to metal flanges in the hull of steel or ferro-cement boats is essential. With moulded GRP hulls the timber beds are usually totally glassed into the hull skin. This glassing must be very carefully done with reinforcing layers strengthening the contact point between bed and hull skin (see page 57).

It follows that the actual construction of the engine beds will vary from boat to boat according to the shape, design and type of motor. It is therefore impossible to offer in detail methods for installing beds to cover all craft and motors. Using these general guidelines plus a little ingenuity should enable you to construct and fit beds to suit almost any type of installation.

Apart from the major structural timber used for the beds themselves, it may sometimes be necessary (particularly in fibreglass, steel and ferro-cement boats) to install inter-costal or cross-members to brace the beds firmly into position. The methods of fastening and the dimensions of these bracing members will vary, but the overall result should be a well-braced unit which will transmit stresses from the motor into the structure of the hull.

With the beds secured into position and the mounting bolts protruding ready to take the motor, pressure plates must be fitted. These are

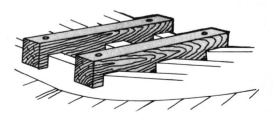

A typical arrangement of timber bearers fitted on a wooden boat's frames or floors.

metal plates which prevent the feet of the motor gouging into the timber of the beds as a result of being bolted down tightly or as a result of vibration when the motor is running. If the engine beds are of steel then pressure plates are not necessary but on all timber beds there must be some metal plate between the feet of the motor and the top of the beds.

This may be in the form of a full length plate or even angle iron, depending on the shape of the motor feet, drilled to accept the mounting bolts and the fastenings for securing the pressure plates to the beds. The larger the pressure plate the less chance there is of it biting into the timber of the beds.

A final check with the motor template should be made to ensure that all is aligned before the installation begins in earnest. Only minor adjustments to alignment can be made after the motor has been mounted. Check particularly that sump and gearbox have good clearance from the hull and that ancillary gear such as generators and starter motor have space around them.

Apart from the convenience of access to dip sticks and other maintenance areas, it is important that the motor has as much space as possible around it to enable it to 'breathe'. Motors, particularly diesels, suffer greatly from restricted air flow and more often than not this problem arises because of the confines of too small a motor compartment and an inadequate allowance for ventilation.

MOUNTINGS

The importance of alignment, already dealt with, is traditionally maintained by bolting the motor down solid on its bearers. This has the advantage of requiring the fewest components, and the transmission is freed of torsional stress. But while this arrangement remains suitable for most petrol engines and the multi-cylinder diesels, the trend towards the single and twin cylinder diesel coupled with the reasonable desire for silence has fostered the increased use of flexible engine mountings.

If the motor is to be allowed to move, then of course we shall no longer be able to maintain the rigid alignment of the shafting, and this must be arranged to absorb that movement. This is achieved by fitting a flexible torsion coupling between the flanges of the gearbox output shaft and the propshaft, and if the latter is less than 2 ft long (to the stern gland) an additional coupling should also be fitted ahead of that gland. The subject of shafting is more fully discussed on page 171.

Flexible mounting feet are designed to absorb the torsional and vibration stresses of the motor, and also to withstand the heavy 'G' loads that are generated in a seaway. Mountings must

Engine beds fitted with flexible mountings ready to accept the motor. Note the cut-away section on the after intercostal to accommodate the gearbox, and the use of a large drip tray.

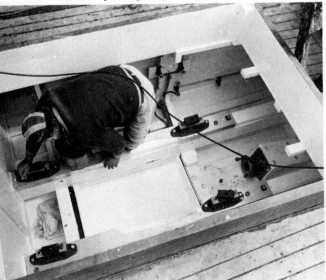

Typical flexible mountings for a marine motor installed on timber beds.

A clean and workmanlike installation of a Cummins V-8 diesel. Note the adjustable flexible mountings, finally set following sea trials.

the propeller end, and at the inboard end a watertight gland around the propshaft. A shaft log dispenses with the rigidity such a housing offers, and so there a short length of flexible hose is interposed between gland and hull fitting.

The two basic methods of fitting a stern tube to the hull are governed by the shape of the hull where it is penetrated by the shaft. In the case of large motor cruisers with flat bottoms, the shaft will be at a fine angle to the hull it penetrates. By contrast, the shaft of most yachts and some displacement-type power craft penetrates the hull at almost right angles through the stern post or transom area.

The first step is to drill out the hull to accept the stern tube and this must be done with a great

Typical stern gland arrangements in a small cruiser. Many glands are fitted with a greaser to expel water, but here the sleeve nut is filled with gland packing, and locked with a nut on the spigot.

therefore be selected with reference to the motor being used, in consultation with a marine engineer. And the same is true for flexible couplings, which are rated by h.p./r.p.m. and torque.

The final alignment of a solid-mounted unit invariably requires the use of shims beneath its mounting feet, but here a further advantage of the flexible variety are the integral screw adjusters. These provide for about half an inch of movement, and they also stress the point that a flexibly mounted motor needs if anything to be even more accurately aligned with its shafting than one solidly mounted. Any misalignment here will tend to be amplified by the system's flexibility, and thus the original advantage may be lost. The decision to fit flexible mountings should obviously be taken early in the design stage so that they are accounted for in the bearer alignment calculations.

STERN TUBE

Stern tubes vary from boat to boat, but the general principle remains the same: that of forming a housing for the propshaft below the waterline, generally with a water-lubricated bearing at

deal of precision if the shaft is to align correctly with the motor. A pilot hole should be drilled as described on page 163, to indicate the point at which the hull is penetrated. In the case of timber craft with heavy skegs, accurate measurement and an auger are required, while in ferro the hole will be cast in. But in GRP and steel the pilot hole will allow any small error to be corrected before the hole is widened to accept the stern tube.

The dummy shaft method outlined on page 163 is a reliable method of establishing the correct angle of alignment for the stern tube, and will ensure that when the components of the stern tube are assembled on the shaft, they and any associated webs or brackets can be fixed in the correct position in the hull. In the case of fibreglass and

An open shaft is carried in a P-bracket on flush-bottomed craft, usually in conjunction with a shaft log.

The shaft log is a flush-mounting plate on the bottom of the hull, and a white metal bearing and sealing gland are carried by the short length of flexible hose.

steel hulls where only the hull skin is penetrated, alignment is relatively easy. Where large skegs are involved the alignment is critical at this stage and a great deal of care must be taken when drilling out the shaft hole.

There are two basic forms of stern tube. The *shaft log* type is used in conjunction with an A-bracket on the outside of the hull and is in effect a total stern tube and gland fitting mounted on a plate on the inside of the hull. This is the system used mostly for motor yachts and relatively flat-bottomed craft where the shaft penetrates the hull skin at an acute angle. The shaft log is usually fitted with a flexible piece of hose to allow for any slight misalignment between the angle of the log and the shaft. The plate is a simple basic fitting which can be bolted through the hull or glassed into position in the case of a moulded hull. It is important, of course, to ensure that the alignment is exact and final securing into position should not be done until the shaft has been connected up to ensure that there is no part of the log or the shaft hole through the hull in contact with the shaft. If used in conjunction with an A-bracket or any other type of shaft bracket the whole shaft unit should be aligned from engine to propeller before the shaft log is finally fastened into position.

The second method involves a tube-like *stern tube* of a more traditional type which penetrates the transom or stern post at a broad angle, often close to 90 degrees. Here again, the stern tube can be purchased as a complete unit with flanges and gland. If necessary, the length of this tube can often be cut to suit each individual boat. Alignment is perhaps even more important with this type of stern tube since the shaft may be encased for some distance as it passes through the skeg and any misalignment will cause severe wearing of bearings. There is also less room for adjustment with this type of stern tube and therefore accuracy in fitting is the only way to ensure success.

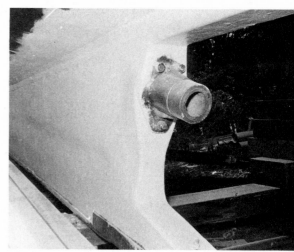

The hollow skeg of a GRP cruiser forms a convenient housing for a propshaft and stern tube, the outboard end of the shaft running in a water-lubricated cutless bearing.

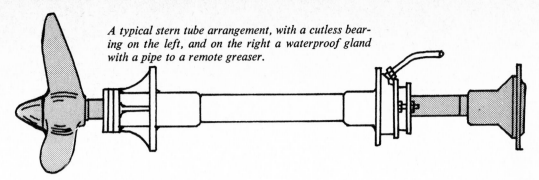

A typical stern tube arrangement, with a cutless bearing on the left, and on the right a waterproof gland with a pipe to a remote greaser.

As a general rule the inboard and outboard bearings have a threaded boss so that they may be screwed on to the tube, thus positively aligning the shaft. The outboard bearing is a seamless tube of internally fluted hard rubber, known as a cutless bearing, and water-lubricated via the flutes, while at the inboard end there is normally a white metal bush with an associated gland filled with packing and waterproof grease. Excessive shaft vibration will make short work of this gland, and where a motor has flexible mountings a short length of rubber hose is interposed between the hull and the bearing and gland.

There are variations on these two basic systems but whatever the type of stern tube fitted, the secret lies in a watertight installation which is in perfect alignment with the shaft and, in turn, with the motor. While it is not beyond the capabilities of a good handyman to construct a stern tube from bits of tubing, in the long run it will probably be false economy since the ready-made units are precision built and, given correct alignment, will function without problems. The whole critical point, of course, lies in the alignment for, as with misalignment of the motor, misalignment of the stern tube will cause wear and tear and vibration which in turn means inferior operation of the power unit and costly repairs at a later date.

Fastening the stern tube in position is no different to securing any stress fitting in place unless it is fitted in an awkward part of the hull. Through bolting with load-spreading plates is the usual system.

PROPELLER AND SHAFT

The importance of the propeller in relation to the type of hull and the propelling machinery was outlined at the start of this chapter, and while it would be of interest to embark on a discussion of the theory involved, that and the experience required in making a correct calculation are really outside the scope of the home builder. Many tables and graphs have been produced, but the essence of the thing is that the propeller manufacturers are using these every day in conjunction with their background of experience on an enormous variety of craft. For that there is no substitute, and in purchasing the propeller it will normally be sized for you free of charge. To do so will require as a minimum the following information:

The dimensions of the boat
The total weight of the boat
The shape of the hull: flat bottom, round bilge, etc
The desired speed
The width of the propeller aperture, or alternatively the distance between shaft and hull
The proposed power
The proposed gearbox reduction
The direction of shaft rotation
The material from which the shaft is made
The shaft diameter, and the taper, if any.

A propeller is a precision designed and built unit which will only obtain maximum performance if all factors relating to it are correct. Therefore in buying a propeller to fit your boat it is important to know that it will be of the right size and pitch to match the design and shape of the hull, and the type of motor installed.

The choice of correct propeller and shaft not only makes for efficient performance, but avoids problems such as vibration damage and corrosion.

Propeller shafts are generally manufactured from manganese bronze, stainless steel or Monel, and propellers from manganese bronze or nickel aluminium bronze. The last of these is the strongest and also the most expensive, and since manganese bronze is lower in the galvanic series this is the most popular material for both shafts and propellers. Whether or not there are material differences in the sterngear, however, it is good practice to fit an adjacent sacrificial anode.

Shaft diameters are governed by the modulus of elasticity of the material, the shaft r.p.m., the torque transmitted, and the unsupported distance between bearings. For example, a 1 in. diameter bronze shaft rotating at 1,000 r.p.m. should have a maximum distance between bearings of 3 ft 3 ins, but in steel this figure may be almost doubled. The need for additional shaft bearings generally only occurs in larger motor cruisers with their engines amidships. For motors up to 30 h.p. with displacement propeller speeds, 1 in. diameter shafting is normally adequate, while for higher powered motor cruisers and planing craft the propeller manufacturer should again be consulted. Clearly the diameter of the propeller shaft will govern the selection of the associated fittings and glands, and so this calculation will be established at the start of fitting out. Corrosion is occasionally a problem with sterngear, and while an anode should always be fitted the following basic guidelines may help in matching hull, propeller and shafting.

Timber Hulls
Propeller—manganese bronze or gun-metal.

Absolute alignment between stern tube and bracket is essential to avoid wear and vibration. Note the sacrificial anode positioned above shaft to reduce corrosion problems.

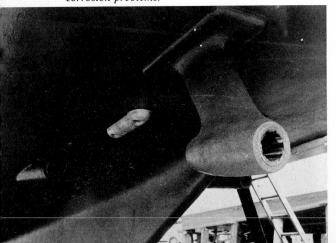

Typical shaft brackets in common use.

Shaft—manganese bronze, stainless steel or monel metal.

Steel Hulls
Propeller—zinc-sprayed cast iron, manganese bronze or gun-metal.
Shaft—zinc-sprayed manganese bronze, stainless steel or monel metal.

Aluminium Hulls
Propeller—manganese bronze (with sacrificial zinc anodes), aluminium alloy.

SHAFT BRACKETS

Where the propeller is snugged up close to the stern tube the outboard bearing holds it in position. Where the propeller shaft extends for some distance beyond the stern tube, however, and particularly where shaft logs are concerned, an A or P type of bracket will be necessary to support the shaft. These brackets are obtainable as a built unit and need only be secured in place. They must always be through bolted as there will be some stress on the bracket during operation and certainly there will be vibration which will tend to shake loose screws, coach screws or similar fastenings.

Since bad alignment between the bracket and the shaft will result in vibration and wear and tear, it is essential that the bracket is correctly mounted at the right angle in order to accept the shaft in complete alignment. The obvious first step is to obtain a bracket as close to the required angle as possible. The bracket must then be packed or padded to obtain the exact angle of the propeller shaft. Probably the best way to do this is when drilling and fitting the stern tube since the method of using a dummy shaft for alignment of the stern tube can also be used for aligning the bracket. The shaft needs to be passed through the hull and bracket bearing, when the bracket can be adjusted both in terms of location on the hull skin, and also with regard to the packing necessary to set the bearing at the correct angle.

Initially, this packing could be a wooden wedge which, when the alignment has been made, can be replaced with metal or polyester filler. It requires some trial and error to ensure that the bracket is adjusted correctly so that when the shaft is threaded through both bracket and stern tube it will rotate absolutely freely without any tendency to bear more on any one part of the stern gear system than another.

Final alignment is made by checking the shaft flange and moving the motor by adjusting shims at the mountings.

FINAL ALIGNMENT

Final alignment of motor and stern gear is best carried out after the boat has been afloat for some days. This applies to almost any type of hull, but more so to moulded GRP hulls where quite considerable change in shape can come about between the boat sitting on dry land and floating in the water. It is also a good idea, providing alignment is as close as it can be made initially, to give the boat a trial shake-down run to work everything into position. Then a final adjustment can be made to ensure that alignment is correct and will be unlikely to change for some time.

The coupling bolts between the shaft and motor flanges should be removed and the shaft turned by hand to check that there is no axial displacement between the faces of the two flanges. Normally this will not be visible to the naked eye, and so the flanges are brought together, just kissing, and *without* rotating the shaft, feeler gauges are used to check the gap around the periphery of the joint. If the flanges are flush there will be little or none, and where the gauge enters indicates the direction of misalignment.

Any misalignment at the half coupling must be corrected by adjusting the shims under the engine feet. This will require a lot of careful trial and error until the exact alignment of the two half couplings is indicated by the feeler gauge. Then the coupling bolts can be replaced and the motor is ready for use.

Misalignment can cause considerable wear and tear on many parts of a motor and its

The crucial test of alignment lies at the coupling. The shaft cannot be adjusted and the motor only slightly. Initial alignment is the key to success.

mountings. It can also create problems in the stern tube and totally wreck the gland. Correct alignment is essential at all times and many boat owners run a check on the alignment of their motors when they do their annual lay-up routine, or at some other advantageous part of annual maintenance work.

FUEL SYSTEMS

Although it is basically one of the simplest of the systems associated with boat motors, the fuel system is very prone to trouble. This is because of the vulnerability of the fuel, particularly diesel,

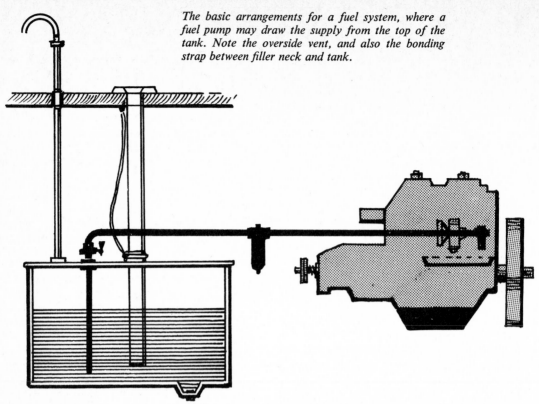

to any foreign matter and also the vulnerability of the system as a whole to leakage. Using the right materials—particularly the right piping—and fitting the system correctly in the first place is the only way to avoid these problems.

Understanding the fuel system and how each part works is perhaps the best way of avoiding problems, particularly when installing a new fuel system and its associated gear. The two principal systems—petrol and diesel—vary in many ways but are similar in others. Obviously much depends on the size of the boat and the motor installed. A simple single or twin cylinder motor may have only a basic gravity feed fuel system, while a sophisticated twin high speed motor will have a fuel system as complex as that of a high performance motor car. Therefore it is impossible to cover in detail all fuel systems under one heading. I shall deal here with the basic small boat system with few refinements—the type of system most encountered in pleasure craft.

Leaving aside the tank, which is described on page 92, the fuel system begins at the point where the fuel is drawn off on the start of its journey to the motor cylinders. The take-off pipe should enter the top of the tank, as this reduces the risk of leakage around the join. The pipe should run

down inside the tank almost to the bottom, leaving space for sediment and foreign matter—particularly water—between the mouth of the tube and the bottom of the tank. If it is not possible to insert the take-off pipe through the top of the tank it should be tapped into the side a few centimetres above the bottom. If there is no alternative but to tap the pipe into the bottom of the tank, its open end must be run up into the tank a few centimetres. All these precautions are to provide space at the bottom of the tank for contaminating matter. A sump on the floor of the tank allows this to be drained off.

Fuel lines for petrol installations should be of seamless copper or Monel, and mild steel may be used with diesels. The use of flexible neoprene tubing should be kept to a minimum, and where for reasons of vibration it is essential, it should be of the type with a reinforced metal braiding. This is normally at the carburetter or fuel pump where it is preferable to the practice of coiling metal tube. Flexible tubing is best fitted with machine-crimped unions, and these maintain the electrical bonding essential throughout the system.

Next in the sequence is the filter bowl. It can be purchased as a complete unit and, like many fuel system fittings, will require brazed nipples at the pipe unions which connect it into the system. Flared fittings are also used. Many boat owners prefer to have filters at other points along the fuel line, notably at the take-off point in the tank. This is all to the good, of course, since you cannot have too many filters providing they do not restrict the flow. But as a rule such filters are aimed at preventing solids entering the pipeline, and only the filter bowl fitted into the system between tank and motor will successfully extract water contamination. As a rule a filter consists of a glass or plastic bowl in which any water can be immediately spotted, and a filter of cloth or wire gauge to remove any solids which may not have been trapped earlier.

Because of the susceptibility of diesel motors it may be necessary to fit even more filters to ensure that only pure diesel fuel finally gets to the injectors. Often the fuel pumps, which are the next stage along the line, are fitted with filters for this very reason.

Not all motors are fitted with fuel pumps, of course. If the tank is above the level of the motor, both diesel and petrol systems use gravity feed to supply the motors. Big motors and yacht auxiliaries with fuel tanks deep in the keel will need fuel pumps to lift the fuel up to the feed area. In some cases small 'header' tanks are fitted which can be kept filled by the fuel pump but which actually feed the motor by gravity. Obviously the system adopted will be the one which suits the requirements of each individual motor. While gravity feed does eliminate one stage in the fuel system, and thus one more thing that can be subject to problems, it requires a tank to be fitted high in the hull and this is not always convenient.

At this point the two fuel systems go their separate ways. In the petrol system the fuel is fed into a carburettor bowl, the level of which is controlled by a float. This is, in effect, a sort of header tank and it is from this reservoir that the fuel is fed into the carburettor intake where it is mixed with air and fed to the motor. Diesel systems require the fuel to be fed under pressure to the cylinders, and thus an injector pump is fitted instead of the carburettor on a petrol motor.

A further difference between a diesel and a petrol fuel system is the injector pump bleed returning unused fuel to the tank. The engine builder should be consulted regarding any specific arrangements here, but in general it is a length of low-pressure tubing which must carry this fuel back to the top of the main tank.

Wherever possible, fuel lines should be routed reasonably high up in the boat and not through the bilge or accommodation. They should be firmly secured with non-abrading clips or clamps, and there should be a clamp within four inches of where any flexible piping is connected. Flexible sections, and all unions, should be reasonably accessible, but likely snags are minimised if these are kept to a minimum. Plan your pipe runs, keep them as short as is practically possible, and with a little ingenuity it is often possible to have just a single length of pipe between tank and motor. Lastly, use only flared pressure fittings or brazed nipples, not the soft-soldered type.

The small diesel auxiliary is also economical, and may therefore have a small integral fuel tank obviating the need for a lift pump.

COOLING SYSTEMS

Fitting a cooling system is a fairly simple task, since most of the system is incorporated in the motor and fitting requires only connection between the hull opening and the intake point on the motor. There is a great deal more involved where a closed circuit fresh water cooling system is involved, as external pipes of the heat transfer unit may be secured to the bottom of the hull. However, this system is not widely used nowadays, and where a closed circuit cooling system is employed, the heat exchanger is usually part of the motor equipment and cooling salt water is pumped in through the hull in much the same way as a direct salt water cooling system.

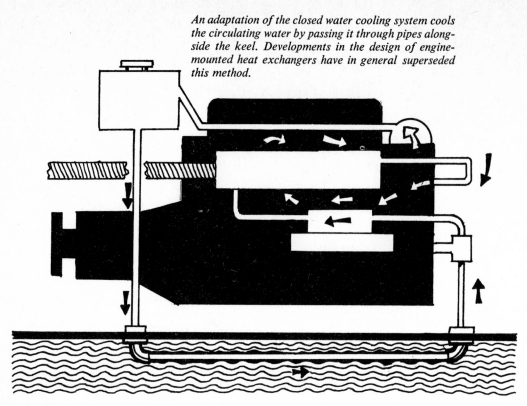

An adaptation of the closed water cooling system cools the circulating water by passing it through pipes alongside the keel. Developments in the design of engine-mounted heat exchangers have in general superseded this method.

These are the two common cooling systems fitted to pleasure craft and are simple and similar to fit. The closed circuit system employs a header tank or heat exchanger from which fresh water circulates through the motor, cooling the relative parts. When this water is returned to the heat exchanger it has become heated from contact with hot parts of the motor and must be cooled before it continues to circulate. This is done by passing it over a grid of pipes containing cool salt water which is being constantly recycled through an intake and discharge system in the hull.

The direct cooling system, as its name denotes, pumps salt water directly through the hull into the cooling system of the motor and returns the heated water back to the sea through a discharge pipe. Thus an open circuit of cooling water passes constantly from the sea, through the motor and back to the sea again. Both systems involve the intake of raw water from ouside the hull, so whichever unit is installed in your boat, the fitting will be similar.

The skin fitting on the hull for both intake and discharge pipes is secured in position as described on page 97. Many small craft discharge the cooling water through the exhaust system in which case only an intake pipe is required. It is common practice to equip this skin fitting with a strainer and scoop so that large foreign matter cannot enter the pipe. However, it is important that the strainer allows free flow of water and usually a finer filter is incorporated somewhere farther along the cooling system—often near the water pump—to remove any smaller matter that has been drawn through the strainer.

The skin fitting must have a stop cock incorporated as it is below the waterline. The hose is attached by ring clips and is usually reinforced plastic or rubber. Copper is also suitable but can produce problems, notably in terms of cracking due to vibration of the motor. If the motor is mounted on flexible mountings then a flexible section of hose will be required at some stage in the copper pipe. It is important when using plastic or rubber piping to ensure that no part of the hose touches the motor as both these materials are easily damaged by chafe or heat.

The connection at the motor end of the cooling line will depend on the fitting on the motor. A ring clip is usually all that is required to secure it in place and when screwed up tight this fitting completes the intake section of the cooling system. As mentioned, many motors discharge

Plastic pipes can be used in the cooling system providing they are good quality and kept clear of heat and chafe.

Where exhaust pipes are not cooled by water injection they must be lagged by asbestos tape to avoid risk of fire. Neoprene and rubber may be used after water has been injected into the exhaust.

their cooling water through the exhaust pipe, but if not, a similar system to the intake line will need to be fitted to carry the heated water back outside the boat. The difference in this line will be that strainer and scoop will not be required on the skin fitting, although the stop cock is still necessary.

EXHAUST SYSTEMS

A number of different types of exhaust system are used in boats, the choice being largely governed by the type and location of the engine. Apart from the obvious requirement of any exhaust system—to safely expel waste gas and heat—the marine exhaust has the added problem of being within the enclosed confines of the hull where it must also be kept reasonably cool. To achieve this the hot gas is first cooled at the manifold, while there are a variety of water cooled silencers.

But before dealing with this aspect, we should look at exhaust systems as a whole for, basically, they are little different to those of any other motor, including that of an automobile. In any internal combustion engine the burning of fuel in the cylinders is followed by expulsion of the waste gases at extremely high pressure and supersonic speed. As each cylinder fires, the gases create a shock wave in the exhaust manifold and with a multi-cylinder motor these shock waves occur many thousands of times a minute.

Between the motor and the exhaust outlet these shock waves must slow down and dissipate until they are at the pressure of the surrounding air, thus reducing the bang of the supersonic

wave to a muffled thud. An idea of the sort of noise that would emanate from an unsilenced motor can be gained from the noise of an aircraft or a racing car's exhaust. Such noise would not be tolerated in normal use, and thus a boat motor, like a car motor, must reduce exhaust noises to an acceptable level before discharging the gas into the open air.

Apart from noise, there are dangers to human life in the gases that leave the motor so that they must be carried away outside the boat where they can be dissipated harmlessly. This means an exhaust system that does not leak and in turn means a system that can withstand the tough wear and tear of marine work. Installation is vitally important in the first place, as is the choice of the correct exhaust system and also the materials used in the system. Certain materials are subject to corrosion from diesel exhaust fumes and others are liable to work-harden in use, creating a risk of cracking and subsequent leaking of fumes into the boat.

And, of course, there is always the risk of fire where a hot exhaust system is concerned. Fire on board a boat is one of the worst kinds of emergencies so it is imperative that the exhaust system is well fireproofed, even more so than its counterpart in a car or other shore-based motor. This means once again the use of the right materials in the system as well as correct installation.

The choice of materials for an exhaust system varies according to the type of exhaust and the type of fuel used. Metal must obviously be used for a 'dry' exhaust, but this is confined to small

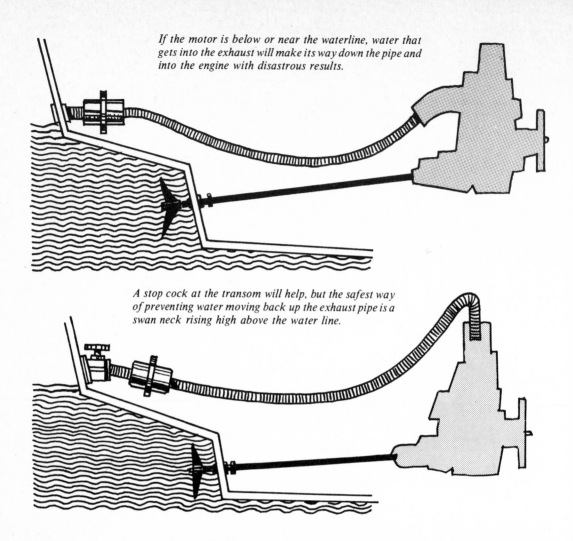

If the motor is below or near the waterline, water that gets into the exhaust will make its way down the pipe and into the engine with disastrous results.

A stop cock at the transom will help, but the safest way of preventing water moving back up the exhaust pipe is a swan neck rising high above the water line.

petrol engines, since a dry absorption silencer cannot be used with a diesel. The general heat problem means that the 'wet' exhaust predominates, and the resultant lower temperatures allow hard synthetic rubber piping to be used safely.

The type of fuel used in the motor is important because some fumes have a corrosive effect on certain metals. As a general rule galvanised iron, copper or brass and synthetic rubber can all be used with wet petrol exhausts, but wet diesel fumes corrode copper and brass and so the choice for this fuel is limited to steel or synthetic rubber. This latter material is perhaps the most popular for wet exhausts of any type as it is flexible, making installation easy and relatively cheap.

But the major problem with fitting an exhaust system is the location of the motor, and the risk of getting water back down the exhaust pipe

when the motor is not running. Many motors are installed below the waterline level and thus any water which finds its way into the exhaust pipe has a downhill run to the motor. If the exhaust port is open the water will enter the cylinder where it will create all kinds of problems, not least of which is the fact that since water cannot be compressed, at the first compression stroke of the piston it will blow the head off the motor!

There are three principal means of avoiding this, the most obvious of which is to raise the motor above the waterline. This is not always practical so it can be discarded for most boats. A flap valve can be fitted to the outer end of the exhaust, permitting exhaust gases to flow outwards but preventing water from flowing into the system. This is frequently used, but on its own it is not totally satisfactory, for it needs only a small foreign object to prevent the flap

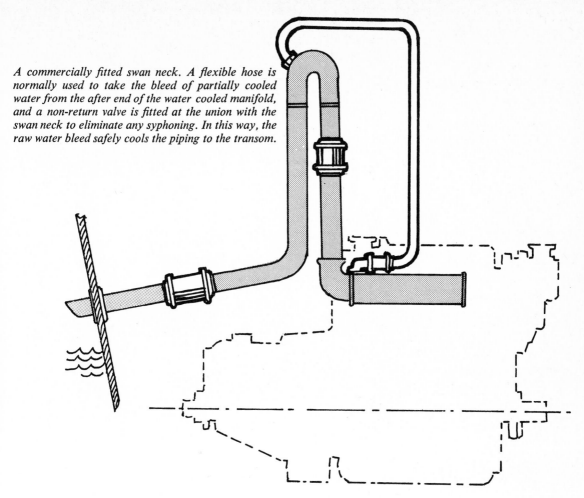

A commercially fitted swan neck. A flexible hose is normally used to take the bleed of partially cooled water from the after end of the water cooled manifold, and a non-return valve is fitted at the union with the swan neck to eliminate any syphoning. In this way, the raw water bleed safely cools the piping to the transom.

valve closing properly and allow water into the motor causing thousands of dollars worth of damage.

The best system is a combination of the valve at the exhaust terminal and a swan-neck in the exhaust pipe near the motor. This comprises a bend in the pipe which carries it well above the waterline level of the boat, and thus prevents any water in the pipe from reaching the motor. It should be as near as possible to the centreline of the boat, particularly in yachts, as a swan-neck near the side of the boat may well be lowered beneath the sea level when the boat is heeled, and its effectiveness thus destroyed.

There are other, patent types of water traps which may be as efficient as the swan-neck, but providing it is correctly installed this method is economical since it involves only an extra metre or so of exhaust pipe and is easily fitted even by an amateur.

Probably the best arrangement, if the fitting of the motor permits, is to locate the swan-neck immediately adjacent to the exhaust outlet. It should be made of 'jacketed' copper pipe, in which the inner exhaust tube is cooled by an outer tube or jacket carrying water from the cooling system. The swan-neck must curve upwards as high as possible above waterline level, the higher the better. At the after end of the curve, as the swan-neck begins its downwards path, the water jacket can be discarded and the cooling water run directly into the exhaust pipe. This makes it a wet exhaust and thus metals need not be used from this point on. Synthetic rubber is the ideal material for the wet exhaust right out to the skin fitting and valve at the transom terminal.

It is important to note that the cooling water cannot be run into the exhaust pipe before the swan-neck is well over the curve or there will be a

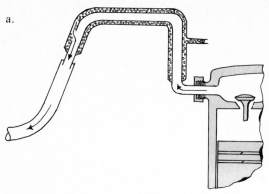
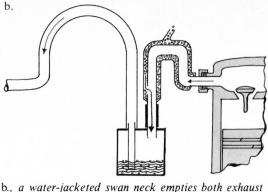

a.   b.

Cross section of two systems of creating a water trap in a water-cooled and silenced exhaust: a., the exhaust gas flows through a water-jacketed pipe over the swan neck, at which point the water is injected into the exhaust pipe;

b., a water-jacketed swan neck empties both exhaust gases and water into a water trap from where it is exhausted through a normal exhaust pipe.

risk of the cooling water being drawn back into the cylinder with the same disastrous results as with sea water. The commencement of the jacketing is also a danger area since copper work-hardens and is liable to crack at this point unless it is annealed fairly regularly. A crack at this point would not only allow gases to escape into the boat but again would run the risk of getting cooling water back into the motor. For this reason, many exhaust components are now made with stainless steel, including jacketing and flexible anti-vibration bellows which may be included in the piping.

Fastening the exhaust pipe in place is relatively simple, bearing in mind that a hot pipe may cause a fire. If a dry system is fitted it must be 'lagged' by winding asbestos tape round and round the pipe until it is totally insulated. Fastening a dry pipe or section of pipe to any but a steel hull is asking for a fire as soon as the motor is run.

Big motors require good ventilation, and special vent ports such as these are common in large motor yachts.

Some motors, particularly those fitted to large motor cruisers, require silencing in addition to the normal exhaust system. A wet exhaust is in itself a form of silencer, but if it is not sufficient then silencers must be installed in the system. These are purchased as a unit and are too varied to detail here. Manufacturer's instructions will be the best guide in fitting a silencer.

Noise, fumes and the dangers of back-water—these are the humbugs of exhaust systems which only correct installation in the first place can avoid. They are serious problems which can endanger the boat so they must receive very close attention.

MOTOR VENTILATION

Motors, like humans, must breathe. Many of the problems associated with boat motors can be traced to insufficient air supply. Particularly is this the case with diesels where often the black smoke seen emanating from the exhaust is due to the motor being too enclosed or in some way being starved of air. Because of the confined space in which many boat motors are mounted a good supply of air may need to be drawn in from outside. In large craft and those with more than one motor, big in-draft ventilators are essential.

Small motors may be able to draw sufficient air for maximum performance from their compartment or from open areas such as the bilge. But since ventilators are easy items to fit there is little point in disregarding this aspect of fitting a motor and good ventilation should be part and parcel of fitting the motor in place. You may just need to open a few holes or apertures in a bulkhead or motor box. On the other hand, to get the most out of the motor it may be necessary to fit good scoop ventilators in the side of the hull where they can force-feed air into the motor compartment.

Fitting of the ventilators is quite simple since they are purchased as a unit and fastened as recommended by the manufacturer. Through bolting will usually be necessary together with a good sealant to make them watertight. However, as these fittings do not usually come under stress, screwing may be sufficient. Each unit will need to be assessed on its location and size.

If the vent is mounted in the side of the hull or some other place where it is open to spray or rain, it will need to be fitted with a water trap, or else have some type of closing mechanism. The former is obviously better since to close off the vent at sea would be to nullify its usefulness to a great extent. There are many patent types of vent available for this job and a visit to the local chandlery will indicate the best for your individual boat.

A number of marine authorities now stipulate that an engine compartment must have positive ventilation, usually employing an electric extractor fan venting on deck or overside, and drawing air from the bottom of the compartment at a rate of not less than 50 cu. ft. per minute.

REMOTE CONTROLS

Most craft, other than very small ones, operate the gearshift and throttle of their motors by remote control. The controls vary from highly sophisticated electric or hydraulic equipment to simple wire or rod activated levers, but basically they all work on the principle that the controls

Single-lever controls combine gear shift with throttle in one lever and simplify handling in close quarters. The unit shown controls two engines, with one cable to each.

are removed from the vicinity of the motor. Two principal requirements are involved in the locations of remote controls: one is that they are in a place where they can be easily reached and operated by hand, and the second that they are conveniently located to other controls—notably the steering wheel—in a position where visibility for manoeuvring is good.

Remote control units may be single or twin, with the gearshift and throttle combined, or each control separate. The design of the unit must allow for easy access for maintenance and lubrication and the transmission should operate smoothly and without jerking or sticking. Where twin units are concerned both controls should be in a position where they can be operated by one hand. The controls should be grouped together with instruments and any other equipment related to the use of the motor.

Electrically operated and hydraulic controls are more complicated to install and service, but permit convenient positioning as the wires and piping can be led into awkward engine installations from the helmsman's position. Rod and link or cable (Morse) units are easy to install and maintain. Since all remote control equipment is subject to breakdowns or similar problems it is a good idea to get to know your gear from the installation stage and thus be prepared for any sudden repair work which may arise during use.

Flexible wire controls are perhaps most commonly used on small to medium sized pleasure craft. They consist of a length of wire which travels around pulleys linking the control lever to the throttle or gear shift lever on the motor. Because most gear shifts operate both ways—forward and back—the wire control is usually supplemented with a rod or tube. This must be firmly fixed in position to prevent any movement when pressure is applied on the control lever.

When fitting this type of remote control it is important to remember a few basic facts. Pulleys must be used whenever there is a change in direction of the wire and these pulleys must be strong enough to withstand the load that will be placed on them, as also must be the anchoring points or fastenings that hold them in position. They must be aligned to give a clear lead so that the wire runs directly onto the pulley and there is no risk of chafe at the housing. The pulley diameter should be at least ten times the diameter of the cable, with a minimum diameter of 50 mm.

Tension must be applied to the cable to enable sensitive adjustments of the control lever to be relayed to the control on the motor. The most common method of doing this is to use small turnbuckles somewhere in the line.

Another type of system used for throttle control is a single cable which is fairly rigid and travels inside an outer tube. This is probably the most common of the remote control cables since it eliminates the need for an extra cable and also the need for pulleys. The only limitation with this type of cable is that it is much less flexible than the pulley type, and therefore cannot be bent around sharp corners. Manufacturers specify minimum radii, while the outer casing of the cable must also be firmly clamped down to maintain the effective push-pull action.

All cables, no matter what type, must be well maintained or problems will occur in operation. For this reason they should be fitted in such a way that access is available for greasing and inspection. Pulleys are usually of plastic and need little lubrication, but the cables will need attention as corrosion or rust may occur, and often with the single cable type, the internal cable gets dry or rusted in the course of use, either of which will create problems. Where rod and tube are used, such as in Teleflex gear, regular greasing is essential for smooth operation and long life of the equipment.

Where there is firm resistance involved in moving the control on the motor—such as on a gear lever—rod and link systems are preferable to wire and pulley. This requires not only well-designed and robustly constructed stainless steel rod, but also well secured fastenings. Considerable pressures come onto rod gear when in use, and these pressures will be transmitted to many of the anchor points along the line, particularly the bellcrank assembly which is a part of the linkage used to turn the transmission through an angle. Failure of the bolts holding the anchor point to the boat's structure means failure of the entire system.

One of the most important aspects to consider when fitting rod and linkage gear is the compression factor that will come on the rod when under load. If it bends or deflects then the rod is too long and/or too light and shorter lengths or heavier gauge rod must be used. Similarly, joints in the linkage must be strong enough to take the load of moving the gear shift backwards and forwards without moving out of alignment. These linkages must be kept well lubricated and free, for stiffness at these points will mean added load on the rod and on the unit as a whole.

DRIP TRAY

Since the drip tray fits right under the motor its measurements will be the inside measurements of the motor beds. The length will depend on how far working parts of the motor extend, for the drip tray, to be totally effective, must underhang every part of the motor which is liable to leak any kind of fluid. The tray can be fitted before the installation of the motor, in which case it is a permanent fixture, or it can be a portable arrangement which slides out from under the motor for ease of cleaning. Obviously, the choice will depend on the type of motor installation since access to the underside is often difficult and a permanent tray is the only choice. In this case some means of cleaning must be devised. Pumping is not usually sufficient.

If the tray is fitted *in situ* it can be glassed in or lightly screwed since there will be little stress on the fastenings. Steel, aluminium or moulded GRP trays can be made up or purchased, or a built-in fibreglass tray can be constructed with woven mat and using the structure of the beds as the form onto which the glass is laid. This is a quite successful and easy method with any type of hull construction, but is particularly popular with fibreglass and timber hulls.

Sophisticated remote controls for small craft operate everything from the one position including trim, tilt, choke, friction control, trailer, electric start and normal throttle, and gear shift.

CHAPTER 8

Masting and Rigging

MASTS AND SPARS

MASTS AND SPARS can be made from a number of different materials but the two most commonly used are timber and aluminium. Even timber, the traditional material for masts, is rapidly being superseded by lightweight aluminium in most modern yachts, particularly racing yachts. Aluminium has a number of advantages over timber, notably lighter weight and greater strength. It is also more durable and less likely to deteriorate due to wind and weather, although chafe, corrosion and fatigue have to be considered. While the great majority of masts and booms are now aluminium, timber spars are still in use, and occasionally made. However, they require skill, space, specialised tools and suitable wood, and are not a job for the average amateur. On the other hand, it is quite feasible to buy a suitable bare section of extrusion and the necessary fittings, and rig one's own mast. With careful planning, adequately sized and well made fittings and fastenings, and a good standard of workmanship, such spars can be entirely satisfactory and significantly cheaper.

This is no place to go into the pros and cons of aluminium *vs* timber as a masting material. Since both are used, and since, perhaps, timber is more of a handyman's material than extruded aluminium, I shall include both materials in this section. However, we are concerned here with fitting out as opposed to basic building, and therefore I shall deal solely with the fitting and rigging of all masts and assume in both cases that the basic mast section is already supplied.

TIMBER MASTS

These come in a variety of forms, commencing with the solid spar which has been the basic form of mast since forests were first decimated to build the old wooden ships. There is nothing wrong with a solid spar, and there are still many to be found among the yacht fleets around the world. However, the hollow section has proved more efficient and generally solid masts are confined to small boats of the centreboard type or large, commercial windjammers. Spruce is the most popular material and is selected for its straight grain pattern which is important if the spar is to have equal strength throughout its length.

One of the main problems with solid masts is the amount of weight aloft. Hollow spars reduce the weight considerably with little reduction in strength. Indeed, a hollow mast of only 10 per cent increased diameter will have the same strength as a solid mast but with obviously much saving in weight. The problems of weight aloft are important since the higher the weight is carried the greater the leverage effect tending to heel the boat.

For example: a weight of 10 kilograms carried 1 metre above the deck will create a heeling moment of only 10 kg/m. The same weight carried 10 metres above the deck creates a heeling moment of 100 kg/m. Since a yacht is at her best when sailed as upright as possible the need to reduce heeling is important and thus reducing unnecessary weight aloft is the principal way of reducing the heeling moment.

Small boats and dinghies which use solid spars find them very effective for racing. Generally speaking, a solid timber mast will bend more

Solid wooden masts are not widely used with modern rigs. The older gaff rig required a shorter mast and thus solid spars could be used without adding too much weight aloft.

than an aluminium one and can thus induce more control into the mainsail. However, the consistency of the bend is better with aluminium since no two timber masts bend alike. Tapering the solid mast will reduce some of the weight aloft, of course, but for most purposes a hollow or built spar is more suitable.

All masts are in compression when under load; the pressure of the wind on the sails is opposed by the tension in the rigging, which, with the inherent stiffness and strength of the mast, prevent bending and collapse. To hollow out a spar too much would be to make the walls too thin to withstand these compression factors and generally the limit which is applied is for the thickness of the mast wall to be not less than one-fifth the diameter of its section. This makes for a fairly rigid cruising mast and is often reduced somewhat if the boat is to be raced.

Built masts come in a variety of shapes, the most common being the rectangular or oval section. This has been found to have good aerodynamic factors and is without doubt the most popular type of wooden spar in use. The simple, basic box shape is usually made of spruce although oregon is also suitable providing it is clear—i.e. has an even grain pattern with no knots. Other forms of hollow masts are either built or merely hollowed from solid timber spars and, because of the long sections required, usually start at some point along their length.

Fittings for a timber mast are little different to those used on aluminium extrusions. The fastenings used are also similar with the exception, perhaps, of pop rivets which may be used instead of screws on aluminium masts. Major fittings are through bolted in both cases

Some idea of the enormous compression strains on a mast under load can be seen from this picture. Compression is the most common cause of failure in a mast.

but one of the advantages of timber is that it is less liable to corrosion problems than the alloy. The only dissimilarity between metals is likely to occur between the fastening and the fitting and the major problem of corrosion with the aluminium is avoided. Generally speaking, most fittings on a timber mast are external while halyards and other running rigging may be fitted internally on an aluminium mast. Once again, this is a relatively insignificant difference, and the basic methods described for fitting an aluminium mast later in this section can be adapted to timber masts relatively easily.

ALUMINIUM MASTS

The principal advantage of aluminium masts is the saving in weight. The thin walls of the alloy plus its lighter weight and considerable strength enable a mast to be built to remarkably light dimensions which will nevertheless incorporate all the strength factors of a heavier section in timber.

Another advantage is its uniform bending qualities and lack of deterioration with use. In the early days a certain amount of metal fatigue was experienced in these spars, but modern extrusions have been improved and metal fatigue, like age deterioration, has been considerably reduced. Providing the correct marine grade alloy is used corrosion is negligible and even this can be reduced by anodising or painting. Electrolytic corrosion can occur where different metals are in electrical contact with the mast wall. Care in selection of fittings and fastenings can prevent this and, where it cannot be avoided, insulating material can be placed between the two dissimilar metals.

Extrusions can be purchased in a number of different forms although a general oval shape is the most popular. Internal or external tracks or luff grooves are optional as also is tapering. Cruising yachts, particularly large craft, usually step a mast of uniform dimension, the tapered versions being more popular with performance racing craft where mast bend will be induced.

One of the advantages of uniform dimensions in the mast is that it can be cut to any length by simply using a hacksaw. This simplifies obtaining heel and cap fittings, which must fit snugly, and in fitting out generally. It also allows the repair or construction of a spar by riveting matching pieces of extrusion through an internal sleeve, which must be a close fit.

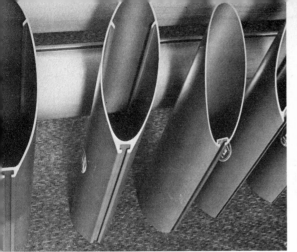

There are aluminium extrusions to fit every purpose. Those with ribbed strengthening and thicker walls are designed more for cruising—others for the bending that is involved in performance racing.

Rigidity and strength is sometimes increased with ribbing extruded on the inside of the mast wall as well as thickened wall sections near the luff groove or track base. Obviously, selection of the right mast for your individual boat is an important factor and one which must be given considerable thought if the maximum benefits are to be obtained with the minimum outlay for the mast.

FITTINGS

Fittings are usually supplied ready-made for most sizes and shapes of masts. With some timber or unusual shaped aluminium masts it may be necessary to have some fittings hand made or manufactured to order, but generally speaking there is a fitting for every mast or one that can be adapted simply. To avoid corrosion problems, the fitting must be of an acceptable metal, particularly if fitted to an aluminium mast. Aluminium and stainless steel are most used for mast fittings, although slight corrosion problems can be experienced with the latter. Brass and similar metals must never be used as aluminium mast fittings unless an insulating material is placed between the two dissimilar metals. Any electrical insulator is suitable, the most common being Tufnol.

The same principle applies to the fastenings whether they be rivets, bolts or screws. They must be electrolytically matched to prevent corrosion problems with the aluminium alloy since, unlike fittings, it is very difficult to place an insulating material between the fastenings

Typical of the problems encountered when mounting fittings of dissimilar metals on an aluminium mast. Insulation between the fitting and the mast wall can reduce this problem.

and the mast wall. The most suitable materials for fastenings are aluminium, stainless steel and monel, which are generally available. Fittings and their fastenings will be dealt with in detail where they occur in this section.

If the extrusion is not of the exact length of the mast it will need to be cut. The sail or rigging plan will indicate the length of the spar, and cutting is a simple process with a hacksaw. Masts and booms will need to be cut to their exact lengths allowing, of course, for any additional fittings which may increase the height or length of the extrusion, such as mast head fittings and gooseneck. The extra length of such fittings would be negligible for anything except a performance racing boat which is carefully measured for handicap or rating purposes. Rough edges must be filed down and the ends of the spars filed flat to take their fittings.

MARKING UP THE MAST

The next step is to mark up the mast and spars for their fittings. This is a very important stage and measurements must be carefully taken from the sail or rigging plan to ensure that stress items, such as the spreaders, are located in exactly the right place. Less critical fittings such as cleats and winches can be placed where convenient, but the designer has located the spreaders where they will be of maximum advantage and they must be fitted in exactly that spot.

The best way to mark up the mast is to have the fitting on hand. Having measured up its exact location, you then check it for comfortable fit and clearance from other fittings. Bear in mind also the need to avoid drilling too close in any one area. Note gooseneck marked out (right).

A jig saw with a metal blade makes light work of cutting apertures in the mast wall. It may need to be started by drilling a hole, although most jig saws can be started by simply angling the blade.

Since there are many different types of fittings available, it is a wise move to purchase your fitting requirements before marking up the mast. The mast cap, for example, can come in many different shapes and sizes, and it would be unwise to mark and cut the extrusion before having the fitting to hand. Apart from measuring directly from the fitting, there is always the chance that a slight discrepancy between the stated and the actual measurements may occur in manufacture, or that the supplier is out of stock, in which case you will need to fit a different type of cap. To obtain a comfortable flush fit, it is always as well to have the fitting on hand so that minor adjustments can be made to ensure that when everything is in place and ready to be fastened it all fits snugly.

Marking up the mast will be very dependent on the sail or rigging plan and all measurements *must* be exact, other than for unimportant fittings. The exact location of each spreader needs particular care. It has to be measured in two directions—along the length of the mast and around the girth of the mast section, which involves measuring around a curved surface. Similarly, the lead from a halyard sheave to a winch, particularly if it is a wire winch, must be accurate or the wire will wind on awkwardly creating riding turns and probably jamming up the winch before the halyard is properly tensioned. All these, and many other factors, must be carefully examined when transferring measurements from the plan to the mast and spars.

CUTTING THE APERTURES

Aluminium masts often have internal halyards, which means that exit boxes must be cut to enable sheaves to be inserted so that the halyards can be led outside to winches and deck leads. Other fittings may also be recessed through the aluminium wall of the mast—certain types of tangs may be internally mounted, for example. Whatever the fitting, the mast wall must be cut to allow access and enable the fitting to be flushed into the mast.

Cutting holes of any type in a mast wall obviously weakens it, so the number and size of apertures must be kept to a minimum. In addition, lines of weakness created by cutting a series of holes in the transverse plane must be avoided, and holes staggered wherever possible. This is particularly the case when drilling the mast for fastenings since a row of holes drilled to enable a fitting to be pop riveted into position is almost tantamount to cutting through the mast section.

The size and shape of the hole will obviously be controlled by the size and shape of the fitting. A drill is usually used to make a hole into which a jig saw can be inserted, and the aperture cut as best as possible with the saw, using a file to shape any awkward areas and to smooth off the rough edges. The best procedure always is to have the fitting at hand when cutting the hole so that by trial and error you ensure a tight, snug fit.

MAST HEEL

The fitting of a mast step or tabernacle is described on page 127, and it follows that the

Filing back the rough edges with a flat file and marking the holes to be drilled completes the preparation for the fitting.

fitting of the heel of the mast must match this arrangement. A wide variety of mast steps are available so the matching fitting at the foot of the mast must be selected at the same time as the mast step. Indeed, they will probably be sold as one unit, although in the case of a channel or U-girder the only fitting may be the through bolts which hold the mast in place. Many mast steps are more complicated, particularly those which pivot the mast so that it can be raised or lowered.

If the mast is stepped on the keel then usually it drops into a cast aluminium socket or some similar mast step secured to the floors. A matching casting, probably in the form of a plug, is inserted into the foot of the mast extrusion and pop riveted or tap screwed.

A similar arrangement may be fitted to the deck or cabin top when the mast is stepped on deck, although stepping on deck allows more flexibility in terms of moving or pivoting the mast and thus tabernacles are usually more involved. Whatever the system used, it will need to be securely fitted to the foot of the mast, and where stress or pivoting will be experienced heavy through bolts of stainless steel will be required.

The channel or U-girder is a popular method of stepping the mast on deck and securing the foot of the mast in position may be done in one of two ways. If the mast is to pivot, a through bolt that holds the foot of the mast clear of the base of the channel is all that is required. Since the full weight of the mast will be supported on this one bolt it is rarely satisfactory for large masts and in any case will need sleeving with stainless steel tube to spread the load.

A more common system is to insert two bolts, one immediately in front of and one immediately behind the mast section, which hold the foot in position, the weight being taken by the base of the tabernacle and thus transmitted to the hull

structure. These are just two of many methods of stepping a mast on deck.

MAST CAP

The cap fitting of an aluminium mast often forms an anchorage for the backstay, forestay and cap shrouds, and as such transfers the heavy compression loads to the tensioned rigging. Its strength and security are therefore crucial. In addition, since it is at the head of the sails, it is usually designed to accommodate three or more sheaves for the halyards and the topping lift.

When the mast is under load, stresses on the mast cap will not be evenly distributed since the weather shrouds will be under stress and the lee shrouds slack. Similarly, there may be different loadings on the fore and back stays depending on the wind direction. For this reason, the mast cap must be very well secured into position; it is general practice to fit the cap in some way into the extrusion itself, either as a sort of plug insert to the top of the extrusion or by cutting out small sections of the extrusion into which the mast cap can be fitted and secured. A typical mast cap used with medium sized craft is an aluminium or stainless steel fabrication which slots into the forward and after ends of the extrusion as well as fitting snugly inside. An overhanging plate carries the various terminals for rigging, halyards and antennae and the whole thing is fastened securely into position to withstand stress from any direction.

In selecting the correct mast cap, apart from taking account of the obvious factors such as rigging terminals and matching dimensions, consideration must be given to the location of halyard sheaves and other working gear. Clear access for halyards to run over the sheaves without chafe is an example of this type of problem. Each individual mast and cap will obviously have its own problems, and these must

Slotting the mast cap fitting into the mast itself adds strength and rigidity.

be sorted out before the mast cap is secured in position. It is wise to make a dummy run with all the running rigging and gear to be attached to the mast cap before a fastening it into position. Alternatively, some boat owners prefer to secure the mast fittings temporarily, then raise the mast, set up the rigging and make a thorough check of all aspects of the mast, spars and rigging before lowering the mast, making any necessary adjustments, and then fastening all fittings firmly into place. This is a particularly good method if you intend to paint the mast since it ensures that no adjustments will be required after the mast has been painted.

Such trial and error work is good practice in any such complicated operation as fitting a mast. There are so many items to be correctly placed in position before a fitting is fastened securely that it is not at all uncommon to find yourself trapped having secured, say, the mast cap before remembering a simple item such as a wire for an antenna or masthead light. Securing everything temporarily and getting the mast fully rigged before final fastening is one way to avoid such problems. Mast caps have, in recent years, become more and more complicated with the addition of instruments and their masthead antennae, to say nothing of recent developments in placing navigation lights at the top of the mast.

Having cut the mast section and fitted the mast cap, fastening into position is carried out in two ways. The tangs for the upper or cap shrouds must be through bolted—this bolt can serve the double purpose of securing both the tangs and the mast cap. All through bolting on the mast should have a compression sleeve or tube fitted

Through bolts hold the cap securely in position. Tangs for the upper or cap shrouds may be part of the cap unit.

inside the section before the bolt is drawn up tight to avoid compression of the mast wall. The remainder of the fastenings around the mast cap will vary according to the design of the fitting and the extra equipment it carries, but generally speaking pop rivets or tap bolts will take care of most fastenings since the through bolting secures the cap well and truly in place. Pop rivets should be aluminium or monel while the major bolt or bolts must be of stainless steel. It is a wise precaution when the tangs are drawn up tight to secure the nuts with a split pin drilled through the bolt|.

SPREADERS

When a camper puts up a tent, he learns to take the guy ropes out from the tent pole at an angle of about 45° before he hammers in a peg and makes it fast. And if he doesn't, and the wind gets up, he's liable to have a rude awakening. The object is to get a good angle of purchase on the pole, and the further away the guy is from the vertical the more secure will it be.

From this simple example of triangulation we can move to the somewhat longer pole that forms the mast of a sailing boat, and its 'guys', the shrouds and stays. Except that now we are no longer encamped with room to move, or to shift the guys, and we have only a deck perhaps 30 feet long and a mere 10 feet wide on which to erect 30 or 40 feet of pole. We are also going to rig a sail on the pole, and so we'd rather it didn't bend, and clearly some extra supporting arrangements will be necessary.

While it may therefore not be possible to rig our 'guys' to get the tent guys' 45° at the top of

The mast cap is the ideal location for antennae and lights, so it must be of adequate strength to cope with them.

the pole, what we can do is stiffen up the pole and set up some struts part way along its length which allow the 'guys', or shrouds, to meet the top of the mast at nearer the 45°. In this way the upper section of the mast may be properly 'guyed', supported on the lower section beneath the base of the triangle which is sufficiently stiff. The shrouds are of course carried all the way down to the deck, and the struts with which they are spread to form the triangle are, logically enough, called the spreaders.

As with the guys for a tent pole, the wider the angle the shroud makes with the masthead the more effective will be the support, but there is normally a limiting factor here with the need to sheet in an overlapping headsail. With the exception of highly stressed racing rigs, therefore, experience has shown that the angle the shroud makes with the mast should not be less than 15°.

The comparative sketch on the right illustrates that by moving the spreaders up the mast this angle might be easily achieved, but it should be remembered that in conjunction with the shrouds they form a triangle that stiffens the mast, and that to do so may expose the lower mast to unacceptable bending stresses. The objective is to spread the load evenly. In the same vein, if the compression loads placed on the spreader by the shroud are imbalanced it will suffer a tendency to bend, and for this reason, as shown in the sketch, it must be set up to bisect the angle it makes with the shroud.

Setting up the spreaders at exactly right angles to the fore and aft line can be a little difficult. There are a number of ways of achieving this; one of the simplest is by using a try square.

1 Make up a plug to fit into the bottom of the mast. With the mast lying horizontal, fit this plug in place and mark on it the exact fore and aft line of the boat which is, of course, an exact dissection of the mast section.

2 Screw into position a batten which has the upper edge along this fore and aft line of the plug and which extends well out on either side of the mast wall.

3 The point at which the spreaders are to be attached—the maximum point of the mast curve—can be marked on the plug and a try square set up so that its base rests along the centreline and its arm extends outwards along the line of the spreader.

In effect, the try square represents the spreader at this point and by aligning it with the actual spreader fitting at the point marked along the

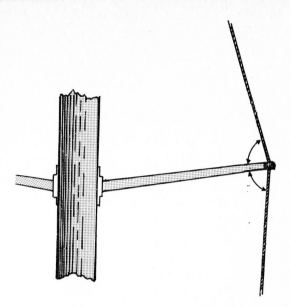

The angle of the spreader to the mast should be such that it bisects the angle it creates in the shroud.

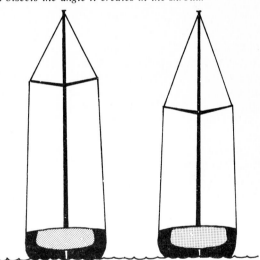

Raising the spreaders may increase the shroud angle at the masthead, but the lower mast will be subject to bending. The right hand rig is correct.

One method of setting up the spreaders.

mast the exact location of the spreader fitting can be found. If, when everything is aligned, the spreader fitting does not exactly fit the shape of the mast curve, then packing or a specially made base may be necessary. So that even pressure is placed on the mast wall, it is imperative that the spreader fitting sits comfortably against the mast wall otherwise a hot spot will be created which may lead to failure when the spreader is under stress.

The spreader fitting may sometimes incorporate the tangs of the lower shrouds, and therefore the through bolt used to secure the tangs may also be used to hold the spreader fitting in place. Often a separate bolt is used which secures the base of the spreaders, but this is a question of individual design, and whether one bolt or two are used at this point, compression tubes will be necessary and through bolting with a split pin to prevent the nuts from becoming undone is essential with each through bolt. It is obviously preferable for one bolt to be used for both fittings, since the more holes drilled in the mast wall the weaker it becomes. Particularly is this the case in the vicinity of the spreaders where enormous pressure is placed on the mast wall due to the spreader being in compression when the mast is under load. Any weakness in the mast at this point may cause failure and subsequent loss of the mast.

A spreader fitting (top) separate from the lower shroud tangs. Its fit to the mast has to be made more precise than it is here. Through bolting is essential, as is a compression tube to prevent the mast wall collapsing under the inward pressure from the spreader.

The same applies to securing other fittings in this area, notably the stainless steel strap which distributes the tang and spreader load. More often than not this fitting is pop riveted in place, which, of course, requires a considerable number of holes to be drilled in the mast wall to accommodate the pop rivets. Wherever possible these holes should be staggered in zig-zag fashion across the mast wall to prevent a vertical or, in particular, a horizontal line of weakness in this area. Most mast failures come around the spreader area and often this is due to weakness created by too much drilling for too many fittings.

With the spreaders in place it is time to look at other load-spreading equipment. Most modern yachts of average size have only one set of spreaders but it is possible in larger craft, and also in craft designed for high performance racing, that another set of spreaders may be required or some similar load-spreading gear such as jumper struts be fitted in the upper regions of the mast. Such equipment can be fitted in much the same way as spreaders with the same care taken not to drill too many holes or create a band of weakness. Wherever fittings of any type are attached to the mast, but particularly where stress fittings are concerned, drilling should always be staggered as much as possible.

SHEAVE BOXES

Sheave boxes, sometimes termed exit boxes, are fittings which incorporate the sheaves over which halyards and other running rigging are carried. There are obviously a number at the top of the mast and a similar number at the bottom, although these may be staggered in terms of location. Exit boxes for all halyard sheaves at the top of the mast will almost certainly consist of metal sheaves mounted in a stainless steel mast cap unit. In the lower regions of the mast the exit boxes will be fitted with similar stainless steel units, but at this point in small and medium sized craft the wire halyard may have been spliced into a rope tail and therefore the sheaves are of plastic, nylon or some other synthetic material.

These exit boxes are purchased as a whole unit ready to drop into place and are almost inevitably internally mounted. This means that a square section of the mast wall matching the sheave unit must be cut out so that the entire exit box can be dropped into place. Care in

A small slot aperture is cut in the mast wall and the exit box, complete with sheaves, fitted into it. As a general rule pop riveting is sufficient to secure the box in place.

The location of exit boxes at the lower end of the mast is a matter of convenience and the location of halyard winches. Holes cut low in the extrusion create less weakness than those higher up.

measuring and cutting is important since, as with all apertures in the mast, the smaller it is made the less weakness it creates. In addition, a flush fit makes for a good firm fastening whereas a loose sheave unit rattling around in an over-size aperture in the mast will be hard to secure firmly in position. The unit is always mounted on a base plate which is pop riveted into place when the exit box has been fitted into the mast aperture.

The location of the exit boxes at the top of the mast must coincide with the direct lead of the halyards concerned to their respective sails. At the foot of the mast, however, convenience is more important and the location of the exit boxes can be adjusted to obtain a good lead from the halyards to their respective winches or, if the halyards are operated from the cockpit, then to the bullseyes or lead blocks leading aft to the cockpit.

The type of exit box must match the type of halyard both at the top and bottom of the mast; in choosing exit boxes, keep them as small as possible while still being compatible with the type of halyard in use. It is obviously wise, as with all fittings, to purchase the exit boxes and align them on the mast before cutting out the hole in the mast section. Some exit boxes are bolted in place and some are held in position with tap screws, but by far the most common method with the average size mast is pop riveting. If there is a possibility of corrosion occurring they may need insulating. Like any other aperture cut or drilled into the mast wall, holes for exit boxes should be staggered both along the length of the mast and also around its circumference so that no line of weakness is created in one specific area.

Some boat owners prefer halyards to lead down from an exit box some height above the deck to the winch in a direct line beneath it, while others prefer the exit boxes at the foot of the mast with the lead of the halyard up to the winch. This is a matter of personal preference, although obviously the lower the aperture the less likely it is to create structural weakness in the mast.

HALYARD WINCHES

Mast-mounted winches are fittings which come under considerable stress and therefore must be securely fastened into position. As a general rule they are mounted on specially constructed pads or bases which fit the curve of the mast wall. They must be bolted into position since pop rivets or tap screws are insufficiently strong to hold the winch in position when under load.

A common type of mounting pad for mast winches. They may be through bolted or tap bolted into the mast wall. The location will be determined by the lead of the halyards. This pad is temporarily secured in place.

Some riggers mount mast winches diametrically opposite one another, with internal spacers and through-bolts from one winch to the other.

The location of each halyard winch will be such that it offers a fair lead to the halyard fall and is at a convenient working height for the crew. On cruisers under 30 ft most halyards are pre-stretched Terylene (Dacron), and may be rove internally and brought out via an exit box at the foot of the mast. But sheaves tend to cripple a wire halyard, and so there is normally one of large diameter at the masthead with the fall taken externally straight to the winch, often with a spliced rope tail for easier handling.

The winch for a wire halyard may have a housing to control the fall, possibly a brake, and all have less gearing than for a sheet. Most winches are stainless steel and should be mounted either on a cast aluminium base or on a pad of some insulating material. The fastenings must always be stainless steel bolts, which may require some juggling to fit the nuts on inside the mast. A long arm or a little ingenuity will usually resolve this problem and that of fitting compression tubes. The latter may require the use of a long line—a halyard if fitted—running inside the mast from top to bottom. The compression tube is knotted into the centre of this line and pulled through until in the approximate position of the bolt it is to carry. Then the juggling begins, twisting the line and pulling it back and forth until it is in position to receive the bolt.

If through bolts are not used, the mast wall can be drilled and threaded to take tap bolts. These are not as secure a fastening as through bolts and should only be used where through bolting is impossible and where the mast wall is thick enough to enable a good thread to be cut.

GOOSENECK

Many sails are provided with a tack downhaul for which a gooseneck must be fitted with a slide. This is often an extension of the existing luff groove in the mast extrusion, or it may be a small separate piece of track bolted or riveted to the mast. A sliding gooseneck is also useful when putting in a reef, and indeed, while the choice of fitting will be dictated by the mast and boom sections, it is well to consider at this stage what type of reefing will be employed and how the gooseneck fittings will be adapted accordingly.

Today's reefing gear is normally one of three types—through-mast roller, worm gear roller, slab and/or points.

Many find the through-mast arrangement the most convenient, where the crew may ease the halyard with one hand while simply winding down the sail with the other. But the necessary fitting is perhaps the most expensive, and must be incorporated as an integral part of the mast/boom assembly.

On older craft open worm gears may still be seen, splendidly cast from bronze or gunmetal, but today's gear is normally a neat enclosed fitting manufactured from stainless steel. It fits tidily between the boom and the gooseneck hinge, as an integral part of the fitting, and no special modifications are necessary to the mast.

The snag with both types of roller reefing is the sail shape that results from rolling the heavy luff rope around the boom, and to counter this there has been a return to modified forms of traditional points reefing. Here sections, or slabs, of the sail are lowered and secured to the boom, for which the sail is fitted with the necessary leech and luff cringles and the boom

The winch will probably need to be dismantled in order to fit onto the mounting pad. Care must be taken to ensure that all metals, including fastenings, are compatible.

Since the gooseneck can exert considerable pressure on the mast wall, the load must be well spread. Here the base of the fitting carries the load out around the mast circumference. Where adjustable goosenecks are fitted the track acts as a load-spreading pad.

with the requisite fittings. On many sails reef points or lacings are added to secure the foot, but on racing craft the boom often has a clew outhaul which provides sufficient tension in the foot for the points to be dispensed with. At the tack there may also be a downhaul, but a more common arrangement is simply a hook: a luff reef cringle is placed over the hook, and then the halyard made up tight.

While these considerations will affect the choice of gooseneck fitting, they are catered for by a wide range of proprietary equipment. The location of the gooseneck will clearly be governed by the overall design of the rig, and the fitting is normally riveted to a metal mast.

The selection of boom fittings will vary according to the type of boat and work she is to do. Light fittings can be pop riveted; those under load must be bolted.

BOOM

The boom is a strut which controls the shape of the foot of the mainsail and forms a mounting for the sheeting arrangements to control the sail. And as described in the previous section, it may have a number of fittings for trimming and reefing.

On the great majority of modern craft the foot of the sail is made with a boltrope which is housed in a channel formed in the top of the boom extrusion.

In a cruising boat the aim is normally simplicity, and where roller reefing is employed the mainsheet is usually taken from a fitting made for the job, at the boom end. The ability to rig the mainsheet more conveniently with respect to the cockpit is not possible with a roller reefed sail unless a boom claw is employed to encompass the reef. A claw is rarely favoured for cruising. Other cruising fittings may include a clew outhaul with its cleats and sheave, plus an anchorage for a kicking strap (vang). With a roller reefed sail the latter will be removed and there are quick-release fittings which enable this to be done simply at sea. Riveting is normally sufficiently strong to fasten the few fittings the boom will need,, and where the load is generally in shear. But except on small craft, this will not be strong enough for the heavy loads placed on the mainsheet, an argument in favour of the fitting at the boom end. Where a mainsheet is rigged mid-way along a boom, either in terms of the cockpit or to more effectively control the sail, the boom may have an extruded channel

to securely accommodate a sliding fitting, or alternatively the fitting is provided with a broad strap which may be strongly riveted to the boom.

The latter is more often to be found aboard racing craft, where with an outhaul and stronger arrangements at the kicking strap, there will also be the necessary fittings for efficient slab reefing. The sail will have requisite cringles in the luff and leech, and coupled with the hooks at the gooseneck previously mentioned will either be reef pendants or permanently rove downhauls at the leech. One needs to get a good purchase on the leech downhaul, and so it is normally run through a sheave to a decent size cleat on the boom, sometimes via a small winch. Double sheaves accommodate the pendants for two reefs. In addition there may also be a luff downhaul. A small tackle is usually employed there, hauling on an eye riveted to the boom, or where the gooseneck is in a slide, hauling the boom down to the deck.

TANGS

Tangs are often incorporated with other fittings, such as spreaders and mast caps. They are heavily stressed points and are therefore through bolted with a compression tube to prevent the mast wall being drawn inwards. There are a number of different types of tangs, some which eliminate the through bolting and depend more on a plate secured to the mast wall. Even this type of fitting must be bolted rather than pop riveted or tap screwed, since the purpose of the tang is to

Tangs may be incorporated with spreader or other fittings, particularly on small yachts. Most require sleeving in order to avoid damage to the mast wall.

transmit the load on the mast to the shroud or stay and it thus comes under heavier stresses than most other mast fittings. By incorporating it with other fittings such as spreaders or mast cap, the load is spread over an even greater area of the mast wall.

OTHER FITTINGS

Depending on the type and size of yacht, the mast may carry a number of other fittings, the most common being spinnaker halyards, topping lifts, inner forestay fittings, runner tangs, etc. Most of these are similar to the fittings mentioned earlier, and the same principles of fitting apply.

Their location will be marked on the sail or rigging plan, and the method of fastening will be indicated by the base plate on which the fitting is mounted. Where the fitting comes under stress, and in particular on large section masts, through bolting is preferable, but for most other purposes pop riveting is satisfactory.

ELECTRIC WIRING

With yachting moving into the electronic age, masts nowadays support the terminals for many instruments as well as navigation lights. As a result, the mast contains, in addition to its internal halyards, topping lifts and other running rigging, a great deal of electric wiring. While it would be ideal to hook all these antennae and lights in to one major circuit running down the

mast, each instrument unfortunately requires its own separate circuit—which means a lot of individual wires running to a lot of individual terminals at various points around the top of the mast. It follows, then, that the best time to fit all this wiring is before the mast is erected.

There is little point in dealing at length with each individual instrument or type of navigation light here, since they are many and varied. Suffice it to say that each is a relatively light fitting and can usually be pop riveted or tap bolted into its required position. The wiring, however, can create problems—if it is left to flap around inside the mast it will almost certainly become entangled with the various items of internal running rigging and become damaged or broken.

There are a number of different ways of securing this wiring, but it needs more than just securing if damage is to be avoided—it needs protection. One of the most satisfactory methods of achieving this is to secure inside the mast a length of plastic conduit tube into which all wiring is run. The conduit can be secured by occasional pop rivets along the length of the mast and the wires fed into it.

Since a long length of wiring is involved, voltage loss due to resistance may be experienced, particularly in the case of navigation lights. For this reason, the wiring should be of heavy gauge as described for internal wiring on page 199. The conduit used should be heavy duty to resist the likelihood of chafe damage from wire running rigging and should be steered around any through fastening that may fall in its path on the way up the mast.

At the foot of the mast the conduit can be brought out through a small cut hole in the mast wall and carried down through the deck without break, thus making a good watertight protection

Heavy gauge cable is required to avoid voltage drop in mast wiring. It must be secured inside the mast—preferably inside conduit—to prevent it fouling internal halyards and bolts.

for the wiring. It may be possible in some cases to continue the conduit down through the mast step, rather than bringing it outside the mast, but this will depend on the individual tabernacle. Whatever the system used, it is good procedure to continue the conduit right into the cabin through a watertight seal; this will also protect it from damage on deck. At the top of the mast the individual wires may be run out to their individual instruments or lights and where a light is fitted at a point somewhere along the mast length, a small hole must be drilled through both mast and conduit to run the wiring out.

STANDING RIGGING

Most standing or fixed rigging uses steel wire rope, commonly stainless steel or galvanised 'plough' steel. Synthetic or fibre ropes are rarely used and rod rigging is restricted mostly to large, high performance racing craft.

The choice between stainless steel and galvanised steel wire will depend on personal choice and the use to which the boat is to be put. Because of its greater strength/diameter ratio, the stainless steel rigging wire is thinner than galvanised steel and therefore creates less wind resistance. Racing boats invariably use stainless steel wire for standing rigging, and sometimes flexible stainless steel wire for running rigging. But stainless steel wire is more expensive than galvanised, and the reduced wind resistance is not significant except in racing. Also, stainless does work-harden over a period of time, which can lead to failure of wire or fittings. On the negative side, galvanised wire tends to chafe as time goes by, damaging the galvanised coating and creating rust spots which not only shorten the life of the wire but also make unsightly marks on any sails which come into contact with it.

The most important factor is probably cost, although when galvanised wire's shorter life span is taken into consideration, the initial saving in cost may be false economy. It would be safe to say that stainless steel wire is much more widely used than galvanised steel wire in modern yachts for a number of these reasons, although the basic fact remains that there is absolutely nothing wrong with galvanised steel wire as a rigging material.

Both stainless and galvanised wire come in non-flexible and flexible forms; the latter is used for certain parts of the running rigging where high strength and no stretch are essential, such as on spinnaker guys on racing yachts, or for headsail and perhaps mainsail halyards. Handling wire is somewhat tricky, and winches and blocks must be properly designed for it. Sheaves which are too small or not set in suitable boxes, poor leads, or chafe can also damage wire, which is costly to replace and splice.

The diameter of the wire used for the standing rigging will probably be specified by the boat's designer, and as a general guide no single wire should have breaking strain less than the all-up weight of the boat. Galvanised plough steel wire has a breaking strain some 15% less than its stainless steel equivalent, but in general it is more ductile. The type of lay employed will largely depend on the choice of terminal fittings.

There are four main types of terminal in use today: Talurit, Norseman, swaged and spliced. Hand-made splices and Norseman terminals have the advantage that they can be made up on the boat with the mast already stepped, while the others require a machine and therefore accurate pre-measurement. This is often done by a trial stepping of the mast, where everything can be offered up, and then taken ashore to the machine. The alternative is an accurate plan of the rigging from which it can be measured and made up beforehand, but such plans, for new or already rigged boats seldom match the true dimensions exactly.

Where any of the machine-made end fittings are used, the construction of the wire will normally be 1 x 19, but if a handmade end is preferred 7 x 7 will be needed in order to make the splices.

Setting up the mast is a tedious but important job. If the mast is out of plumb the performance of the boat will be affected.

Both lays are available in stainless or galvanised. Norseman terminals grip the splayed end of the wire around an olive, and while they may be used with either of the above lays, care must be taken to ensure that this pressure does not cripple the wire. There is less likelihood of this with machine-made ends, but these *must* be of the correct size for the wire in use. Swaging is normally only offered by a specialised rigger, but numbers of waterside chandlers have Talurit machines.

The rigging screw, also known as the bottle-screw or turnbuckle, may be in stainless or galvanised steel, and while it will be sized in accordance with the above criterion it does no harm to err on the side of caution. The spade end should be connected by a shackle to the chainplate, and the forked end by a rigging link (toggle) to the shroud or stay. These fittings will obviously affect the completed length of the individual wire, and so must be taken into account when measuring up, as also the thimble in the made-up eye. Good practice requires that proper toggles are also used at the upper ends of the shrouds and stays, between the wire and the tangs or cap fitting. The use of these links permits each component of the rigging to move freely and take up a straight-line position under strain. Once set up, the rig will require little adjustment, and the freedom of movement of the components will place them in tension, for which they are designed, without any tendency to be bent. The long-term effects of vibration and fluctuating strain will be reduced, with longer life and less liability to failure through metal fatigue or work-hardening.

The two lower shrouds close to abeam of the mast should be cut to exactly equal lengths. The question of raising the mast will depend on its length and weight, for a crane or purchase may be needed for longer sections. When the mast is in place on the tabernacle, the two shrouds should be tuned to equal tension, thus setting the mast up exactly plumb in the thwartships plane. This can be checked by hanging a plumb bob from the top of the mast, when it should come to rest on the centreline of the boat providing, of course, that the boat has been levelled correctly.

The fore and back stays can be checked in much the same way, using the plumb bob again. When the mast is exactly vertical in all planes the plumb bob should rest exactly against the foot. The measurements for the rigging can now be

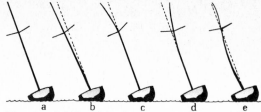

Mast bend induced by incorrect cutting or tuning of standing rigging shows up when the rig comes under load: a), *correct rigging;* b) *and* c), *acceptable distortion if moderate;* d) *and* e), *certain failure of the mast when under load.*

made and the terminals swaged into place, keeping the turnbuckles as open as possible to allow maximum take-up for stretch. This is only one of a number of ways of measuring rigging for a new mast, but for amateurs it may be the best since it is fairly straightforward and eliminates the sort of errors that can arise with other methods. At least with the mast in position and secured you will be able to measure *exactly* the span of each individual stay. It is well worth the effort of stepping the mast to avoid having to recut rigging.

If the mast is to be painted it is wise to do a dummy run on the rigging beforehand—otherwise, the rigging process will scratch the new enamel on the mast making it necessary to touch up the paintwork when everything is in place. With all the rigging measured and the fittings located with temporary fastenings, the rough work has been done.

Initially the rigging should be tuned to a taut but not 'twanging' degree of tension with the mast plumb. Providing the turnbuckles have a reasonable amount of take-up in this condition, tuning and taking up any stretch will be a simple matter when required.

Setting up the rigging is an important part of fitting the mast and associated equipment. While the basic purpose of the shrouds and stays is to hold the mast in position, this position must be maintained not only when the boat is stationary, but also when the gear is under load. A mast which is nicely plumbed when the boat is sitting at the wharf may become grossly distorted and suffer compression failure when the load comes on the sails while sailing. Setting up the rigging correctly can avoid this to a great extent. Initially, as described above, the mast is plumbed vertical and the rigging set up to a moderate degree of tautness. The shape of the mast when

Above and below: *ratlines are easily secured to the lower shrouds and make work aloft easier.*

Shrouds must be secured where they pass over spreader ends to prevent them coming adrift when slack on the leeward side. They must also be capped to prevent chafe damage to large headsails.

the load comes on it will depend partly on the rigging and partly on the thickness of the mast section. A solid, heavy spar will often hold straight no matter how it is rigged. A lightweight mast, by contrast, will bend to a certain degree even if the rigging is set up correctly. The important thing is to ensure that this bend is controlled and is in the direction required.

RUNNING RIGGING

There is little effort involved in fitting running rigging. Since the fittings will all be in place, the sizes of the various halyards, sheets and other ropes can be measured to match and then cut to required lengths. Most running rigging consists of flexible wire and synthetic fibre ropes and these must, of course, match the fittings over which they run, or to which they will be attached. It is pointless, for example, running a wire halyard over a plastic sheave designed for fibre ropes—the sheave will be cut to pieces in no time.

Halyards leaving the mast must be led through blocks and deadeyes located to offer as smooth a run on the rope as possible.

At all points on the mast and spars where running rigging is fitted, a smooth flow of rope must be ensured by selecting the right rope for the fittings and obtaining as direct a lead as possible between sheaves and winches or cleats. Chafe or similar damage to rope and wire always comes about where sharp corners occur or where the fittings do not match the size and type of rope used. Halyards which do not lead directly to winches and cleats which are at the wrong angle to the rope they hold will cause stress on the fitting and damage to the rope before the boat

197

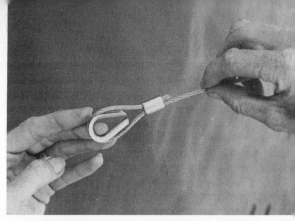

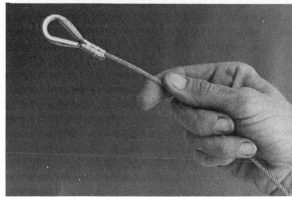

Combined wire and rope halyards are common in small craft.

The simplest form of eye swage can easily be done aboard. The metal collar must be matched to the wire or corrosion will quickly cause deterioration. A pressure tool clamps the collar in place.

has had much active use. These are only two examples of many cases that occur in running rigging, and care during fitting out will avoid these problems.

RIGGING TERMINALS

There are a number of different ways in which the end of a piece of rigging wire can be formed into an eye or some patent fitting which secures to the terminal at the tang or chain plate. The most basic eye is formed by bulldog clamps, but this is unsightly, cumbersome and unsafe. Some form of splicing or permanent method of creating an eye is necessary if the standing rigging is to be trouble-free.

Eye splices in wire rope are uncommon nowadays, most eyes being made by machine. The splice is effective, but difficult to make in 1 x 19 stainless steel wire, and in addition, loses about 25 per cent of its strength in the splice. The most common and certainly the easiest system is the Talurit swage which is formed by pressing a metal collar around the wire under pressure.

Usually a simple press tool—not unlike a pair of bolt cutters—is used to compress the collar or sleeve around the two wires which form the eye. Care must be taken to ensure that matching metals are used or corrosion will take place between the sleeve and the wire.

Another method is to make a 'hot' socket swage. This involves using a special fitting into which the rigging wire is fitted, then molten zinc poured in to make a very strong fitting. This system is usually restricted to galvanised steel wire because electrolytic action is set up with stainless steel wire. Other methods involve the use of fairly expensive machines and in this case careful measuring of the wire is essential with allowance made for the length taken up in the fitting.

Eyes formed in wire rope should always be fitted with a thimble to ensure an even curve and prevent the eye collapsing under pressure. A little practice will make perfect, as always, and fitting a terminal eye to standing rigging is just one fitting-out job which will soon show good results after a few practice runs.

CHAPTER 9

Wiring, Plumbing and Finishing

WIRING

Electric circuits

MODERN YACHTS OFTEN HAVE quite complex electrical circuits. Apart from lighting and such everyday services as water supply and fan ventilation, electricity is used for a wide range of navigational equipment, refrigerators, communication systems, alarm units and so on. Indeed, motor yachts in the luxury class often have as many electrical outlets as a modern home and power a similar dazzling array of electronic equipment, including stereophonic sound and television.

Although the average family-sized yacht rarely goes to this extreme, nevertheless the electrical circuit is still called on to supply a number of outlets which are important to both the safety and the comfort of the boat. Recent years have seen developments in the field of navigation lights—to quote one relatively small area—so that you can now light up your craft like a Christmas tree with legitimate lights—and would be well advised to do so in any crowded waterway. This is a far cry from the old low-powered port and starboard lights that were once the sole drain on the boat's battery during night sailing.

Radios, RDF and depth sounders are common electronic equipment on all offshore craft, and many yachts carry involved sailing instruments for wind and speed indication. Add to this the interior lights and services which provide the comfort in the boat and even in a modest-sized craft you have a fairly extensive circuit with a great number of outlets. Fitting such a circuit into the boat would at first appear mind-boggling to the average amateur, but providing you follow a few basic rules, it is a relatively easy task which should not daunt even the most un-electronically minded boat owner.

Batteries

The way in which to select and install a battery to suit the intended circuit is described on page 202. A simple mathematical addition of the require-ments of the lights and instruments to be installed indicates the battery or batteries required and their capacity. It is always wise to install two separate power sources in case of mishap, and each should be capable of supplying full power to the circuit.

Wiring

The first and perhaps most important factor in boat circuitry is the size and capacity of the wiring. Because of the low voltage, a large gauge copper wire must be used to reduce voltage drop to a minimum. The size of the cable can be found by calculating the number of amps it will be required to carry. Thus the wire at the end of the circuit feeding a 2-amp light, for example, need only be of 2 amp capacity, whereas the main cable from the batteries to the switchboard which may, at capacity, be required to carry 80 or 90 amps should be of at least that capacity. To avoid confusion and offer an average figure as a guide, most small craft would probably get away with two sizes of cables—a 50 amp or greater between the batteries and the switchboard and something around 20 amp cable for the wiring from the switchbox to the outlets throughout the boat. This is only a guide, however, and you should work on your individual requirements, albeit keeping the cables to two sizes to make purchasing easier.

While it follows that the heavier gauge cable used the less the voltage drop in the circuit, costs

Wiring should be run through a conduit where possible with junction points fitted where required. All wiring must be in place before liners or locker facings are fitted.

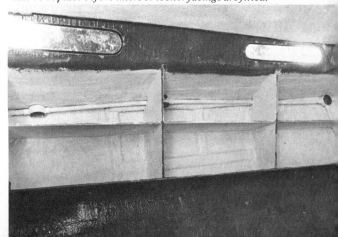

can rise astronomically if you start using very heavy gauge cable. In addition, really heavy cable becomes hard to install as it will not bend easily and if you are fitting it through conduit it will take up most of the space in the conduit, leaving little room for other cables. So careful selection of the gauge of the wire is called for, and at this point a second important factor must be considered—the type of wire. Solid core cable must never be used since it will work-harden and break as a result of vibration or movement when the boat is in use. Stranded copper wire is the best, and it should be double-insulated along its entire length. If you are fitting through conduit you may get away with single insulation, but in steel boats in particular, and preferably in all craft, the cable should be double insulated.

Switches

Every circuit should have a master switch, generally termed an isolating switch, in the cable joining the battery to the switchboard. This cuts off power to the entire boat circuit—an important factor when the boat is left for any length of time, as a minor short could drain the batteries (and ruin them) in no time. There are patent switches available but it is hard to beat the old-fashioned 'knife' switch for complete security.

Each individual circuit must have a switch so that it can be isolated and operated independently of any other circuit. These switches must be of D.C. pattern (fast make and break). The number of circuits in your boat will be an individual choice since some boat owners prefer to have individual circuits for small numbers of outlets while others put, say, most lights on the one switch.

Switches and fuses should be located conveniently at hand (lower left).

As a general rule, each circuit should cover an individual system. For example, the circuit for the radio should be independent of other circuits and thus you have one circuit for one outlet, while the cabin lights may all be hooked into the one circuit and you will have half a dozen outlets operating through the one switch. Then again you may decide to break down the circuits for each cabin so that the lights for the forward cabin, bathroom and main saloon are on independent circuits. The power drain will have some importance in deciding the number of outlets per circuit since you will not want to overload the capacity of the wire, but generally convenience is as much a guide as any as to how many and which circuits are wired independently.

Fuses

Each circuit must have at least one fuse. Timber and fibreglass yachts will usually require only one fuse in the positive side of the circuit, but steel and sometimes ferro-cement craft will require a fuse in both the positive and negative sides of the circuit. This is because the hull can act as a conductor in the event of a failure in the cable insulation, thus shorting out the entire circuit.

As a general rule, the fuse is connected directly to the main supply cable (positive) before the circuit switch. Since fuses vary in design and capacity from place to place it would be best to ask your local auto-electrician or someone else familiar with low voltage systems about the most efficient type of fuse for your purpose. Some local authorities also specify standards for this equipment, so to deal with it on a general basis here might be misleading.

Connection box

While the positive side of the circuit is led into the switchboard, it is generally common practice to lead the negative cable direct from the isolating or master switch to a connection box. This is merely a junction box with input of one heavy duty cable and output for a number of lighter gauge cables, each of which provides the negative end of each individual circuit. Since boat circuits cannot be earthed through the hull, all wiring is dual (both positive and negative) with the positive side going through the switchboard and fuses, the negative side via the connection box. Both wires are then run out into the boat to form each individual circuit.

A well laid out switchboard showing each switch with its associated fuse. Dividing up the circuits so that each has its own switch and fuse makes trouble shooting—and fixing—easy.

Switchboard

Because a number of separate circuits are involved, the tidiest way to fit the electrical system is to draw everything together at a switchboard. Here the fuses and circuit switches are neatly placed in order and labelled for quick reference. As a general rule the board is incorporated in a neatly finished box or cabinet that enhances the decor of the cabin with one side hinged so that it can be opened for ease of access. Behind the door the fuses, switch wiring, connection box and perhaps even the master isolating switch are grouped, nicely concealed from view, but readily accessible in the event of a blown fuse or for other repair work.

The number and type of fittings on the switchboard is obviously an individual preference, since some boat owners may like all their electrics stowed away here, with ammeters indicating battery charging and other parts of the motor electrics incorporated. Others like only the neat row of switches, with or without the fuses in sight, set into an attractive teak fascia, to complement the rest of the cabin furnishings.

Circuits

When the positive wire on the switchboard leaves its circuit switch it joins the negative wire from

the connection box and sets off on its journey around the cabin to its outlet or outlets. Where there is only one outlet the connection is simply a matter of joining the positive and negative wires to their respective terminals at the instrument. Where the circuit involves more than one outlet, then each item must be connected up in parallel.

To the uninitiated this is best explained as follows. The positive and negative wires travel the length of the circuit unbroken, but at each outlet they are both tapped and a positive and negative wire led from the main cable to the terminals of the instrument or light. Probably the cabin lights offer the best illustration of this. The circuit for the lights will travel around the cabin unbroken and will be tapped by leads to the terminals of each light. Since most lights have individual switches as part of their design, the positive lead is always connected to the switch and the negative to the bulb terminal.

Circuit diagram

The circuit diagram illustrated is a simple circuit for an average family-sized boat with a number of instruments as well as light circuits. It is not intended to be anything but a basic guide, and you will need to adjust it to suit your own craft before commencing the wiring procedure. Using this diagram as a guide, then, a rundown on the

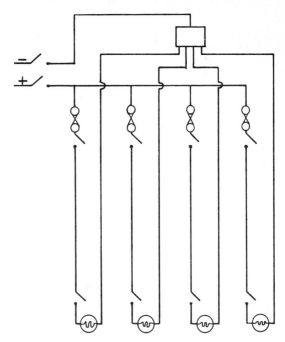

A typical circuit layout for a 12-volt boat system.

procedure for wiring the boat circuits would be as follows:

1 Connect the positive cable from the isolating switch to the first of the circuit fuses on the switchboard. Continue this lead, connecting each fuse until all are hooked up.

2 Connect the negative cable from the isolating switch to the connection box.

3 From the connection box lead off the required number of negative leads (smaller gauge cable) for the circuits.

4 From the fuse connect a wire (positive) to the circuit switch on each circuit. Lead a similar wire from the other terminal of each switch for the circuits.

5 Draw together a positive wire from each switch on the switchboard and a negative wire from the connection box and lead them off to their respective circuit.

6 Connect the battery to the isolating switch (both positive and negative) with heavy duty cable.

Batteries

There is not much point in fitting a flamboyant system of lights, fans, radios and so on unless you provide the power to operate them. Unlike the system at home, where you can just keep on adding items as long as there are plug outlets to feed them, the electrical system of a boat is dependent on one source—its batteries. Unless the batteries can cope with the power drain of the electrical fittings they will quickly lose power and probably suffer damage at the same time.

So it is important before hooking up an electrical circuit to work out how much power you are going to need. There is no reason to limit your luxury or labour-saving items as long as you provide sufficient power, both in terms of battery capacity (number and size) and the generator to run them directly, charge the batteries, or both. This may be on the main engine or separately powered, and the amount and duration of electrical demand has to be balanced by the output and running time of the generator, and the battery storage capacity, in designing the system. Realistic estimates of power use and priorities, and of people's tolerance to generator noise, are needed.

The best way to approach this is to draw up the total electrical power your circuit will require by adding the total wattage of all equipment. This is the power required to operate the circuit. The flow of current from a battery on the other hand is termed 'amperes' and each battery has a life of a certain number of ampere hours. That is to say it will discharge at a steady rate of so many amps for so many hours.

There is a basic method of converting watts into amps simply by dividing the watts by the voltage of the battery. Since most boat battery systems are 12 volt, this would mean dividing the total wattage by 12 to arrive at the amps. This figure then divided into the ampere hours of the battery will indicate the number of hours the battery will power that circuit.

Let's take an example: we work up the total wattage of our fittings as follows:

Navigation lights	(5 @ 10W) =	50W
Deck lights	(2 @ 10W) =	20W
Interior lights	(6 @ 20W) =	120W
Water & bilge pumps	(3 @ 40W) =	120W
Radio	(1 @ 60W) =	60W
	Total load =	370W

Converted to amps (370W ÷ 12V) = 30.83 amps
Assuming we have a 250 amp/hour battery, then the battery would service the circuit (with all units in use) for (250 ÷ 30.83) about 8 hours. Since it would be very unlikely that all fittings would be in use at the same time for the full

As important as the power supply is the means of recharging the batteries. The motor instrument panel should be well equipped to indicate the charging rate on each bank of batteries. A hydrometer should be used to indicate the state of charge of the battery.

Outlets must be planned well in advance and fitted in the circuit before the furniture or liners close them in. Wiring should always be kept high up the boat's side.

period, we might expect 12 hours reasonable running time from this battery. This allows a little in hand for other uses, but means that the battery must be recharged every 12 hours while in use.

Wiring

Using incorrect or insufficient wiring can lead to all kinds of problems, some of a very dangerous nature. One of the best ways to explain the basic principles of wiring is to liken it to plumbing. Assume we have a plastic hose through which we are running a flow of water. Providing the pressure of the water meets the capacity of the hose all will be well, but if excessive pressure is applied, then the hose will probably burst.

So with an electrical cable. If it is of a size that can carry the current adequately all will be normal, but when the pressure of electricity builds up to the point where the cable cannot cope with it, the excess pressure will cause failure and although it will not burst like the hose, it will probably overheat and start a fire.

The cable or wiring must therefore be big enough to carry the load and this can only be determined by consulting a table of standards set down by an electricity authority. Suffice it to say, from our example of the water pipe, that wiring should be of large diameter for preference and constructed to meet the requirements of the authorities mentioned above. The insulation and sheathing should also be of a type suitable for marine use, a common type being PVC insulated cable sheathed with polychloroprene (PCP).

If electric wiring is to be concealed it must be put in place fairly early in the fitting-out process. If a hood liner or any other form of lining is used, then the wiring should be behind it with outlets at the points where the light fittings or switches are to be located. This calls for a certain amount of planning and it is a wise procedure before commencing the wiring, or for that matter commencing any interior work, to draw up a wiring diagram to cover all the boat's electrics. Invariably, if this is not done, something is forgotten and when the interior of the boat is just about finished it has to be hacked about to insert more wires.

Bonding with a small GRP tack over the wire will secure it at intervals along any part of the hull, although it can also be secured to timber hulls by driving wiring clips into structural parts of the boat. A problem can arise where the wiring has to run across a series of beams or similar structural members, but providing it does not weaken the structural member a hole should be drilled so that the wire can be passed through and not have to loop round each individual beam. Passing the wire through a series of these holes will hold it in place without any further tacking. Steel and aluminium may be more difficult although fibreglass will take to the steel provided it is properly cleaned, but failing that, as may be the case with ferro-cement, parts of the boat's construction may need to be drilled and a fastening secured in place. Resin glass is a good insulator, so can be used liberally, even where joins in the wire are concerned.

It is good practice to keep the electric wiring high up, preferably behind hood liners or near the hull/deck join, as this reduces the risk from water which may be sloshing around in the bilges. Plastic conduit should be used and a number of wires fitted through the one conduit, and a junction box fitted at take-off points. Where wire is taken through decks or any other area open to the weather, it must be well waterproofed by use of resin or some type of sealant. Where it is unavoidably exposed to view in the cabin it can be covered with light timber trim.

Lights

There are two basic forms of lights used aboard boats—external and internal. The former are mostly concerned with navigation regulations and therefore are made to exact specifications in terms of screening and of output. Internal lights, by contrast, are of no specific construction, being both normal tungsten bulb and fluorescent and constructed in any design suitable to the layout and decor of the interior accommodation.

Navigation lights

In order to meet the regulations, navigation lights must be mounted in such a position and manner that the light they throw falls across a specified arc of the horizon and is screened so that it cannot be seen from elsewhere. In most cases, the navigation lights of motor yachts are mounted on the cabin, with the white steaming light elevated on a short mast, the regulation distance above the two sidelights. Smaller power craft may carry these three lights as a combined lantern, and sailing yachts may carry them on deck or at the masthead. Location and screening of these lights is of prime importance when fitting them and the screening will need to be adjusted to suit their location.

For example, some yachts mount their sidelights in the rigging, in which case specially constructed screens must be built around them to throw the light solely in the required direction. Similarly, specially constructed brackets may be necessary for the lights fitted to a sailing yacht's masthead. The only light common to all types of craft is the stern light which is attached onto or near the transom and, in terms of construction and screening, is similar in all types of power and sail craft, although in some larger boats the output may vary.

The regulations do not specify the exact height above water at which the navigation lights must be carried. What they do specify, apart from the angle of the horizon over which the light must show, is the relative height between the sidelights and the white steaming light, and in some circumstances the height above deck.

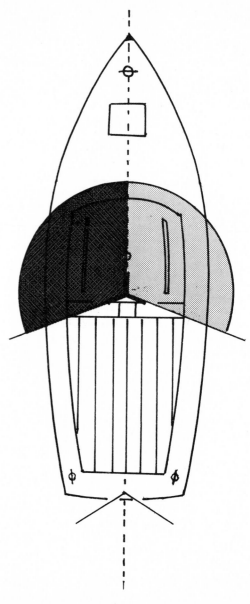

Navigation lights must be correctly designed and totally waterproof if they are to operate over the required range and arc through all weathers.

Illustrating the 112·5° arc of each sidelight, and the 135° arc of the sternlight.

In recent years there has been increased emphasis on requiring yachts, whether power or sail, to comply with the relevant Rules in the International Regulations for the Prevention of Collisions at Sea (1972), although in local waters of some countries variations are permitted or local rules apply. Before planning the navigation lights for your boat, it would be well to ascertain the requirements for the waters in which you will be sailing. The following basic definitions, from the Collision Regulations, should be learned as a first step.

Masthead light or *steaming light:* a white light placed over the fore and aft centreline of the vessel showing an unbroken light over an arc of the horizon of 225° and so fixed as to show the light from right ahead to 22·5° abaft the beam on either side.

Sidelights: a green light on the starboard side and a red light on the port side each showing an unbroken light over an arc of the horizon of 112·5° and so fixed as to show the light from right ahead to 22·5° abaft the beam on its respective side. In a vessel of less than 20 metres in length the sidelights may be combined in one lantern carried on the fore and aft centreline.

Sternlight: a white light placed as nearly as practicable at the stern showing an unbroken light over an arc of the horizon of 135° and so fixed as to show the light 67·5° from right aft on each side of the vessel.

All-round light: a light showing an unbroken light over an arc of the horizon of 360°.

Flashing light: a light flashing at regular intervals at a frequency of 120 flashes or more per minute.

Vessel includes every description of water craft, including non-displacement craft and seaplanes, used or capable of being used as a means of transportation on the water.

Power-driven vessel: any vessel propelled by machinery.

Sailing vessel: any vessel under sail provided that propelling machinery, if fitted, is not being used.

Vessel engaged in fishing: any vessel fishing with nets, lines, trawls or other fishing apparatus which restrict manoeuvrability, but does not include a vessel with trolling lines or other fishing apparatus which do not restrict manoeuvrability.

Underway means that a vessel is not at anchor, or made fast to the shore or aground.

Length and *breadth* of a vessel means her length overall and greatest breadth.

Restricted visibility: any condition in which visibility is restricted by fog, mist, falling snow, heavy rain storms, sandstorms or any other similar causes.

The arc over which these lights must show is governed by regulation and must be very closely adhered to. As a general rule it is best to purchase the lanterns with the lights already mounted and screened to specification. Careful alignment with the boat's fore and aft centreline will be necessary to ensure that the screened arc is correctly located.

Unless the location of the boat's navigation lights are specified on the plan it obviously will require a little thought and planning before fitting them in position. Apart from meeting the regulations, the wiring between the switchboard and the lights should be concealed as it travels around the cabin and up the mast. As mentioned before, cabin wiring should be concealed behind liners and thus will need to be in place before the liner is fitted. Internal wiring of a mast also needs to be fitted in the early stages before the mast is erected. Where possible, the lights should be mounted fairly high up as they are difficult to see when fitted low on a small boat, particularly in a seaway. This applies more to sailing yachts than any other type of craft since, for example, a sidelight mounted well down on the hull will be virtually immersed when the boat is heeling to that side. It may also be partially covered by a big genoa headsail or similar sail whose foot carries low to the deck.

The ideal place for the lights of a sailing yacht is at the masthead where they can be seen clearly no matter how the boat is sailing. However, additional lights are required when the yacht is under power as the all round lantern at the masthead can be used only when under sail. These are the sort of factors which must be borne in mind when planning the location of the navigation lights to ensure that they can be clearly seen at all times and are not obstructed by any other part of the boat's superstructure or fittings. Once the location has been decided, and the lights correctly aligned for regulation screening, they can be hooked up to the wires pre-run from the switchboard. As with all deck openings, however small, the hole through which the wires are led must be well waterproofed and a special waterproof fitting or a heavy layer of sealant used to attain this. The normal navigation light units merely require screwing into place as there is little stress placed on them in use.

Decklights may be fitted to assist with night work, particularly changing sails on a sailing yacht. The most common place for these is on the underside of the spreaders, in which case the wiring is run internally up the mast and out into the spreader arms where the light fitting, which can be of any required design providing it is thoroughly waterproof, is fastened into place with pop rivets. It is important to ensure a good seal between the light fitting and the spreader surface or water will collect inside the light bowl and eventually damage it. The spreader lights and any other working lights carried on the boat should be hooked up separately to a fuse and switch on the switchboard, and where a number are carried it may be necessary to connect them to separate switches. Spotlights and floodlights, if fitted, are usually completely self-contained and sealed units and are merely bolted into place and hooked up to the circuit as for any other electric fitting.

Interior lights

The choice of interior lighting is completely personal. Apart from the choice between fluorescent and tungsten lighting, there are a myriad designs to select from. Providing the wiring is ready to hook up to the lights, fitting is a question of simply screwing the fittings in place and connecting the terminals. As described on page 203, the wiring should be concealed where possible, particularly in the main saloon, and should therefore be in place before any liners are fitted. The points at which lights are to be fitted must be pre-determined and wiring from the concealed circuit brought through into the cabin at these points. Some light fittings have their own switches, a good idea where power is at a premium. All lights, however, must go through a fuse and switch on the switchboard separate from other circuits such as instruments, navigation lights and decklights. Fluorescent lighting is hooked up in exactly the same way as tungsten lighting, the only difference being in the light fitting. However, special care must be taken with these lights to ensure correct polarity.

Concealed lighting can add good atmosphere to the interior of a main saloon, and one way of doing this is to insert the light fittings in the deckhead before the hood liner is fastened in place. The lights can be inserted between beams or in a specially made box, the outer face of which is fitted with opal glass to diffuse the light evenly. Timber trim around this glass finishes off an attractive recessed light fitting which costs next to nothing to install. Care must be taken in fitting the hood liner to ensure that the location of the holes cut to match the recessed lights are in the correct position or the whole hood liner will have to be removed again to make adjustments. As with so many fittings, use of a template can avoid this problem.

Interior lights can be recessed into the structural work of the deckhead or sides of the boat.

Small lights are often fitted at the mast head to illuminate burgees or wind-direction indicators.

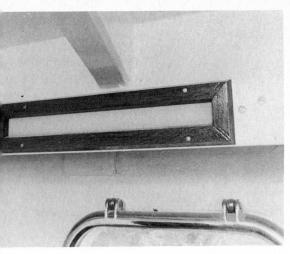

When the liner is fitted, ground or opal glass surrounded by timber trim, gives a neat finish to recessed lights.

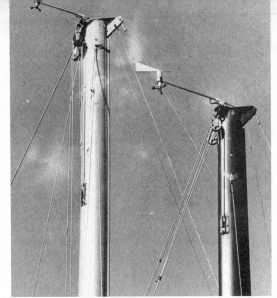

Wind instruments may be visual or electrically connected to dials in the cockpit. High-performance racing craft carry a complicated mass of antennae at the masthead.

There is little more that can be said about fitting interior lights since the choice is so wide and the fittings so different. Bear in mind, however, that the basic principle is the same in all cases—the wiring must be left pulled through any liner before it is fastened in place and the circuit passed through a fuse and switch on the switchboard. Since most boat circuits are 12 volt, small bulbs such as those in cars can be used, and some of the lights adapted for boat interiors. Such small lights fit in with the principle that sleeping and work areas (galley, chart table, engine) should be lit separately, and interior lights not dazzle cockpit crew. Bunk and chart table lights need to illuminate a limited area and be usable without disturbing sleepers or affecting night vision.

Instruments

The number and type of instruments fitted aboard a boat depend to a great extent on its size, its available power and the sort of work it will do when in use. A medium-sized sailing yacht, for example, may have no instruments at all since many purists believe that instruments are not necessary for sailing and if the boat is not to be used in coastal waters navigation instruments will not be necessary either. By contrast, a large motor cruiser will probably have a dashboard resembling the cockpit of a big jet with every instrument ranging from simple tachometers through to Omega or similar sophisticated navigational gear. Thus the fitting of instruments is a subject which could quite easily fill a whole book of similar size to this and can in no way be dealt with in depth here. Most instruments, in any case, come complete with specialised fitting instructions from the manufacturer and these will vary from the type of instrument to its location in the boat. An impeller-type log, for example, will require the hull to be punctured and the impeller fitted through the skin, while engine instruments may require nothing more than connecting up the terminals on the motor to the respective terminals on the dashboard instrument. Even fitting similar instruments can be approached in different ways, and the impeller log which requires a hole to be cut in the hull will obviously need different fitting to the trailed log which streams astern and requires no aperture in the hull, merely a bracket on which the recording part of the instrument can be mounted somewhere near the transom.

Like lights, instruments must be tapped into the main electrical circuit and hooked up via a fuse on the switchboard. This requires careful advance planning so that leads can be located through cabin liners in the correct location for instruments.

As a general rule, navigational instruments such as radios, depth sounders, RDF and similar instruments are located near the chart table or at least somewhere in the cabin where they have reasonable protection from the weather. A yacht's wind direction and speed instruments will most likely be located in the cockpit where

Motor and navigating instruments are vitally important to the safety of the boat and must be correctly installed for easy reading.

they are visible to the helmsman, while the engine instruments for a motor yacht will be located close to the steering and throttle controls. Where flybridges are concerned, a duplicate set of instruments will probably be run from the main instruments at the steering position, so that full control of the boat can be taken on the flybridge.

Most small craft instruments are designed to operate on a 12-volt power system and can therefore be hooked directly into the main boat circuit, taking care not to overload the circuit. Plan to obtain sufficient power from the batteries to operate all instruments, lights and other electrical equipment without running the batteries down too quickly. Small positive and negative leads can be left protruding through the liner when it is fitted in place, to provide a hook-up for any number of electrical instruments; if these are not used then the hole can be simply plugged with the wires behind it, thus offering easy access should you fit another instrument in this location at some future time. Outside antennae, which may be fitted to the top of the mast or at deck level or even under the waterline, will have special fitting instructions with them since, apart from through bolting, which is the most common general system in use, there are many patent methods of securing such equipment in place. Bear in mind most importantly the question of making the aperture in the deck—or wherever the antenna is fitted—waterproof.

PLUMBING

Piping

There are three principal types of piping used aboard small craft—copper, plastic and rubber. You should ensure that all piping, whether for fuels, liquid, gas, water or waste, complies with local statutes and trade and insurance standards, both for safety and to maintain the value of your boat. The materials and jointing methods must both suit normal use and in case of fire not burn, melt or come apart to release fuels or cause flooding and perhaps sink the boat.

Most piping carries fuel or water to service outlets which are scattered throughout the boat. Since tanks are generally low in the hull, a good place to conceal piping is beneath the cabin sole. This allows good access and catches leaks. So that it does not abrade or strain unions, all piping should be firmly fastened down and run clear of sole boards, shafts, ballast etc.

There is only one basic maxim to bear in mind when fitting pipes through the hull of a boat—keep them running in as straight a line as possible. Particularly is this the case with plastic hoses which kink easily when bent through too tight a curve. Slow curves should be easy to lay when the piping is laid through the bilge area as there is usually plenty of room underneath bunks and other interior furniture to allow wide sweeps.

Where piping is laid through the bilges, take-off pipes will run upwards to service outlets wherever they may occur. These pipes should be run up the hull alongside a frame or similar structural member if possible so that they can be

Some of the more useful types of piping for use on boats can be seen here. The large diameter rigid plastic pipe acts as a filler for the bottom tanks while reinforced plastic attached to copper pipes provide the take-offs. The corrugated piping in background is a ventilating duct.

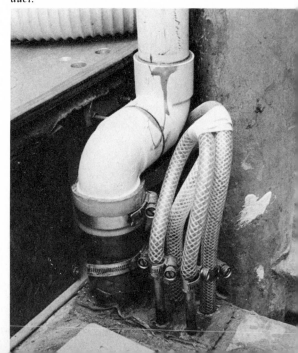

A combination of piping can be used with ring clips providing the fastening medium. Where reinforced plastic pipes are used, short lengths of copper must be fitted to provide rigidity where a stop cock or take-off pipe is connected.

Passing the piping through holes in interior furniture or floors beneath the cabin sole conceals it and holds it securely, yet allows easy access in the event of problems.

secured along their length. Pipes which are not secured slop around when the boat is moving in a seaway and cause leaks at joins or chafe against some nearby object which will eventually damage the pipe. T junction pipes are let into the main fore and aft pipe to fit take-off pipes. Stainless steel ring clips must be used at all pipe joins where plastic or rubber hoses are used.

Copper is widely used, but the tubing and unions can fracture from work-hardening, usually due to vibration. Special flexible, fire-resistant tubing for fuels (Armourflex) is available and also has a metal braid to maintain electrical bonding, essential in fuel systems as a safety measure. The bonding must be continuous through the unions.

All piping must be carefully secured at joins and connections to prevent leakage, but nowhere more so than when the pipe carries LP gas or petrol fuel. Both these substances are highly inflammable and a leak will cause fumes to gather in the bilges, creating a high risk of explosion. Where these types of fuel are piped through the bilges a sniffer alarm should be fitted to indicate any leakage.

Flexible pipes such as rubber and plastic must be kept away from moving parts and from heat. While chafe caused by rubbing against a moving part will soon damage these pipes, heat will destroy them even more quickly. It is important, as described in the section on fitting motors, to

take particular care with these pipes when they are in the proximity of the motor, since there are many areas here where the pipes can be damaged in this way.

Filler pipes leading from the deck to tanks should be of larger diameter and heavier material than those used for take-off from the tank. The deck opening should be on the gunwale outside the deck or cockpit, to drain overboard.

Filters and strainers

Almost all plumbing systems need some form of strainer or filter. The most obvious case is when seawater is pumped into the boat. Since there is always a certain amount of foreign matter or marine life in seawater, valves or pipes in the plumbing system can easily become blocked unless the water is strained when it is drawn through the skin fitting. There are two basic methods of straining water—a filter fitted internally to the plumbing system near the skin fitting, and a strainer placed over the intake hole on the outside of the hull.

By far and away the most common and the simplest to fit is the strainer on the outside of the hull. It has one big disadvantage, however, in that a clogged or blocked strainer is difficult to clean unless the boat is slipped or someone goes over the side. An internal filter, by contrast, is easily cleaned without getting even your feet wet. Nevertheless, filter systems have their own problems, so the best system is one which incorporates both the filter and the strainer.

209

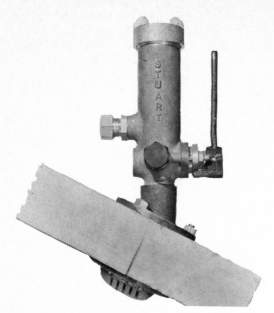

A typical skin fitting, combining exterior strainer with interior filter and stop cock, seen through the hull section.

The strainer may take a number of different shapes, the most common of which is that of an inverted colander or convex metal plate perforated with small holes. By keeping the curve of the fitting low, the flow of water around the hull skin is not disturbed excessively and thus speed is not affected.

These strainers are almost invariably fastened through the hull skin and in many cases are an integral part of the skin fitting. Securing them into position is a simple matter of screwing and bolting and using a sealant. The strainer will need to be anti-fouled to prevent growth attaching to it and clogging the perforations. It is as well to paint inside the fitting with anti-fouling composition as well, and with this in mind many strainers are equipped with easily removable covers.

The filter system on the inside of the skin fitting may take a number of different forms and there are a number of patent types. Each has its own method of attachment and fitting them is a question of following the manufacturer's instructions. Skin fittings are not always located in the most convenient position for a filter, particularly if access is difficult. In this case, they may be placed somewhere along the pipeline from the intake aperture, but this of course will depend on the design of the filter unit itself.

Good access is important since the filter will need to be changed or cleaned at regular intervals if it is to operate efficiently. So that there is no flooding when the intake pipe is opened for filter cleaning, the sea cock must be placed between the filter and the hull.

Strainer, skin fitting and filter, if they are an integral unit, can be easily fitted and hooked up to the piping inside the hull. If they are separate units, the skin fitting and strainer will need to be secured through the hull and sealed. The filter can often be fitted later.

Pressure water supply

As with the same fittings in a house, taps used on boats come in a variety of designs and shapes. Generally speaking the choice of tap is a personal one, although hand pumps do not offer much variety in terms of aesthetic appeal. Pressure fed taps can be as artistic as in any well-designed bathroom.

There is nothing complex involved in fitting a hand pump. The whole unit is screwed and glued or bolted to the sink and the supply pipe fitted to it and secured with a ring clamp. The water is pumped up by hand so there is no further fitting to be done. This is without doubt the simplest system and the one least prone to problems. However, it is not always the best system, particularly with showers and the like where a steady flow of water is required. Here an electrically operated pressure system is needed. Since most commercially produced pumps can cope with more than one tap it is not uncommon

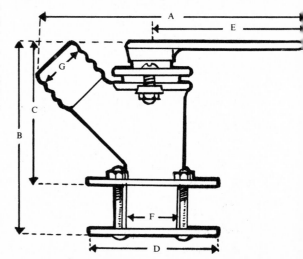

A typical filter stop cock used on skin fittings aboard small craft.

to have the entire bathroom—or for that matter the entire plumbing system in the boat—hooked up to the electric pressure supply.

The pump can be purchased as a unit and fitted beneath the sink or some other out-of-the-way spot, since these units are quite small and easy to fit. Manufacturer's instructions must be followed as the pump will only have a certain capacity depending on the power supply and its ability to raise water from tanks in the bottom of the boat. The length of piping and the number of outlets vary according to the power of the pump and the height the water has to be raised.

Pumps are made in a number of voltages but the most common is the 12 V range where a variety of outlets—say up to five or six—can be fitted providing the head (the distance and height the water has to be pumped) is not excessive. They are wired directly to the boat's power supply and are activated by turning on the tap. A pressure water system is ideal for a boat but it is also very expensive on water and fitting an electric system almost invariably means fitting bigger water tanks. The hand pump, which is all that is needed for galley and handbasin use, is far less wasteful and cannot be left running, though it has limited lifting capacity. Most sinks and basin units come complete with holes for fitting the tap and most tap units come with

Plumbing arrangements beneath a bathroom sink look complicated but are quite easily unravelled. The pressure water pump is fitted to a bracket in the centre, so is as easily accessible as the rest of the plumbing.

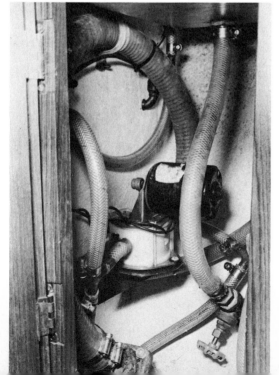

either bolting or threaded ring arrangements for securing in place. In the case of a built galley or bathroom unit it may be necessary to cut a hole in the top to allow access for the tap. This can be simply done using a keyhole or jig saw. Matching the diameter of the water supply pipe with that of the tap is the only requirement and ring clips (always stainless steel) are all that is needed to secure the pipe in place. When the tap is bolted or screwed into place it should be bedded firmly in a sealant to ensure that dripping water cannot seep into the unit below the sink.

Showers

As with most plumbing fittings, showers come ready-made in units and their installation is mostly a matter of selecting the right spot and connecting up according to manufacturer's instructions. However, there are a few more details involved with showers than with other equipment and these are worth looking at before placing the whole unit into position. Firstly, hand pumping is not a very satisfactory way of feeding a shower. In the close confines of a boat not only does one get spasmodic spurts of water but there is a strong tendency to bump elbows or catch fingers in swinging the pump lever back and forth at a rate fast enough to give a good supply. Pressure water from electric pumps is more suitable and just as easy to fit.

Space is a problem with showers as with many other fittings. Using a complete compartment for a shower that will be used probably only once a day is a waste of space, particularly on small craft where space is so limited. One widely used compromise is doubling the toilet area as a shower compartment. This is not as silly as it sounds for both units are only used spasmodically. The shower unit is fitted above the toilet, probably the best type being the 'personal' shower on the end of a flexible hose rather than the type which is permanently fixed to the deckhead or bulkhead. A fine rose is essential for water economy. A handhold placed to suit users of the toilet or shower will be useful.

When the toilet is in use the shower remains up on its clip. When it is required the toilet seat is closed and the shower switched on. The shower can be taken either standing in the toilet compartment, if headroom allows, or sitting on the closed toilet.

It is important to keep the toilet area uncluttered and sealed. Toilet paper and tissues,

A small float pump in the bilge area operates as water levels rise and provides an ideal discharge unit beneath the sole in the bathroom or shower area.

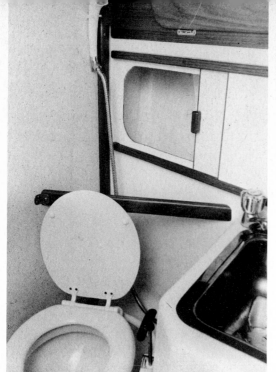

As bathroom space is always at a premium, careful use of space is essential. Here the toilet has a shower above and sink beside it. Note how lockers can be closed off to keep toiletries dry when shower is in use.

for example, will need to be placed in a cupboard or somewhere else where they will not get soaked, and the bulkheads and floor of the compartment will need to be lined or fibreglassed to make them waterproof. This is no great problem, however, and the result will enhance the appearance of the compartment. Laminex is the ultimate material, although if the compartment is big enough tiling is by no means out of the question and is often used to good effect on larger craft.

Draining away the shower water can create problems, particularly in small craft and even more particularly in motor yachts which have relatively shallow bilge areas. One of the most effective systems is to seal off the shower area with a thwartships lip across forward and after ends and a drainage hole in the lower corner of the tray thus formed. The shower water can be led off from this drainage point either directly into the bilge or to a tank from which it can later be pumped overboard. Water should only be drained into the bilge if it is then pumped overboard immediately since bathwater lying in the bilge areas tends to create unpleasant odours if it is left too long. An ideal arrangement is to fit an automatic bilge pump which discharges

immediately any water that makes its way into the bilge. A grating instead of the tray makes just as good a floor for the shower compartment but is rather more difficult to clean unless it is completely removable. In any case the floor beneath the grating will still need to be waterproofed and fitted with a strainer.

By using this system even small yachts can be fitted with showers without taking up any more space than that already occupied by the toilet. Indeed, the only addition to the toilet compartment is the shower head which is easily placed out of the way when not in use, particularly if it is of the portable variety.

Hot water systems

One of the most difficult service systems to fit in a boat is a hot water system. This is because the power source required for heating large volumes of water is difficult to obtain, and also storage of heated water means adding considerable tank capacity. With a 12-volt electrical system and limited storage capacity, small craft are hard put to fit an effective hot water system. Large motor yachts can often utilise the engine heat of their constantly running motors to provide hot water but this arrangement is virtually impossible in sailing yachts where only small auxiliary motors are fitted and used only infrequently.

The heat exchange method is quite widely used and can provide a very efficient hot water supply. Cold water is passed around or through the motor or a specially fitted heat exchanger which raises its temperature to the required degree. Since most equipment of this type is fairly specialised and follows no specific pattern, de-

Motor yachts of this size usually have twin motors providing an adequate supply of hot water through heat exchangers. If the motors are stopped for a lengthy period, an auxiliary system such as LPG must be employed.

A solar generating panel on the deck or cabin top offers a good potential power source, particularly in tropical waters.

pending to a great extent on individual design and the brand of motor used, the only way to fit such a hot water system is to follow the manufacturer's instructions. Some use fresh water, some salt, some tap off the cooling system of the motor, some have a separate heat exchanger. Whatever the basic method used, a large motor which is run consistently is essential if the supply of hot water is to be adequate.

There are a number of other systems for heating water, of which the most commonly used in small craft is the LP gas system. This works in much the same way as normal gas water heating systems onshore and can be obtained as both instant-heat or storage systems. The latter is not popular because of the lack of storage capacity on a small boat. The most successful system is instant-heat hot water in which the water is drawn through a gas 'furnace' which operates on the same tap that controls the water supply. The water is heated instantly so there is no wastage of gas, nor is there a need for storage other than for the supply of cold water which feeds into the heater.

Hot water systems of this type can be purchased under a number of brand names and once again, fitting them will depend on each individual manufacturer's instructions. A supply of LP gas and cold water will need to be piped to the heating unit and pressure supplied by an electric pump if one is not already fitted as part of the unit. This system is not only economical in terms of gas and water, but often provides hotter water than a storage system.

Electric heating systems are rarely successful unless the boat is provided with a high voltage system and a generator to produce the required amount of power. This is not the case with the usual 12-volt system fitted on medium and small craft and thus electric hot water systems can be discarded in all but large motor cruisers, and even then there are problems in terms of constant power supply. Because of the drain required by a water heating element, batteries are quickly flattened unless there is a back-up system whereby they are recharged immediately.

Solar heating has a potential as a cheap power source, but involves water storage which, as mentioned before, is not always convenient. Large capacity storage tanks not only take up a lot of room but influence the trim of the boat according to whether they are full or empty and there are sufficient problems with normal fresh water supply tanks in this regard without adding hot water storage. In addition, solar water heating systems usually require a back-up system activated by some other power source to compensate for times when the sun is not out and the solar unit not operating. Although it is possible that solar water heating units may become more sophisticated, it does not at this stage appear to be a suitable system to fit aboard small craft.

So the choice boils down to LP gas heating or heat transfer from large motors. Of these, small to medium craft and sailing yachts will invariably opt for the gas system since their small and relatively infrequently used motors do not provide sufficient heat.

FINISHING

Finishing work is of vital importance for two reasons—the appearance of the finished job and the protection of the materials used. Poor finishing can make an otherwise first class fitting-out job look amateurish, and this in turn can affect the value of the boat since there is a natural buyer resistance to anything that appears to be an amateur job. Even though this may apply only to the interior, a prospective buyer will see it as applying to the whole.

But outside the aesthetic appeal, finishing is vitally important to the protection of the timbers and metals used for fitting out. This is obviously more important above decks than below, but is nevertheless important in all areas, for interior furniture with a badly finished or deteriorated surface will not only look bad but require maintenance and even, ultimately, replacement if it deteriorates badly. Varnishes, paints and similar finishing materials are available and are easy to apply so there is no excuse for a poorly finished job. Skimping at this stage in the fitting-out work will result, like the proverbial ha'porth of tar, in the ruination of the boat. The best finishing materials and quality workmanship are as important at this stage as they are at any point in the fitting-out process.

Since there are many good books which deal with finishing work in great depth, I shall only describe here the principal materials and techniques used to finish fitting-out work, and then only as far as is required for the average fitting-out job. There are many finishing materials which I may not mention which may do the job as well as those described here. Modern developments in the synthetic paint and varnish field have produced an enormous range of high quality products and it is impossible to cover them all. Suffice it to say that providing you are sure of quality material, and are versed in the techniques of using such material, there is no reason why you should adhere closely to the finishing materials described here if you can achieve a similar or better result with other materials.

For the relative beginner, however, there is a lot to learn about finishing if the job is to have the aesthetic and practical features described above. Painting, for example, is not just a question of wielding a brush if the best quality finish is to be attained. And no matter how good a varnish, it will not produce that deep, magnificent timber

The finish can make or mar the fitting-out job. Professional-looking work not only adds to the appearance of the boat but increases her resale value.

glow unless great pains are taken with the preparation. A little knowledge may, proverbially, be a bad thing but in the case of finishing work it is better than no knowledge at all!

Paints and varnishes

Most finishing is done with paint or varnish. Particularly is this the case with timber, but it applies almost equally to steel and ferro-cement, while aluminium and fibreglass are sometimes left in their natural state, but also frequently coated with some protective material. Broadly speaking, paints and varnishes are available in two principal forms—oil-based and synthetic. The oil-based paints and varnishes are the traditional coatings used on boats for many decades, the synthetics have come in relatively recently and, like so many synthetic materials, made rapid inroads into the markets of the old traditional oil based coatings. This is no place to go into a discussion of which is best since both have advantages and disadvantages. However, like most modern materials, the synthetic paints and varnishes would appear to have the edge. Experience will prove that for the type of work described in this book a synthetic finish is preferable to an oil-based finish in nearly all cases, always providing, of course, that the synthetic is of high quality.

Preparation

Proper preparation of the surface plays a large part in the success of a finish. A poorly prepared surface will inevitably result in a poor finish, and in many cases no finish at all. Where a veneer or laminex is being laid, for example, a surface which is not correctly prepared may not take the glue which holds the laminate in place. Similarly with painting, an unclean surface can result in

Much of the interior timber will be varnished to retain the warm appearance of the grain. Fine wet and dry sandpaper is the best medium for preparing the surface.

the paint blistering off almost as soon as it is dry. Preparation means removing dirt, moisture, grease, rust, loose old paint, roughness and pits, by cleaning, filling and sanding. Then correct primers and undercoats are essential.

Quite apart from these obvious cases, it is essential to prepare any surface correctly to obtain a high quality finish, particularly with paint or varnish. It does not matter whether oil-based or synthetic finishes are used, if the surface preparation is poor then the finish will be poor.

Timber

Like all surfaces, timber must initially be free of any dirt, grease or moisture before paint, varnish or veneer is applied. Dirt can be removed by washing off with soapy water òr sandpapering, allowing time for the surface to dry before applying any coating. Grease can be removed with spirits, and moisture by drying out thoroughly. No coating will adhere satisfactorily to a damp surface so even if the painting has to be postponed for a day or two it is vitally important that the surface is clean. The area surrounding the surface should also be clean, and where an interior is being painted or varnished it should be vacuumed out thoroughly to make sure that no dust or sawdust from previous fitting out work is hovering around ready to settle on the newly painted surface.

New timber should be sanded with a fine sandpaper, wiped thoroughly clean with a damp rag and allowed to dry before the first coat of paint or varnish is applied. Old paintwork must be rubbed back thoroughly with wet-and-dry sandpaper, washed clean and allowed to dry.

Fibreglass

The same preparation applies to fibreglass as to new timber, although the final sanding need only be light in order to give the surface a key. Since an etch primer is used with fibreglass, the need for a hard rub-back at this stage is eliminated. However, the surface must be clean and a thorough wiping down with soapy water, or white spirit if grease is present, is important. If the surface has recently been removed from a mould the release agent must be totally wiped off—again white spirit is best for this.

Metals

New steel and aluminium need no preparation other than cleaning prior to a primer being applied. Corroded or rusted areas must be thoroughly sanded back to the bare metal and a rust inhibitor or anti-corrosive agent applied. Again, cleaning is very important.

Ferro-cement

Cleaning is more important than ever with ferro-cement hulls due to the absorbent quality of the surface. Sanding should not be necessary in terms of preparation unless there are ungainly protrusions in the plaster. When thoroughly cleaned the surface must be coated with a sealer before finishing work can commence.

Painting
Timber

The secret of successful painting with timber is the use of wet-and-dry sandpaper between each coat. With the surface prepared as described earlier, the first coat of primer is applied by brush. When thoroughly dry, the surface is rubbed back using a fine-grade wet-and-dry and building up a good slurry. When the slurry is washed off, any bare patches which are revealed should be patched up again with primer and also rubbed back when dry. The undercoat is then applied; one coat is seldom sufficient. However, follow manufacturer's instructions.

When thoroughly dried, the undercoat is rubbed back with wet-and-dry to a smooth surface. As the second undercoat is applied the process is repeated. Undercoat can be applied by brush or spray, the former probably being more practical.

The topcoats can be applied by brush or spray, but in this case spray painting offers far and away the best results providing it is done properly. It is an easy technique to master, but requires lots of practice to obtain a really top quality finish. The spray gun should be moved constantly backwards and forwards and the coating of paint kept as light as possible to avoid runs. The number of topcoats is not important, and the manufacturer's recommendations should be followed, but it is important, once again, to thoroughly rub back with wet-and-dry between each coat. Only by continuous hard rubbing will a firm, mirror-like finish be built up. As a general rule, no less than two topcoats should be applied, and more if using a spray in preference to a brush.

Fibreglass

After preparation of the surface as described earlier, GRP must be primed with a special etch primer. This creates a key on the shiny surface of the synthetic material, providing a base on which individual coats of paint can be built up. Generally speaking, synthetic paints such as polyurethane are preferred for painting fibreglass, but the principle of painting is the same as that for timber. After the etch primer, an undercoat is laid, preferably by brush, and rubbed back with wet-and-dry paper. Spray painting is sometimes best with polyurethane paint and the number of topcoats required will depend on the finish required as well as the manufacturer's recommendations. At least two or three coats will be necessary and, if the surface has not been painted before, more may be required to obtain a quality finish.

Metals

As with GRP, aluminium requires a special etch primer. With steel, particularly after treatment with anti-corrosive or rust inhibitor, a special

Preparation is as important in painting GRP as it is with any other material. The surface must be absolutely clean before application of any paint. Acetone is the best cleaning medium.

metal primer must be used. The old fashioned red lead is a poorer primer than many more modern paints, and very slow drying. Zinc chromate and the more modern synthetics will make the work faster while being just as effective.

On top of the primer, specially recommended undercoats can be used with a follow up of topcoats according to the manufacturer's recommendations. Apart from the primer, the build up of coats on metal is much the same as that of any other material and once again spray painting is always preferable to brush or roller painting.

Ferro-cement

Paint systems for ferrocement have received attention from paint companies, and there are special coatings for under and above water use such as epoxies and epoxy-tar compounds. It is well worth obtaining the technical information freely available from major paint manufacturers on traditional and newer paints, application and compatibility, for all materials —wood, metals, GRP or ferro.

Melamine plastics

Known in various parts of the world as Formica, Laminex or some other trade name, melamine plastics are widely used on boats as the ideal means of providing easily cleaned surfaces, particularly in areas such as bathroom, galley and tabletops. For convenience I shall refer here to Formica instead of using the clumsier term 'melamine plastics'.

An attractive deckhead for a timber yacht, easily maintained and cleaned, can be made by interspersing varnished deck beams with Formica covering the normal deck head. Since varnishing a deckhead is a major job this not only reduces the work to merely varnishing the deck beams, but also offers an attractive, clean finish which, if white plastic is used, can lighten what might be otherwise a dark interior.

Whatever the use of the plastic finish, its application is similar to that in the kitchen of a house. The surface to which the Formica is to be attached must be well cleaned off, with particular attention to removing any grease or dirt. A template is essential to ensure a good fit, otherwise you may end up with a scraggly edge of Formica which doesn't quite match the area it is meant to cover. The template can be made of literally anything, but cardboard is ideal.

The template is transferred to the top or hard surface of the Formica and the outline traced

This combination of melamine plastics and timber (teak) trim make an attractive and practical door for a bathroom compartment.

When drilling formica to secure fittings, cover the drilling area with sellotape or some similar material to prevent the plastic cracking and chipping.

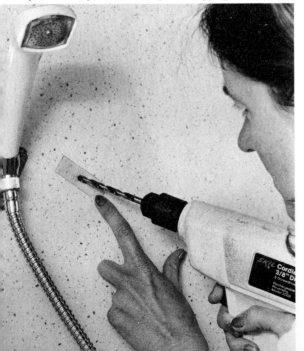

onto it. Formica can be cut either with a fine tooth saw or, preferably, with a special knife called a Formica blade which cuts the plastic much as a glasscutter cuts glass. The surface is brittle so care is necessary when tracing over the outline of the pattern with the point of the knife blade. Easy, gentle cutting at first with a number of passes over the surface is best, since the surface is so smooth that the knife can easily wander and if too much pressure is applied an incorrect cut may be made. Straight lines should be followed with a metal rule and curves must be followed carefully until a reasonable groove has been scored in the surface.

When you are quite certain that the outline is evenly grooved into the surface, place the sheet of Formica on the edge of a table. Pressing down firmly on the part to be fitted, bend the outer edge of the Formica upwards with the first finger and thumb, folding the outside edge back onto itself until it snaps off. Repeat this carefully all along the outline, breaking off only a small piece at a time. Ragged edges must be filed off, taking care not to chip the top surface. When the entire sheet has been broken away to leave the outline of the piece to be fitted, final trimming can be done with the knife or file.

Contact glue is the best for securing the Formica in place. Both surfaces should be evenly covered with the glue which must then be left to dry. One of the secrets of correct use of contact glue is to ensure that both surfaces are well dried out before pressing them together.

Fitting the two surfaces together takes a great deal of care, since once the contact glue adheres it is very difficult to undo. One way of avoiding the problem is to insert a piece of paper between the two surfaces until the Formica is correctly aligned, then gradually withdraw the paper holding the two surfaces firmly in contact. When all paper is removed the Formica is well rubbed down, working from the centre outwards to remove any air pockets.

If the fit is snug round the edges, you may prefer to leave the finish as is and, indeed, this is probably the best way. Where the edge is ragged or needs tidying or where appearances will be improved by it, a light timber trim can be glued and nailed around.

Timber veneers

Timber veneers, like melamine plastics, are in effect stick-on surfaces used for covering less attractive materials. They are not uncommon in

Timber veneers offer a cheap way of achieving a quality-looking job. They must be carefully applied and glued if the appearance is to be effective.

at this point that some materials do not lend themselves to use on small boats where water, particularly salt water, is liable to find its way below decks. A classic example is denim which, while being an excellent material for the sort of wear and tear that will be experienced on board a boat, tends to shrink badly when wet, and stains when in contact with salt water.

From experience I have found the most practical and attractive fabric for use in interior furnishings, particularly for bunk cushions and covers, is a woven wool fabric. While at first glance it would not seem to be a very 'boaty' material, in practice it wears well and resists shrinkage or staining from salt water. If it is sprayed with a synthetic waterproofing spray when first fitted, it will offer long use under hard conditions without great signs of wear and tear. It can be easily washed; therefore, cushions should be fitted with plastic zippers running the full length of the inside edge of the cushion. Plaid designs or something similar tend to show marks less than plain or checkered materials and piping is not necessary unless personal taste dictates otherwise.

Another material widely used for covering bunk cushions is vinyl, because of its waterproof qualities and its ease of cleaning—but remember, if it is waterproof on the outside, it is likewise proof to any water which may gather on the inside. A gradual seepage of moisture into the

Vinyl and other plasticised fabrics are ideal for use on small boats and make excellent covers for cockpit cushions.

finishing work, particularly in boat interiors where they create a pleasant timber appearance to what would have otherwise been a rough and perhaps unattractive surface. They are glued in place under pressure, and for large areas it is best to buy ply which has already been veneered rather than to attempt the job. The wood veneers now incorporated into Formica-type plastics are much easier to handle and come in a wide range of grain and colour.

Fabrics

Since this book is not intended to be a manual on interior decoration, it is hardly the place to discuss fabrics in any sort of detail. In any case, the material used for furnishing the inside of a boat will obviously be the owner's personal choice, particularly in terms of colour and design. However, it is perhaps worth mentioning foam of the cushions will be trapped inside the vinyl covering and become very hard to dry out. Although many people find that vinyl is an uncomfortable material in very hot or very cold weather due to its clinical, plastic finish, a lot of boat owners like vinyl as a cover for bunk cushions. When piped, it certainly looks attractive.

It is worth mentioning at this point that the material used inside bunk cushions, while not being a fabric, must be both waterproof and of reasonable density. Kapok, and similar stuffing materials, will become clogged with water if they get wet. Rubber or plastic foam is ideal but it should be high-density foam in preference to the normal material in order to keep the thickness down and yet retain a comfortable feeling when sat upon. High density foam around 10 cm thickness is adequate for most bunk cushions, whereas normal plastic foam would need to be almost twice that thickness to achieve the same comfortable support. Apart from the cumbersome appearance of the thicker material, it sags much more than the high density foam and thus tends to stretch the covers after a period of time, making them appear unsightly.

Many bunk cushions are awkwardly shaped, particularly in forward cabins or quarter berths, and covering them can be a pretty tricky business unless you are expert in soft furnishings. A ham-handed job may well spoil the total aesthetic appearance of the interior of the boat, so this is one place where you really should call for the experts.

Index